Middlebrow Queer

Middlebrow Queer

Christopher Isherwood in America

JAIME HARKER

University of Minnesota Press

Minneapolis • *London*

Material from Christopher Isherwood's archives copyright 1940, 1944, 1945, 1946, 1947, 1948, 1949, 1950, 1953, 1954, 1955, 1956, 1957, 1959, 1960, 1965, 1967, 1972, 1974, 1975, 1976, 2009, 2013 by Don Bachardy.

Interview with Don Bachardy copyright 2013 by Don Bachardy. Printed by permission of The Wylie Agency LLC.

Quotations from letters owned by Gore Vidal are reprinted by permission of the Estate of Gore Vidal.

Passages from W. H. Auden letters are reprinted by permission of the Estate of W. H. Auden.

Passages from Stephen Spender letters are reprinted with permission of the Estate of Stephen Spender.

Passages from Glenway Wescott letters are reprinted by permission of Harold Ober Associates, Inc.

Passages from John Rechy letters are reprinted with permission of John Rechy.

Passages of Dodie Smith letters are reprinted by permission of the Estate of Dodie Smith.

Every effort was made to obtain permission to reproduce material in this book. If any proper acknowledgment has not been included here, we encourage copyright holders to notify the publisher.

Selections of chapter 1 were first published as " 'Look Baby, I Know You': Gay Fiction and the Cold War Era," *American Literary History* 22, no. 1 (2010): 191–206.

Published by the University of Minnesota Press
111 Third Avenue South, Suite 290
Minneapolis, MN 55401-2520
http://www.upress.umn.edu

Library of Congress Cataloging-in-Publication Data
Harker, Jaime.
    Middlebrow queer : Christopher Isherwood in America / Jaime Harker.
    Includes bibliographical references and index.
    ISBN 978-0-8166-7913-3 (hc : alk. paper) — ISBN 978-0-8166-7914-0 (pb : alk. paper)
1. Isherwood, Christopher, 1904–1986—Criticism and interpretation.
2. Homosexuality in literature. 3. Gay culture in literature. 4. Homosexuality and literature—United States—History—20th century. 5. Literature and society—United States—History—20th century. 6. Gay men—Identity. I. Title.
    PR6017.S5Z675   2013
    823'.912—dc23

                                                        2012038000

Printed in the United States of America on acid-free paper

The University of Minnesota is an equal-opportunity educator and employer.

20 19 18 17 16 15 14 13   10 9 8 7 6 5 4 3 2 1

Contents

Acknowledgments

The Rare Book and Manuscript Library, Columbia University, the Bancroft Library at the University of California, the New York Public Library (main branch and the Lincoln Center), the British Library, the Boston University Archive, and the Huntington Library generously granted access to their collections.

The University of Mississippi supported the research and writing of this book through summer research grants and a sabbatical.

The University of Minnesota Press provided both enthusiasm and feedback, and made this a better book.

I thank colleagues and friends for their contributions to this book, with apologies to anyone I may have inadvertently forgotten: Erin Smith, Theresa Starkey, Kacy Tillman, Jill Anderson, Pip Gordon, Robert Caserio, John Howard, Wayne Gunn, Sue Hodson, Ivo Kamps, Doug Armato, Danielle Kasprzak, and especially Alida Moore. Special thanks to Don Bachardy for his generosity.

Christopher and His Readers

C HRISTOPHER ISHERWOOD'S *CHRISTOPHER AND HIS KIND* (1976) begins with queer bravado. Explaining why he really went to Berlin in the 1930s—in a word, boys—Isherwood frames his homosexuality defiantly: "Girls are what the state and the church and the law and the press and the medical profession endorse, and command me to desire. My mother endorses them, too. She is silently brutishly willing me to get married and breed grandchildren for her. Her will is the will of Nearly Everybody, and in their will is my death. *My* will is to live according to my nature, and to find a place where I can be what I am . . . But I'll admit this—even if my nature were like theirs, I should still have to fight them, in one way or another. If boys didn't exist, I should have to invent them" (12). Isherwood's memoir embraced the defiant spirit of gay liberation and inspired a younger generation of gay men. He became a link to a hidden history of gay men *and* a rebellious rebuke to the pre-Stonewall closet. Gay publications rushed to interview him and claim him as an honorary grandfather of gay rights.[1] Armistead Maupin's comment about Isherwood suggests his role in gay liberation literary circles: "No other figure in my life made me feel more connected to a past I had never known and a future I had yet to realize."[2]

Isherwood used gay liberation rhetoric repeatedly during the 1970s and 1980s, and Isherwood scholarship, a small but robust body of work, has followed his lead, interpreting him as a pioneer of gay rights and of what we now call queer modernism. This mode of inquiry has been particularly illuminating for a writer whose political and literary interests intersect with key moments in twentieth-century history and aesthetics. Isherwood was interested in evolving theories of gay identity, staying at Magnus

Hirschfield's Institute of Sex Research in Berlin in the early 1930s, reading Alfred Kinsey's famous report on male sexuality in 1948, participating in Evelyn Hooker's groundbreaking research on gay men in the 1950s, and buying texts on gay liberation in the early 1970s. He even seems to anticipate some of the oppositional energy of queer theory; Isherwood insisted on using the term "queer" to describe his own sexuality, embracing the pejorative to emphasize his own distance and dissent from mainstream culture. Isherwood's conversion to Hinduism enhances this convergence with queer theory, because Hinduisim refutes the notion of a unified autonomous self as false masks of identity that obscure a deeper complexity and chaos. This rejection allies Isherwood with queer critiques of identity categories as disciplinary regimes.

Isherwood's personal connection to writers who have subsequently become foundational to queer modernism—including Virginia Woolf, E. M. Forster, Somerset Maugham, and W. H. Auden—connects him to another contemporary critical discourse. With his third novel, Isherwood came to the attention of Bloomsbury; partly through the intervention of friend (and rival) Stephen Spender, *Mr. Norris Changes Trains* was published by the Hogarth Press. Isherwood didn't cultivate these relationships as carefully as Spender and was often critical of the Bloomsbury group.[3] Nevertheless, some identification with British modernism was important to Isherwood. His role as a prototypic metronormative writer, from London to Berlin to New York to Los Angeles, made an oppositional stance toward the "general public" almost obligatory. These gestures continued throughout his writing career. In *Christopher and His Kind,* he quotes from Virginia Woolf's diary as an oblique way to establish his cultural capital: "Isherwood and I met on the doorstep. He is a slip of a wild boy: with quicksilver eyes: nipped; jockeylike. That young man, said W. Maugham, 'holds the future of the English novel in his hands'" (325). Isherwood's insistent relationship with such queer figures makes him a natural fit for queer modernism as articulated by scholars like Heather Love.[4] His rejection of identity politics and his multiple queer networks, then, make him seem presciently ahead of his time. But the brilliance and appeal of these critical narratives may obscure the Isherwood who did not simply anticipate our own critical obsessions.

I was introduced to Isherwood through *Christopher and His Kind* in a 1993 graduate seminar. Separated from those heady days of gay liberation, I found the book a bit flat, but reading *The Last of Mr. Norris* aloud on a cross-country trip, I was smitten with Isherwood's charm, his campy humor, his deft sentences, and his nuanced accessibility. Isherwood scholarship's focus on his role in the modernist canon and, more recently, his queer credentials, failed to captured Isherwood's appeal for me. *Middlebrow Queer* constructs a different literary genealogy, one that doesn't assume traditional notions of cultural capital and literary merit but articulates different standards to assess style, value, and cultural significance. Indeed, Isherwood's connection to both queer modernism and queer theory becomes a bit more fragile on closer examination. Isherwood's enmeshment in mainstream popular culture concerned critics in the 1930s even before his immigration to the United States; in 1938, for example, British critic Cyril Connolly criticized Isherwood for rejecting the formal innovations of the Bloomsbury group for a colloquial realistic style. Isherwood's "fatal readability,"[5] Connolly sniffs, placed him in unwelcome company. Connolly elaborates in a passage that veers quickly into highbrow tantrum:

> This, then, is the penalty of writing for the masses. As the writer goes out to meet them half-way he is joined by other writers going out to meet them half-way and they merge into the same creature—the talkie journalist, the advertising, lecturing, popular novelist.
>
> The process is complicated by the fact that the masses, whom a cultured writer may generously write for, are at the moment overlapped by the middle-class best-seller-making public and so a venal element is introduced.
>
> According to Gide, a good writer should navigate against the current; the practitioners in the new vernacular are swimming with it; the familiarities of the advertisements in the morning paper, the matey leaders in the *Daily*

> *Express,* the blather of the film critics, the wisecracks of
> newsreel commentators, the know-all autobiographies of
> political reporters, the thrillers and 'teccies, the personal
> confessions, the *I was a so-and-so,* and *Storm over such-
> and-such,* the gossip-writers who play Jesus at twenty-five
> pounds a week, the straight-from-the-shoulder men, the
> middlebrow novelists of the shove-halfpenny school, are
> all swimming with it too. For a moment the canoe of an
> Orwell or an Isherwood bobs up, then it is hustled away
> by floating rubbish, and a spate of newspaper pulp.[6]

I love the rhetorical excess to which Connolly's disgust leads him—
beneath the Menckenesque disdain, he paints the enemy so viv-
idly that one cannot help but be interested in these "gossip-writers
who play Jesus." Indeed, Connolly's detailed list shows a minute
understanding of the "river of print" that defined interwar English
literary culture, including modernism, despite his insistence on
modernism as a oppositional aesthetic. Recent scholarship shows
how modernist writers participated in the same celebrity culture
that glorified "middlebrow novelists" and movie stars; they were
published by mainstream presses, chosen by book clubs, and
marketed extensively (and sometimes, these modernist writers
even wrote their own ad copy).[7] Yet the myth of modernism as
pure and oppositional persists.

Isherwood himself invoked it when it suited him, but his authorial identity had much broader influences and was thoroughly
enmeshed with Connolly's populist river of print. Isherwood
may have socialized with British modernists, and he may have
approved of their cultural rebellion, but he didn't embrace their
commitment to formal experimentation in his own writing. He
praised Proust and Woolf, but loved Dickens and George Moore.
He read hundreds of volumes of poetry and enjoyed mystery novels and sex paperbacks. He loved movies, worked as a Hollywood
screenwriter for decades, and socialized with actors and direc-
tors. Though he wanted the emerging cultural capital of modernism, he was deeply interested in work that has been dismissed as
pulp and Victorian. Isherwood addressed this diversity of reading
in one of his college lectures from the 1960s: "I was asked by one

of you who was kind enough to write to me why, if I liked Forster, had I, on other occasions, expressed a preference for melodrama of another kind and, in fact, rather like Dickens, rather like Balzac. Of course, the answer is that one is not bound to any one way of doing things. And though one's admiration goes out in many directions, when it comes to trying in a small way to be an imitator or disciple, one chooses one master rather than another. One owes a great deal to many masters."[8] It is in Isherwood's catholic appreciation of multiple styles, even those that prominent modernists denounced as old-fashioned and reactionary, that his ambivalent relationship to cultural hierarchy becomes evident. Isherwood moved beyond form to define great writing as "a joy that accepts the whole of the human experience."[9] A writer "must be passionately engaged in the action" but he must also "look down on the action with . . . compassion."[10] That somewhat mystical quality cannot, he insists, be located simply in style or scope or emotion, because writers with defects in all three can yet be considered great novelists. Isherwood's own writing merged popular and middlebrow forms in a readable style that always claimed a secure place in the mainstream literary marketplace.

Nor, on closer examination, does Isherwood anticipate queer theory in its radical rejection of heteronormativity and identity politics. Certainly, one can find provocative statements in his 1970s interviews and his private letters, but his public persona during the Cold War was much more circumspect. Though he included gay characters in his fiction and incorporated camp into his style, he never declared himself during the Cold War, talking about "homosexuals" as a category that didn't include him. In addition, despite his rejection of a coherent self, Isherwood remained committed to the idea of gay identity as a meaningful category; his discussions of his "tribe" or his "kind" suggest a gay universalism that is distinctly unfashionable in contemporary queer theory. While Isherwood sometimes used the term as a critique of mainstream society, he used it more commonly simply as a synonym for "gay." In other words, Isherwood's "queer" is not our "queer."

Because I want to highlight Isherwood's distinctive relationship to both literary value and gay identity, I have chosen an intentionally provocative title: *Middlebrow Queer.* No one would be more hor-rified to be called middlebrow than Christopher Isherwood, who saw the bourgeoisie and its sorry moral and aesthetics codes as the enemy—except, perhaps, the many literary critics who have worked diligently to raise his status in the academy over the past forty years. The term "middlebrow" emerged as a pejorative dur-ing the interwar period, as Isherwood was beginning his writing career; it can mean middle class, mediocre, reactionary, melo-dramatic, feminine, sentimental. Indeed, middlebrow is used as shorthand for conservative mainstream, and the term's connec-tion to eugenics and to inferior aesthetics has led some critics to avoid its use altogether.[11] I use the term "middlebrow" because of its role in American literary history and its potentially destabiliz-ing critical valence. New York intellectuals like Dwight Macdon-ald and Clement Greenberg railed against the "middlebrow" in the late 1940s and early 1950s for "fatal readability," and one can see the results of this critical invective in Isherwood's negative book reviews during the period.

But middlebrow isn't simply a useful historical term; as Janice Radway argues, the middlebrow is an ongoing mode of reading and writing emphasizing emotion and intense identification. In my first book, I argue that middlebrow also embodies an ongoing mode of *authorship,* one valuing identification, emotion, and a symbiotic relationship between reader and writer.[12] These values were increasingly important to Isherwood in his American autho-rial incarnation, and using the term "middlebrow" acknowledges modes of writing that are not legible in modernist aesthetics. Like "queer," middlebrow is a pejorative used to dismiss cultural in-terventions deemed illegitimate, inferior, and feminine. And like "queer," it is a term that can potentially destabilize a host of bina-ries that continue to frame literary and cultural studies: art and trash, innovative and derivative, hard-boiled and sentimental, radical and conservative, and, I want to add, gay and mainstream. Queer theory frames heterosexuality as an institution that could only be created through the foil of "the homosexual"—a new crea-tion that codified simple binaries about sexual identity. Similarly, modernism, and other systems of fixed aesthetic hierarchy, can also be destabilized by the middlebrow, clearing the way for the much more vibrant, diverse, and interesting cultures of letters in twentieth-century American writing, including the complex negotiations and aesthetic exuberances of Cold War print culture.

Eve Kosofsky Sedgwick argued for queer literary readings that "explore the extremely varied, dynamic, and historically contingent," "queer reading that can attune it exquisitely to a heartbeat of contingency."[13] *Middlebrow Queer* uses Sedwick's advocacy of contingency to reconsider categories of "gay" and "lesbian" not as transhistorical essences but as culturally and historically contingent constructions in need of their own nuanced excavations. Through Christopher Isherwood, I reconstruct the complex networks of readers, publishers, and authors that made up Cold War queer print cultures and their complex intersection of highbrow, middlebrow, and lowbrow. In addition to analyzing his Cold War novels, I examine correspondence between Isherwood and agents, editors, fellow writers, and readers and analyze multiple and discarded drafts of Cold War novels, thus reconstructing the evolution of his authorial identity. Isherwood is a particularly promising figure for this kind of excavation, because after his immigration to the United States in 1939, he immersed himself in American culture and tried to construct an authentic American authorial identity. The Cold War would seem to be a bad time for a gay Englishman to acclimate himself to American culture; many Cold War scholars have painted a devastating portrait of conformity and homophobia. More recent scholarship, such as Michael Sherry's *Gay Artists in Modern American Culture*, suggests robust, diverse, and surprisingly visible gay reading and writing communities during the Cold War. In this book, I detail a number of queer networks and print cultures that Isherwood appreciated, observed, and enjoyed, and that show up in his Cold War novels in unexpected ways. From gay protest novels of the late forties and early fifties, through early sixties gay novels, popular culture mashups, and out gay pulp, Isherwood's American career is a revealing road map of Cold War gay cultures of letters.

Writing about gay identity for a mainstream audience seemed an insurmountable problem for a number of gay writers in the twentieth century; both external and internal censors wielded considerable power. Christopher Nealon's suggestion that pulp novelist Ann Bannon was "groping for solutions to the problem of how to 'represent' lesbians and tell a story about them"[14] applies more broadly to queer authorship during the Cold War. Two recent biographies—Wendy Moffat's *A Great Unrecorded History: A New Life of E. M. Forster* and Justin Spring's *Secret Historian: The Life and Times of Samuel Steward, Professor, Tattoo Artist, and Sexual Renegade*—demonstrate the conflicting challenges of gay authorship. Forster, thoroughly identified with middle-class respectability, stopped writing novels and short stories for public consumption because he didn't feel he could write openly about gay experience and keep his role as chronicler of middle-class life. Samuel Steward, involved in rough trade, wanted to write about explicit sexual experience and was forbidden to do so by censorship laws. Both biographies—the gentle Cambridge fellow and the adventurous tattoo artist—draw haunting portraits of strangled voices.

Isherwood, who was friends with both Forster and Steward, avoided the perils of each. Like Forster, he was a respected mainstream writer who longed for domestic space. Like Steward, he was a cultural rebel who rejected monogamy and saw himself as an outsider to mainstream society. Writing about gay experience became increasingly important to Isherwood during the Cold War; he includes gay characters in all of his American novels. Finding a satisfactory solution for doing so was an ongoing challenge, because Isherwood wanted neither to demonize gay experience nor to sentimentalize it. His novels, which emphasized domestic gay spaces, were a particularly delicate Cold War negotiation, for while he was mainstreaming gay content for heterosexual audiences, he was also, covertly, writing for gay audiences—encouraging identificatory reading practices and constructing a symbiotic relationship between reader and writer.

Isherwood's immersion in New York gay culture was essential to the merger of middlebrow and queer that informed all his Cold War literary productions. Perhaps most important to Isherwood was "camp," both the term and the aesthetic mode it suggests. "Camp" is a notoriously difficult term to define; it tends to inspire lists, aphorisms, and colorful examples, and it has a vigorous and contradictory theoretical genealogy. Various theories have defined it as a hysterical sign of postmodernism, a means of queer resistance, an apolitical escape from activism, a style, and a structure of feeling. Isherwood's understanding of camp, which I discuss throughout *Middlebrow Queer*, informed his authorial identity during the Cold War; he is often credited with being the first to define camp publicly, in *The World in the Evening* (1954). His understanding of camp evolved during the Cold War and circulated through his novels.

Although camp is often set in opposition to the middlebrow, Nicola Humble suggests that camp and the middlebrow are intimately connected through the queer pleasures of reading.[15] Both camp and the middlebrow have a particular relationship to sentimentality: camp considers it "as spectacle," while middlebrow sees it "as viewpoint"—a difference, Sedgwick suggests, that is "powerfully charged for textual performance."[16] Isherwood's middlebrow camp often seems to inhabit both simultaneously, identifying with and ironically commenting upon its queer characters and contexts. His symbiotic relationship with gay readers, and the complex, layered form of writing this relationship entailed, constructed a mode of writing that extends the critical boundaries of both gay fiction and middlebrow fiction. It is this evolution of Isherwood's authorial identity, simultaneously American and queer, that *Middlebrow Queer* explores.

Isherwood's American Incarnation and the Gay Protest Novel

WHEN CHRISTOPHER ISHERWOOD AND W. H. AUDEN SET sail for New York in 1939, it seemed to most like simply another adventure. Ever since purposely failing the Tripos (a cumulative two-year exam) at Cambridge and leaving the narrow confines of his upper-crust upbringing, Isherwood had been a wanderer. His most profound attachment had been to Berlin, despite, or perhaps because of, his mother's continued outrage at Germany for her husband's death in World War I. When the Nazis took power in 1933, Isherwood traveled around Europe, looking for a new nationality for his German boyfriend, Heinz Neddermeyer; he also began to establish both his reputation as a novelist and his public persona as a leftist. After Heinz's arrest and return to Germany in 1937, Isherwood's journeys expanded; he and Auden traveled to China (a trip documented in their *Journey to a War*), then returned to England through New York, which offered such tantalizing delights that both were eager to return.

The move to the United States, for Isherwood, was a quest for personal, spiritual, and literary reinvention. Isherwood's journeys always had a profoundly domestic streak; though he later claimed that he went to Germany "for boys," his European travels were to save one particular boy, by finding a permanent home for them both. When he lost Heinz to the German war machine, Isherwood rethought his allegiance to abstract political systems; he embraced first pacifism and then Hinduism, withdrawing from the public leftist allegiances of the 1930s. In the United States, he made a home with a different boy, Don Bachardy, and he remained in the United States more than half his life, becoming both an American citizen and a self-invented American writer.

Yet, as James Berg observes, "for most critics studying the overall arc of American literature in the twentieth century, Isherwood simply does not appear."[1]

If we read Isherwood within the arc of twentieth-century American literature, specifically during the Cold War, when his American novels were written, we discover a complicated process of assimilation and often-overlooked queer reading and writing cultures. Isherwood's move to the United States caused a profound identity crisis, because American Cold War politics and literary culture were difficult for him to navigate. Isherwood eventually constructed an American identity through gay culture and framed his authorial persona through the Cold War gay protest novel, which provided him with a model, and foil, for working both within and against American culture.

Authorship and American Identity

From his association with older writers like E. M. Forster, William Plomer, Somerset Maugham, and Virginia Woolf, through his close friendships with Stephen Spender and Auden, Christopher Isherwood was thoroughly enmeshed in 1930s English literary culture. Outside the queer fraternity of English writers, Isherwood found himself adrift. Not long after moving to the United States and receiving "a bundle of letters from England . . . and a copy of *Horizon*," Isherwood wrote that "*Horizon* makes me feel homesick for what is, after all, my only real home, 'the gang.'"[2] He remained connected to England throughout his American sojourn, publishing in English periodicals, tracking English reviews of his novels, collecting the English editions of his books, and following English sex scandals and literary movements. In the United States, he maintained friendships with a number of English expatriates, including Auden, the writer Dodie Smith (who would become famous for her children's book *The Hundred and One Dalmations*) and Alec Beesley, her pacifist husband, and Chris Wood, Aldous Huxley, and Gerald Heard. This latter group sustained Isherwood financially (a loan from Wood helped Isherwood settle in Los Angeles) and spiritually; Heard introduced Isherwood to Swami Prabhavananda, which led to Isherwood's conversion to Hinduism and his unsuccessful sojourn as a Hindu monk. Even Isherwood's American networks, which I discuss later, grew out of those English attachments: Lincoln Kirstein and Glenway Wescott had met members of Isherwood's set while traveling in Europe.

Despite these continuities, Isherwood's move to the United States was a conscious break from England, one that became a public scandal in England once World War II began. In 1939, Isherwood wrote in his diary, "If I were told that somebody else had 'run away from England,' I should ask, 'What did "England" mean to him?' 'England' to me meant a place that I stayed away from as much as possible during the past ten years. From a strictly patriotic standpoint, you can be 'disloyal' in peace as well as in war."[3] Isherwood wanted to separate himself culturally as well as physically; he planned to become an American writer. Looking back on his immigration, he wrote, "[I] saw myself as a natural citizen of the go-getters' homeland. Oh I'd talk faster and louder than any of them. I'd learn the slang and the accent, I'd adapt like an Arctic fox. Before long, I'd be writing the great American novel. I was very sure of myself."[4] Toward that end, Isherwood tried to "use American idiom, pronunciations and intonations in his speech," even going so far, as his biographer notes, to switch to American spelling "after almost half a lifetime of using British spelling."[5] His Americanization extended to writing in Hollywood, where he joined other American writers such as Anita Loos and Dorothy Parker; socialized with Greta Garbo, Charles Laughton, and other stars; attended parties hosted by Marion Davies and David Selznick; and worked on adaptations of popular writers such as James Hilton. Isherwood's embrace of Hollywood earned him the disdain of his English peers, who worried he was becoming a facile California phony.

To defend himself against the rising chorus of criticism during World War II, Isherwood invoked noblesse oblige. He wrote to Stephen Spender in 1940, "Why have I decided to become an American citizen? Because I believe that the future of English culture is in America, and that the building of this future will be assisted by the largest possible cultural emigration. The two elements have got to mix."[6] Isherwood's self-dramatization as defender of

English values in a colonial outpost was a bit much for Spender, who endured German bomb raids while Isherwood, in his view, had expensive lunches with movie stars on the beach: "To me, this remark is just a meaningless noise. As long as England exists and is having a history, it is absurd to talk about culture emigrating. Culture isn't something which is quite separate from the lives of the people."[7] Biographer Peter Parker is similarly dismissive.[8]

What both miss, however, is how Isherwood echoes D. H. Lawrence. Lawrence traveled to the United States after World War I because, as Donald Pease describes it, "he believed the great passional life of Europe, what he called its 'spirit,' had already migrated to America. While in Europe, this great westering spirit had resulted in great artistic and cultural achievements; but they belong to Europe's past."[9] Lawrence's Eurocentric triumphalism is notable, but so, too, is his belief that the history of Europe was not only irrelevant but harmful to the "westering" spirit. America becomes a kind of dreamscape, an imagined refuge, and the "west" becomes a symbol of freedom and liberation. Isherwood was disgusted by his mother's worship of the past and had fantasized about desecrating the family estate, Marple Hall (something he achieved indirectly, years later, by signing over the property to his mentally disabled brother). Lawrence's appeal was irresistible; "the real America, for me, was the Far West," Isherwood explained: "All my daydreams were based on D. H Lawrence's *St. Mawr*."[10] He traveled by Greyhound bus to California so that he could see the "Far West,"[11] and his diary includes many references to the journey as pioneer quest. Later, he made a pilgrimage to Taos, New Mexico, to see the setting of *St. Mawr* for himself.[12]

Isherwood's American reinvention, then, was mediated by Lawrence, who defined a mythical "westering" spirit as the essence of modern America. Lawrence guided Isherwood's understanding of an American canon, as well; he had Lawrence's *Studies in Classic American Literature* in his library, as well as many of the writers Lawrence championed: James Fenimore Cooper, Herman Melville, Henry David Thoreau, and Walt Whitman. He also embraced the individualism and freedom such writers have come to represent: he wrote in his diary in 1940, "I love this country. I love it just because I *don't* belong. Because I'm not involved in its traditions, not born under the curse of its history. I feel free here. I'm on my own. My life will be what I make of it."[13] Lawrence led Isherwood to define American identity in terms that Cold War intellectuals were making famous during the 1940s and 1950s. Unfortunately for Isherwood, much of that definition of American character explicitly excluded limey buggers like him.

During the 1940s and 1950s, Cold War intellectuals sought to establish the United States culturally as well as politically (and many did so with covert CIA support for key literary journals).[14] The discipline of American studies—established in books by Leo Marx, F. O. Matthiessen, Richard Chase, and Leslie Fiedler— sought to establish a mythic American spirit; critics in the *Partisan Review* contrasted the freedom of highbrow aesthetics with the niggardly realism of totalitarian regimes. These cultural interventions were marked by an aggressive masculinity;[15] any deviance was denounced as aesthetically compromised and un-American. Literary criticism implicitly enforced conservative gender roles and betrayed anxiety about inordinate cultural influence of women and gay men in the United States, an anxiety alleviated through prescriptive and narrow literary norms.

In the interest of enforcing cultural boundaries, many Cold Warriors denounced middlebrow culture for its nefarious, feminizing influence. Dwight Macdonald's influential essay "Masscult and Midcult" defined middlebrow as mass culture for the educated, a kind of intellectual slumming with devastating consequences for the sedentary mind. "A tepid ooze of Midcult," he warns, "is spreading everywhere" (54), and it must be resisted because middlebrow "pretends to respect the standards of High Culture while in fact it waters them down and vulgarizes them" (37). This accusation of pretense, or infiltration, animates most Cold War critiques of middlebrow; Clement Greenberg claimed that "middlebrow culture attacks distinctions as such and insinuates itself everywhere, devaluating the precious, infecting the healthy, corrupting the honest, and stultifying the wise."[16]

If the middlebrow was dismissed for its fecundity, gay men were dismissed for their "sterility." Michael Sherry's *Gay Artists in Modern American Culture* points out that gay visibility was high in the late forties and early fifties: critics warned of a nefarious lavender menace undermining the masculinity and virility of American culture, a concern that acknowledged the number of Cold War American artists who were gay, including Aaron Copland, Samuel Barber, Stephen Sondheim, Leonard Bernstein, Tennessee Williams, Edward Albee, Truman Capote, James Baldwin, and Gore Vidal. Their presence led to an "imagined conspiracy," exemplified by the circulation of the term "Homintern," a playful coinage by Auden, a twist on "Comintern."[17] It was, for Auden, Isherwood, and their friends, clearly a joke; homosexuals were almost universally vilified and criminalized, and had neither the political organization nor, in the thirties, the inclination to carry out a guerrilla campaign against straight culture. The playfulness of a term like "Homintern," however, was completely lost when it made its way into mainstream criticism.

Critics, Sherry tells us, were equally dismissive of "both women's and gay men's creativity," attributing "shallowness, decorativeness, shrillness, and lack of authenticity" to both; real "culture," these critics believed, was "made by real men" (63). He suggests that "the conflation of women and gay men drew strength from the coding of the arts as feminine and of queer men as gender inverts" (64). Building on Sherry's observation, I want to suggest that Cold War culture was consumed by both homosexual panic and middlebrow panic, two impulses that were intertwined in Cold War cultural hysteria.

Isherwood, then, constructed an American authorial identity in a culture with an obsessive fear of perverse sexuality, foreign influences, and accessible writing. No wonder he struggled to find a place within Cold War confines. His sense of the American literary tradition was defined by what Nina Baym calls "melodramas of beset manhood": Ernest Hemingway, Raymond Chandler, Theodore Dreiser, William Faulkner, Henry Miller, and John O'Hara. Isherwood once met O'Hara, who snubbed him. When he complained of it to Dodie Smith, she elicited an astonishing confession: "I asked if he wanted to provide himself with an American clique as a substitute for his lost English one . . . and he admitted that this was exactly what he did want. 'I shall talk to them,' he said with a very little St Christopher look and tone of voice. 'Hemingway, Faulkner, Dos Passos, Steinbeck—I shall talk to them all.'"[18] Isherwood, floundering in his new environment, sought community with writers who barely spoke to each other, and whose competitive masculinity was antithetical to his own ethos.

The Cold Warriors presented a formidable barrier to Isherwood's attempted Americanization. During the war he wrote, "My voice is changing, like a choirboy's, and I can't find the new notes. But I am more certain than ever that something is happening inside (surely it is to everyone who isn't a stone, these days) and there will be something to show for this exile."[19] Isherwood's metaphor is telling; to be American was to leave adolescence behind and write in a virile, masculine voice. For Isherwood, a slight gay man with "an effeminate British voice,"[20] such a transformation was as unlikely as it was undesirable, and indeed, trying to find an American voice through the hypermasculine preening of the era contributed to his postwar writing block. When he finally developed an American voice, it came not through the Cold Warriors but through the subversive voice of gay culture.

Isherwood's notion of American gay culture was filtered through an English genealogy. Edward Carpenter, a mentor of Forster, met Walt Whitman and read his works as frankly homosexual.[21] Forster, Isherwood's first and most important literary mentor, embraced this interest in Whitman and passed it on. Isherwood particularly loved Whitman's poem "O tan-faced prairie boy":

O TAN-FACED prairie-boy!
Before you came to camp, came many a welcome gift;
Praises and presents came, and nourishing food—till at last,
    among the recruits,
You came, taciturn, with nothing to give—we but look'd on
    each other,
When lo! more than all the gifts of the world, you gave me.[22]

Whitman's all-male camp, an embodiment of the "manly love of comrades," may have influenced Isherwood's own, humorous, poem, "On His Queerness," when he rejects a visit to the Aquarium

in favor of "that old, old Roman Camp."[23] The "tan-faced prairie-
boy" became Isherwood's model of the American boy, one he found
in a variety of boyfriends: "Vernon Olds," Jim Charlton, Bill Caskey,
and finally Don Bachardy.

In the United States, Isherwood quickly found mentors in his
gay Americanization who counterbalanced the hypermasculinity
of Cold War intellectuals. New York's artistic and literary scene
was markedly gay during the Cold War.[24] Isherwood disliked
New York, but through Auden, and later Don Bachardy's artistic
networks, he had access to New York gay culture and made his
own friendships within it. Glenway Wescott and Lincoln Kirstein
were particularly important mentors for Isherwood, roughly the
same age, and each in his way explained the United States to him.
Wescott had been a promising novelist in the 1920s and 1930s;
Hemingway satirized him in *The Sun Also Rises,* and he was a
fixture of expatriate circles in London and Paris. By the 1940s,
Westcott had stopped writing fiction and was best known for his
friendships, his insatiable appetite for gossip, and his voluminous
correspondence, a Who's Who of influential New Yorkers.

Perhaps his most important influence (besides flying to Hollywood to read Isherwood's diaries) was his advocacy of Alfred Kinsey. Wescott became intimate with Kinsey in 1949, after the 1948
publication of *Sexual Behavior in the Human Male,* a book that
scandalized postwar American culture with its vision of diverse
and taboo sexual acts. Wescott's letter about a dinner party with
Kinsey and Forster suggests why Kinsey interested this group of
gay men: "K. is the strangest man in the world—his face very good
and sagacious, but with a haunted look: fatigue, concentration
and (surprising to me) passionateness. . . . Just now he is working
specially on artists; . . . he appears to have in mind a fundamental
pattern, relating art and eroticism of imagination. Here the scientific findings have given startling indications: responsiveness to
concepts, exaggerations, imageries, indecencies, all seem a part
of maleness."[25] Kinsey, for Wescott, unites all male sexuality, gay
and straight, through artistic creation. This sense of fluidity across
hetero- and homosexuality for men was illustrated by Kinsey's
claim that 37 percent of all men have had sex with other men,

even those who identify as straight. Certainly, Isherwood's English gay circle, and his American one, demonstrated that fluidity. Both Kirstein and Spender married, despite their primary attraction to men; at least two of Isherwood's American lovers, "Vernon Olds" and Jim Charlton, also married. This notion of fluid male sexuality continues to crop up in Isherwood's Cold War writing, which could suggest Kinsey's influence.

It isn't entirely clear how enthusiastically Isherwood embraced Kinsey's ideas, however. Wescott reports in his diary that Isherwood called Kinsey and himself "the saints of sex,"[26] but Isherwood resisted having his own sexual history taken by Kinsey, despite Wescott's repeated entreaties to do so. He was also reading letters from Kirstein, who described Kinsey as "a disgusting old Voyeur [whose] entire work is a scientific fraud."[27] It is safe to say, however, that Kinsey's image of a homoerotic America, in which all-American boys have homosex, tempered the hypermasculinity of American literary culture.

Lincoln Kirstein, especially in Isherwood's early years in the United States, was an even more decisive influence. Best known for his patronage of George Balanchine and key role in establishing the New York City Ballet, Kirstein was also a novelist and an aspiring poet when Isherwood met him in 1939. But more important, Kirstein was a hilarious interpreter of American life. In 1944, for example, Isherwood wrote Kirstein to ask about Hollywood's "obsession about virility":

Why does it haunt them so? They can't *all* be queer? I wish you would explain it to me. Because virility is the one thing which really makes me feel a stranger in my adopted land. They go on about it like crazy. Odets did, too. Shakespeare was virile, roistering, swashbuckling, etc etc., until I could have vomited. What puzzles me, in my innocence, is that, to me, most Americans do seem quite adequately virile (whatever it means) or at any rate like virile boys. Even the queens could tear a European tapette in half. So what is the trouble? You will think me very naïf; but please answer, because you are the only person who really elucidates

America for me. I remember, when I asked you why the skyscrapers, and you replied "Just nervousness," which immediately explained everything.[28]

Isherwood's suggestion that those obsessed with virility are actually queer is an interesting commentary on the politics of Cold War America, and explains the homosexual panic that gay artists inspired. That Isherwood turned to Kirstein for such explanations indicates his important role in Isherwood's American reinvention.

Kirstein's reply to Isherwood exemplifies what biographer Peter Parker terms the "broad streak of camp in his character":[29]

Now, listen Cwissy, and I'll tell you about sex. It is not in the least complicated. It is because the Americans as a whole are entirely immature about everything. . . . No American cares about pleasing a woman, essentially. Ask any GI whore. What we really want is to Come (quick if possible), have a good wash and then steak and French fries. . . . As for Odets thinking that Shakespeare was "virile" swashbuckling etc. you also forget that we are uneducated and do not understand any classic unless its been pre-digested. . . . We are a wonderful, sympathetic and generous people but the men are rarely grown to puberty, and the cycle of Freud, auto, homo and hetero-sexuality has just got to first base. This makes it awful for most American woman *[sic]*. . . . I think we overestimated, quite a lot the, as Twig, used to say, the er gay world. It's a backwash rather than an institution, although I certainly feel psychically they are far more advanced, even though they are stopped.[30]

Kirstein's frank dismissal of American men for immaturity and sexual inadequacy runs counter to the standard narrative of Cold War sexuality, which, as Michael Sherry explains, framed gay men as immature and straight men as both virile and wise. Kirstein isn't necessarily sold on gay men's superiority, but they are "far more advanced" than straight men.

This combination of facetious humor and cultural critique marked Kirstein's understanding of camp. Isherwood and Kirstein use the term "camp" constantly in their letters during the early 1940s; for example, Kirstein described a novel as a "serious camp about Reform Laws."[31] Isherwood assured Kirstein that their divergent war experiences wouldn't separate them, "I suppose because we have something in common on an entirely different plane: the camp that passeth all understanding."[32] Kirstein answered, "It is certain that we, I mean you and me and Fido and Paul and Goop will always be friends and lovers, and as for me the war has not only untouched me, it has peeled years from my hide and I am polished to a rare peak of camp. It is fortunate there is no one here to scream with."[33]

Kirstein's notion of camp is firmly grounded in gay New York culture (excavated by George Chauncey in *Gay New York*)—the drag balls, the cruising, the replenishing supply of beautiful young boys from the provinces, the exaggerated public behavior of "camping." Isherwood's understanding of camp, as I discuss in the next chapter, isn't quite the same, but Kirstein's tutelage about "camp" was nevertheless important to Isherwood. The term became essential to his aesthetic and sexual identity and led to his famous definition of camp in *The World in the Evening*, articulated by a character explicitly modeled on Kirstein.

Writing *The World in the Evening* was a tortured process that took more than ten years. Of course, Isherwood's life went through dramatic changes from 1939 to 1954, when the novel was published. After his conversion to Hinduism in 1940, he was classified as a theology student, edited *Vedanta and the Western World*, translated the Bhagavad-Gita and other Hindu religious texts in collaboration with his swami, and tried living at the monastery as a monk during World War II. It didn't go well; he picked up tricks on the beach during his attempt at celibacy, and socialized with a group of gay men that included Denny Fouts (who would later appear in fictional form in *Down There on a Visit*), Bill Harris (with whom Isherwood had an ongoing affair while in the monastery), and William Caskey (with whom he set up house after leaving the monastery—right after World War II ended in August 1945—and with whom he would continue an off-again, on-again relationship until 1953, when he met Don Bachardy). He did complete one novella while in the monastery, *Prater Violet*, a novel influenced by his Hollywood work but one that he dismissed to his friend Edward Upward as a rehash of his old themes, not an example of his new American authorial identity.

After 1945, however, Isherwood found that American literary culture produced a phenomenon that would give him a model for an American idiom. Kirstein's campy commentary on American life prepared Isherwood to appreciate the gay publishing boom of the late forties and early fifties, the creation of the gay protest novel.

The Cold War Gay Protest Novel

Gordon Hutner notes that "among the most surprising features of the postwar literary landscape is the number of novels that focus on the veterans' experience with African Americans, homosexuals, Jews, and assorted criminals, really a catalogue of the dispossessed."[34] Hutner is one of the few contemporary critics to note that homosexuals were part of the larger interest in "the dispossessed" that marked the late 1940s and early 1950s. That postwar explosion of gay-themed fiction hasn't remained in our critical consciousness,[35] but Cold War commentators noticed; in 1958, Leslie Fiedler referred to it directly in an article titled "The Un-Angry Young Men." In an otherwise dismally bland American literary field there was a "staunch" exception to this rule: "the homosexuals." "One feels sometimes," he writes, "that homosexuality is the purest and truest protest of the latest generation, not a burden merely, an affliction to be borne, but a politics to be flaunted" (11). This protest, grounded in key literary texts, assaults the conservative familial politics of the era: "The earliest work of Truman Capote—or more strikingly of Carson McCullers—. . . seem in our context to be conquests of new areas of feeling. . . . Implicit in the whole trend is a certain impatience with the customary taboos and restraints; . . . the celebrations of homosexual sensibility implies [sic] a rejection of the ideal of the monogamous family and of men who are men (i.e., Gary Cooper). It is, perhaps, more than that, too: the last possible protest against bourgeois security and the home in the suburbs in a world where adultery is old hat" (12). Fielder's identification with this fiction as protest is significant, I think, given how protest novels had fallen into critical disfavor by 1958. The protest novel is a key genre in the middlebrow lexicon; during the late 1930s, the protest tradition was recognized as positive and distinctively American, and its values in literature were no longer dismissed as hysterical dogma. *Uncle Tom's Cabin* became a touchstone as an exemplary American novel of protest, and reviewers and critics respected protest novels as a form that needed to be evaluated on its own terms.[36]

Postwar, protest novels fell into critical disrepute. Taking aim at *Uncle Tom's Cabin,* James Baldwin famously dismissed the protest novel as a bastion of "the ostentatious parading of excessive and spurious emotion"; sentimentality, for Baldwin, is "the signal of secret and violent inhumanity, the mask of cruelty."[37] "The aim," he concludes, "has now become to reduce all Americans to the compulsive, bloodless dimensions of a guy named Joe."[38] For Baldwin, and for the larger critical establishment, the apparent sympathy of protest novels masked a cruel oversimplification, a production of a consumable stereotype that rendered violence to the full humanity of its subjects.

What this Cold War dismissal of the protest novel overlooks, however, is how terms such as "sentimental" and "propaganda" are imprecise invectives that say more about cultural capital than about the features of a particular text. Any piece of writing that evokes emotion can be rejected as sentimental, particularly if that emotion comes from subjects deemed unworthy. The feminist recuperation of the sentimental came from an awareness that societal prejudices had, in Jane Tompkins's words, "taught generations of students to equate popularity with debasement, emotionality with ineffectiveness, religiosity with fakery, domesticity with triviality, and all of these, implicitly, with womanly inferiority."[39] The label "propaganda," like "sentimental," is used to dismiss any perspective that differs from the mainstream. Reductive, dehumanizing stereotypes that were accepted as normal—such as Cold War images of Communists, tramps, and queers—rarely got called propaganda, particularly when they appeared in the works of establishment figures like Norman Mailer, Saul Bellow, and John Updike.

James Baldwin himself was to discover this the hard way when his own essay was used against him; critics scorned both *Giovanni's Room* and *Another Country* as sentimental propaganda. This has everything to do with the gay themes in both. In the late 1940s, Cold War intellectuals lumped together and pathologized all novels that touched on gay themes. By choosing to write about gay themes in such an environment, the writers I discuss here challenged the status quo and insisted on the shared humanity of their subjects. As Isherwood argued, "There are certain subjects—including Jewish, Negro and homosexual questions—which involve social and political issues. There are laws which could be changed. There are public prejudices which could be removed. Anything an author writes on these subjects is bound, therefore, to have certain propaganda value, whether he likes it or not."[40] So despite the considerable differences in style and content, I believe it makes sense to talk about this group of gay novels in the late forties and early fifties collectively as the gay protest novel.

The Cold War gay protest novel had some important precursors, including Radclyffe Hall's 1928 *The Well of Loneliness* and a group of American novels from the 1930s that detailed New York gay life, including camping, cruising, and drag balls.[41] They exposed middle-class readers to sensational, decadent, and ultimately tragic images from a hidden, exotic underworld. But like *The Well of Loneliness*, they also encouraged readerly sympathy through the suffering of the main characters. These strategies would recur in the Cold War gay protest novel. Postwar gay novels insisted that "we" are just like "you," creating new images of gay men as all-American boys who just happened to be gay: the protagonists came from all parts of the country—the South, the Midwest, the West Coast, New York. Postwar writers domesticate homosexuality, claiming it as a legitimately American phenomenon, rather than a decadent, foreign import. One can read this Americanizing influence as a continuation of the Popular Front's discovery of America; instead of learning about forgotten regions, or ethnic minorities, readers were finding out that gay people were all around them, playing tennis, chopping cotton, making movies, fighting wars.

These novels provide a new "norm" for gay experience, one articulated most succinctly by Gore Vidal in *The City and the Pillar*:

It starts in school. You're just a little different from the others. Sometimes you're shy and a bit frail; or maybe too precocious, too handsome, an athlete, in love with yourself. Then you start to have erotic dreams about another boy—like yourself—and you get to know him and you try to be his friend and if he's sufficiently ambivalent and you're sufficiently aggressive you'll have a wonderful time experimenting with each other. And so it begins. Then you meet another boy and another, and as you grow older, if you have a dominant nature, you become a hunter. If you're passive, you become a wife. If you're noticeably effeminate, you may join a group of others like yourself and accept being marked and known. There are a dozen types and many different patterns but there is almost always the same beginning, not being like the others. (98)

As Vidal's passage demonstrates, much of this literature aims to make gay life intelligible, and through that translation, help to make it sympathetic. Of course, it also makes gay life lurid, suggesting that visibility doesn't necessarily lead to acceptance. And indeed, Vidal's coming-out template contains numerous stereotypes: of effeminacy ("shy and a bit frail," "passive," "noticeably effeminate"); of narcissism ("too handsome, an athlete, in love with yourself"); of predatory gay sexuality ("sufficiently ambivalent . . . sufficiently aggressive," "dominant nature . . . a hunter"); of traditional male–female role playing.

Such stereotypes recur in gay protest novels. Vidal's own novel ended with a gay murder (and the original ending, a gay rape, wasn't much of an improvement in terms of gay stereotypes). Suicide is another theme; *The Folded Leaf,* by William Maxwell, ends with an attempted suicide, and the threat of suicide hangs over a number of these novels (notably Charles Jackson's *The Fall of Valor* and *The Lost Weekend*). Absent fathers and smothering mothers abound. Yet if negative stereotypes occur in many of these novels, counteracting images of sympathy and tenderness also emerge. John Horne Burns provides one such unexpected image of a gay bar in *The Gallery.* Never named as "gay" or "homosexual," the bar is described through the eyes of its Italian owner, Momma, who describes her "boys" with great affection and sympathy. In response to harassment from an MP, Momma is mystified:

> Momma couldn't decide what grudge the MP's had against her. There had been occasional fights in her bar, yet the other bars of Naples had even more of them. Her soldiers were gentle. All she was trying to do was run a clean bar where people could gather with other congenial people. Her crowd had something that other groups hadn't. Momma's boys had an awareness of having been born alone and sequestered by some deep difference from other men. For this she loved them. And Momma knew something of those four freedoms the Allies were forever preaching. She believed that a minority should be let alone. (133)

Burns's rhetoric here is ingenuous; by invoking Cold War political rhetoric, he makes an oblique case for the innate rights of Momma's gay customers, and even indirectly lauds their individualism, even as she points to their "deep difference from other men," just as Vidal did. This embedding of argument in interior monologues or conversation is a common strategy of protest novels and appears in a number of gay protest novels. In Burns's novel, the contrast between rough heterosexual bars and the "gentle" utopia of her gay bar runs against common stereotypes of a rough gay underworld.

Gentle men are often the bogeymen of the Cold War gay protest novel, particularly when they can be characterized as queens. Cousin Sebastian, in Capote's *Other Voices, Other Rooms,* is the epitome of the queen stereotype: dressed in kimonos, secretly haunting the house in drag, pale, unhealthy, and insinuating. Yet sometimes the queens of these novels are extraordinarily insightful, frightening protagonists who want to remain anonymous. In Jackson's *The Lost Weekend,* for example, Don encounters a gay nurse in his brief stay in the alcoholics' ward of the hospital, "a big strapping fellow around thirty, broad and well-built but far from muscular. With a frame like a hammer-thrower, he was yet soft, just this side of fat. He stood looking down with a half-smile on his face, and the impression he gave was that of an enormous sleepy tomcat, indifferent, self-sufficient, yet predatory" (134–35). The nurse calls him "baby" and subtly flirts, with great self-possession and alarming insight into Don's self-delusions. Don watches him walk away, "with a noiseless casual tread as if in carpet-slippers on his way to his own bathroom at home, indescribably nonchalant and at ease. It was infuriating. But you didn't have to watch him, did you? He lay on the mattress face down, refusing to look further" (139). Don cannot seem to resist the fascination of this confident queen, who somehow senses that Don's heavy drinking is related to his suppressed sexuality (Don began drinking after he was kicked out of his fraternity for a too-intense friendship with a fellow fraternity brother, though he never makes this connection):

> They went along the corridor in silence till the nurse stopped and pushed a button in the wall. Then he leaned against the wall and looked at Don.
>
> Never had he felt so much on trial in his life—on trial for what, he didn't know. He went hot with exasperation and embarrassment as he felt the nurse's eyes looking him over. He didn't know where to turn, where to fix his own gaze. He waited in a foolish suspense—unreasonable, outlandish, bizarre. In all his life there was no precedent of behavior for such a moment. If that guy so much as spoke to him, uttered a word of advice, told him to take it easy— He felt the odd smile and fought to resist. But it was no use, he couldn't help himself any longer. Involuntarily, he raised his eyes and looked back.
>
> "Listen, baby." The voice was so low and soft he could scarcely hear it. "I know you." (154–55)

That moment is perhaps the key to understanding the gay protest novel. These texts insist that their readers can know and identify with gay characters, who are no longer other, but just like us, even the queens who act as scapegoats in so many of these novels. If queens are gazed at, they gaze back with enormously powerful responses.

That phrase—"listen, baby, I know you"—recurs in one of the

most famous gay novels of the 1950s: James Baldwin's *Giovanni's Room.* The narrator sees a beautiful, sailor, who shoots him "a look contemptuously lewd and knowing," a precursor to an imagined pickup line: "some brutal variation of *Look, baby, I know you*" (122). The casual recurrence of this phrase suggests how well known gay protest novels were. In a 1964 interview,[42] Baldwin revealed that *Giovanni's Room* was a rewrite of an earlier novel titled *Ignorant Armies,* based on the 1944 murder trial of Wayne Lonergan, who, according to a *Time* magazine article, was a "handsome, six-foot, crop-headed Royal Canadian Air Force aircraftman charged with murdering his socialite wife."[43] Baldwin followed the press coverage closely, which, if *Time* magazine is any indication, included salacious details of Lonergan's conquests (including his wife's father) and pseudo-Freudian discussions of homosexual perversion. The court case has many of the elements of gay protest novels, including the tragic ending and the normal, all-American queer. Baldwin explained that the character based on Lonergan became David of *Giovanni's Room* with few changes.[44] Baldwin was writing this novel as gay protest novels were receiving unprecedented coverage in the literary press, suggesting his own unacknowledged debt.

Many gay protest novels are set during World War II. Novels like Richard Brooks's *The Brick Foxhole* and James Barr's *Quatrefoil* show both the opportunity for gay relationships that the war provided and the social difficulty that surrounded such relationships. The eroticization of the soldier also animates many of these novels. Jackson's *The Fall of Valor* exemplifies this trend, when Ethel Grandin comes across a newspaper photograph of a marine, hidden under her husband, John's, desk blotter. All the subsequent revelations of the novel are buried in this moment:

> He wore a wrinkled shirt open at the throat and loose
> tropical shorts exposing thick bare thighs and knees,
> slightly hairy and probably dirty. He had a couple of days'
> growth of beard so that a potential mustache of some size
> and width was plainly outlined. His eyebrows were raised,
> his eyes closed in sleep; his nose was short, almost pug;
> the mouth was wide and attractive, with tightly closed

lips; the chin was strong. He was a very rugged, masculine, and mature-looking young man. . . . The relaxed curling hand showed a dark fuzz on the back; the rifle must have rested heavy on the weary shoulder and in the crook of the arm. . . . The photograph had a compelling beauty; realistic in the extreme, yet poetic, it evoked the *Drum-Taps* poems of Whitman of which her husband was so fond *(O Tan-Faced Prairie Boy).* (55–56)

Jackson explicitly eroticizes the soldier (even evoking Isherwood's Whitmanesque myth of the tan-faced prairie boy). World War II provided the opportunity for a number of gay men to form communities in coastal cities, and gay protest novels set in the war complement Allan Bérubé's argument in *Coming Out Under Fire.*

In addition, some gay protest novels feature adolescent coming-of-age themes that construct a queer agrarian ideal. Thomas Hal Phillips's *The Bitterweed Path* features two Adams in the Garden of Eden, a paradise from which they are banished. In these agrarian bildungsromans, protagonists struggle to create language for sexuality that cannot be named without shame. Yet the descriptions of same-sex erotics in these novels are strikingly beautiful. The opening scene of *The Bitterweed Path,* for example, describes two naked boys in a locker room—a scene ripe for sensational expose—and transforms it into a holy communion: "Suddenly he caught his breath and the bundle slipped a little in his hands. Hardly three yards away from him a boy stood smiling; he was very still and naked and the light seemed to bounce away from the pale fullness of his loins. Along the lean body the neat muscles moved faintly. Darrell's gaze measured the body slowly, cautiously; it was almost the size of his own, not quite so heavy or so brown. The eyes before him were a little lower than his own and the head of short, dark hair was clean and tangled and soft. They stared at each other and slowly their faces began to redden" (4). "Listen, baby, I know you" indeed. The novel embraces queer sensuality as implicitly natural, if necessarily adolescent, and agrarian gay novels from the period similarly construct some of the Cold War's most moving images of gay desire.

Cold War gay protest novels have been largely forgotten in

American literary history, but Christopher Isherwood knew them very well. In *Lost Years,* Isherwood's reading list from the late 1940s includes a wide range of these novels, including many forgotten tomes from this tradition: Willard Motley, *Knock on Any Door;* Burns, *The Gallery;* Vidal, *The City and the Pillar;* Capote, *Other Voices, Other Rooms;* Carson McCullers, *Reflections in a Golden Eye;*[45] William Goyen, *The House of Breath;* and James Barr, *Quatrefoil*[46] (a novel for which he declined to provide a blurb). Isherwood not only read these novels but advocated for them publicly. In a talk prepared for the BBC in 1952, he named six promising young American writers: Ray Bradbury, Truman Capote, William Goyen, Speed Lamkin, Norman Mailer, and Calder Willingham.[47] Three of these writers—Capote, Goyen, and Lamkin—were gay, and Calder Willingham's first novel, *End as a Man,* included two gay characters and was often discussed in the postwar gay publishing trend. He was, in other words, creating a distinctly gay Cold War canon.

Isherwood wrote a fan letter to Willard Motley (and received a disappointingly generic postcard in return, since Motley clearly had no idea who he was),[48] but he became close friends with three key figures of the gay protest novel: Truman Capote, Gore Vidal, and Speed Lamkin. His infamous "love at first sight" meeting with Truman Capote is a case in point. He described the appearance of Capote at Random House as an almost mystical encounter:

> Christopher was prepared for the honor by one of the Random House partners, who assured him that this young man, whose first novel, *Other Voices, Other Rooms,* was soon to appear, could only be compared to Proust. And then the marvelously gracious little bony personage itself appeared; Truman sailed into the room with his right hand extended, palm downward, as if he expected Christopher to kiss it. Christopher didn't, but, within a few moments, he was quite ready to—having been almost instantaneously conquered by the campy Capote charm. To hell with Proust; here was something infinitely rarer and more amusing, a live Ronald Firbank character! Christopher came home and raved about him.[49]

Ronald Firbank, master of camp and artificiality, was a key touch-stone for Auden and a familiar figure in Isherwood's English cir-cle; Auden once advised Lincoln Kirstein to treat World War II as if it were a Firbankian farce.[50] For Isherwood, finding the embodi-ment of Firbank in an American environment queered the Ameri-can literary scene for him. The delight was mutual; according to Capote's biographer, Capote viewed Isherwood as a link to gay British modernists like Somerset Maugham and Virginia Woolf; he entertained Capote and his friends with stories and provided them with a transatlantic gay heritage.[51] Finally, Isherwood was in a position to lead the younger American gay writers of the Cold War, as he had always imagined his role in American culture.

Gore Vidal was another intimate of Isherwood's, though his relationship was somewhat more complicated. Vidal was ambi-tious, boastful, and disingenuous; Kirstein described him as "a spoiled, ambitious little industrious boy, too dainty for this old crab, and stuff with envy. He has a nice complexion, and, as far as I'm concerned is good for one thing."[52] Peter Parker suggests that Vidal flirted with Isherwood to gain his mentorship while privately dismissing him as too old.[53] Vidal's capacity for feuds is limitless—early feuds with Truman Capote and the Beats marked his literary life, one like Norman Mailer's in its irascibility. Still, Isherwood valued his friendship and, particularly during the fif-ties and sixties, read his work and reviewed his novels.

Speed Lamkin was, like Capote and Vidal, a member of the younger generation who became intimate with Isherwood. He first came to Isherwood's attention through Lincoln Kirstein: "There is a new Louisiana girl called Lamkin, whom Wystan has, or shares; he is 19 plus (about 5 years), and has written 2 plays, 3 novels, 4 epics and 5 poems. He is fierce; he was in the Amedican Embassy in Paris for a year; why he got out I don't know, but he is the latest menace."[54] Glenway Wescott described him as "a huge youth with a baby face, indeed one might say a piggy face, but in a pedigreed way. Of the Southern plutocracy, though he com-plains of insufficient means. . . . The talk has been that he kindly takes people to bed with him a good deal."[55] Lamkin was young, attractive, ambitious, and enormously productive as a writer (as Kirstein's ironic list suggests); his first novel, *Tiger in the Garden*, was published when he was only twenty-two. His second novel, *The Easter Egg Hunt*, about William Randolph Hearst and Marion Davies, sent Lamkin to research in Hollywood, thus linking Isherwood's New York gay life with his Hollywood one. He became a friend (and sometimes a lover) of Isherwood, and later, Lamkin read multiple drafts of *The World in the Evening* and influenced its evolution.

Isherwood thus became a genial uncle to this younger generation of gay writers, a link to the "Auden circle" and older gay writers such as E. M. Forster and Somerset Maugham. He worked with Glenway Wescott to help Willam Goyen and Donald Windham (authors of gay novels *The House of Breath* and *The Dog Star*, respectively) to receive writing fellowships. This networking extended institutionally as well, through Isherwood's relationship with Random House. Robert Linscott, a senior editor for the firm, oversaw a number of gay writers, including Christopher Isherwood, Gore Vidal, Truman Capote, Stephen Spender, Paul Cadmus, Tennessee Williams, and William Goyen. Linscott was married and seemed to be connected to old money (he summered away from New York and had a country home), but Isherwood's then-lover William Caskey referred to him as "Miss Linscott,"[56] so it is possible that Linscott, like Lincoln Kirstein, was both married and gay. Certainly, he seemed to relish the campy letters of Truman Capote, trading gossip about witty cocktail party putdowns and William Faulkner's fey preparations for the Nobel Prize acceptance ceremony,[57] and howling with delight over Capote's International Daisy Chain—essentially a naughty version of "six degrees of separation" that connected all members of New York society through a chain of affairs.[58] Linscott's gay authors inquire after each other, write blurbs for each other's books, and offer praise. William Goyen's first novel is a case in point. Stephen Spender, Goyen's "friend," let him stay with him and his wife, Natasha, to finish the manuscript for *The House of Breath.* Isherwood sent a blurb to Linscott and conveyed encouragement to Goyen through Linscott. Linscott sent news of Isherwood's travel book *The Condor and the Cows* to Truman Capote while he was in Italy.

Despite these friendships, however, and his familiarity with the gay protest novel, Isherwood had reservations about these novels. In his letters with Lincoln Kirstein and William Caskey, he shows an acute awareness of their themes and their shortcomings. For example, Isherwood wrote Kirstein, "What is Sppeedd Lambkin's novel's name? No—let me guess. Knock on Any Nude? Grandpa was a Hustler? The Glass Streetcar? End in a Man? The Tree of Doors? Are You Receiving Me? The Alligator Boy and the Girl from the Rue Jacob? Getting warm—getting cold? I give up."[59] Isherwood's complex play with the titles of gay novels (including Willard Motley's *Knock on Any Door*, Tennessee Williams's *A Streetcar Named Desire*, and Calder Willingham's *End as a Man*) shows that gay protest novels were a known commodity. William Caskey wrote (in a letter enclosed with Isherwood's) that "I am writing a queer novel. . . . It's quite a bit about me as well, to say nothing of all the nasty queens I know who will be brilliantly described in the torrid tome. After all I see no reason for Miss Capote and Miss Vidal to get all the gravey *[sic]* with their perverted ideas. I shall call it The City and the Prick or Other Drag Shows, Other Camps! Promise me you'll buy a copy."[60] Caskey's campy rewriting of Capote and Vidal suggests that the "queer novel" is already, by 1948, an obvious genre to be satirized.

These novels' shortcomings were also clearly an ongoing topic of conversation. Kirstein asked Isherwood to "please cable Pig-fig [Caskey] why they always have to KILL and BURN? My theory is that its all arranged by the Gore-Vidal Foundation to corroborate the finale's [sic] of Charles Jackson novels to prove they are life-or rather, deathlike."[61] Kirstein's humorous commentary notes the impression that many of these gay protest novels insisted on tragic endings.

Isherwood's letters showed his own problem with the tragic element of many of these gay novels: "I've just written two boosts: one for Truman's Other Vices, Other Wombs, and the other for Vidal's City and Pillar. You won't agree, I fear—but I do think Truman's style, not his content, is remarkable, and Vidal is such a welcome change after Jackson and all those wistful books about folded leaves and primrose men that I feel it ought to be encouraged, though the style is Satevepost."[62] Isherwood has no patience for Jackson's tragic agony; his reference about "folded leaves and primrose men" refers, at least partially, to William Maxwell's *The Folded Leaf,* a novel in which gay desire is nascent and never consummated, but still requires a suicide attempt to exorcise. The open discussion of homosexuality in both Capote and Vidal earns his praise. (The description of Vidal's style as "Saturday Evening Post" suggests that he still clung to highbrow distinctions in his literary assessments.) Isherwood wasn't entirely satisfied with Vidal's novel, however, for the same reason he was annoyed by Charles Jackson's—the tragic ending. In an oft-quoted letter to Vidal, Isherwood articulated his objections, showing a keen awareness of postwar protest novels:

> I am sure that you, personally, would wish to see the homosexuality laws repealed or at any rate revised? Very well, now the question arises: how will your novel affect public opinion on this matter?
>
> This brings me to your tragic ending: Jim's murder of Bob. . . . What I do question is the moral the reader will draw. This is what homosexuality brings you to, he will say: tragedy, defeat and death. . . . But there is another side to the picture, which you (and Proust) don't show. Homosexual relationships can be and frequently are happy. Many men live together for years and make homes and share their lives and their work, just as heterosexuals do. This truth is peculiarly disturbing and shocking even to "liberal" people, because it cuts across the romantic, tragic notion of a homosexual's fate.[63]

Note Isherwood's appeals here for "normative" and long-lasting gay relationships, the emphasis on happiness and emotion, the focus on changing legal status. Isherwood's sense that these novels could change people's minds, and that, as a gay writer, one had the obligation to present the "truth" of long-term relationships, so as to "[cut] across the romantic, tragic notion of a homosexual's fate," suggests that despite his impatience, he was clearly sympathetic to the middlebrow aims of the gay protest novel. His own contribution to the genre came with his nearly decadelong struggle with *The World in the Evening.*

◈ 2 ◈

"Too Queer to Be Quaker":
Gay Protest and Camp

T*HE WORLD IN THE EVENING* HAS BEEN PANNED CRITICALLY since its publication in 1954; even Isherwood's friend Dodie Smith, after reading the novel, claimed that America was "destroying his sense of values and even his taste" and "has almost ruined his talent."[1] Isherwood disavowed the novel almost as soon as he had completed it, and continued to trash it whenever he got the chance. During his university lectures in the 1960s, for example, he was so critical of the book that his students asked him if he wasn't being too hard on himself.[2] His most telling comment, though, was his earliest, to Edward Upward: "*The World in the Evening* is a failure. But an interesting one, I hope, and a necessary one, I'm *sure*, for me."[3] This idea of "interesting failure" provides a way to reassess the novel, particularly through analyzing its evolution, which may be more interesting than the final product. Isherwood's struggle to reinvent himself as an American novelist, his desire to incorporate openly gay content, and the discouragement he received resulted in an uneven final product. Isherwood didn't quite solve the problem of incorporating gay content, but his attempt to do so—through a merger of gay protest and New York camp—marked a significant moment in his evolution as an American gay novelist. The novel he wrote, and the novel he shied away from writing, are both essential to understanding *The World in the Evening*.

Gay Protest and *The World in the Evening*

Christopher Isherwood's fourth novel is divided into three sections. The first, "An End," introduces us to Stephen Monk and his wife, Jane, at a Hollywood party. Stephen catches his wife with Roy

Griffin, runs away to Philadelphia and his childhood nanny, Sarah, and has an accident that leaves him in a cast for ten weeks. The second section, "Life and Letters," features Stephen's friendships with a German refugee, Gerda (whose husband is in a concentration camp), and a gay couple, Bob Wood and Charles Kennedy. This part also features flashbacks to Stephen's past, prompted by rereading his late wife Elizabeth Rydal's letters. Through these flashbacks, readers learn of Stephen's marriage to Elizabeth, his affair with a young man, Michael, and his affair with Jane before Elizabeth's death. In the third section, "A Beginning," Stephen sees off Bob, joins the military, congratulates Gerda on her husband's escape from the Nazis, and becomes friends with his ex-wife, Jane.

The structure of the novel, at first glance, may not seem like other gay protest novels of the Cold War era, but reviewers recognized it as part of the genre. A prim English reviewer "deplore[d] Mr Isherwood's lapse into a fashion of today's writers of detailed dwelling on homosexuality,"[4] suggesting contemporary awareness of the gay protest novel. Howard Jones, writing in the *Saturday Review of Literature,* explains that "the apologia for the homosexual . . . is the theme of the book"; "the plea of the book," he concludes, "is for a more compassionate understanding of this particular phenomenon."[5] V. S. Pritchett went further, commenting wryly that "the fashionable homosexual theme appears in its Sunday suit."[6] The "cleaned-up" version of gay life speaks to the novel's middlebrow intent.

Pritchett's biting comment made an impression on Isherwood,[7] because he did incorporate many protest conventions in *The World in the Evening.* One scene from the novel mimics Gore Vidal's gay road map in *The City and the Pillar* to humorous effect:

> "Let me tell you something, Bob. There was a guy *I* liked, once. In that way, I mean. . . ."
>
> "Sure, I know," Bob grinned ironically. "Some kid in school. And afterwards you hated yourselves. And now he's married and got ten children."
>
> "No. This wasn't in school. . . ."
>
> "Well then, it was in some low bar in Port Said, and you were drunk, and you got picked up, and it was horrible. . . ."

"It wasn't in Port Said, and it wasn't in the least horrible. It didn't just happen once, either. I told you, I liked this guy. He's one of the best people I've ever known. . . . And now, will you stop treating me like a public meeting?" (102)

Isherwood's mockery of the "standard" coming-out story—one that Gore Vidal writes about explicitly in *The City and the Pillar*—demonstrates a clear familiarity with Cold War gay protest novels.

Isherwood's witty depiction of the two options for sex in the gay protest novel—adolescent phase or sordid assault—explains his own approach in *The World in the Evening*. He includes two gay sex scenes, and while neither was particularly explicit ("In the darkness I remembered the adolescent, half-angry pleasure of wrestling with boys at school. And then, later, there was a going even further back, into the nursery sleep of childhood with its teddy bear, or of puppies or kittens in a basket wanting only the warmness of anybody"; 184), it is still clearly sex between men, something he had been coy about in his Berlin writing. His treatment of straight sex is more explicit but no less transgressive; he writes not only about adultery but also prostitutes, venereal disease, and abortion. Even his friend Dodie Smith admitted "the sex is a mite too wild for me."[8]

It is through the narrator, Stephen Monk, that Isherwood queries many of the cultural stereotypes about homosexuality that gay protest novels both circulated and disavowed. An American expatriate with Quaker roots, two marriages, and multiple homosexual affairs, Stephen is brought to a crisis by the failure of his second marriage when he catches his wife, Jane, with "Roy Griffin, that film-fairy, that pansy male-impersonator who fooled nobody but himself, stuck with a very expensive nymphomaniac. . . . The poor miserable little pansy bastard" (19). Stephen, in other words, dismisses Roy as a prototypic queen, and projects all his own self-loathing onto Roy. Stephen's anxiety about being perceived as a queen himself recurs throughout the novel. He fears "the dreaded test of his manhood" (71) and resolves to "be a real, masculine, all-providing husband"(141). He is aware, in other words, of his masculinity as a performance, and not a particularly successful one.

Stephen is a checklist for homosexual pathology: promiscuous, unfaithful, narcissistic, infantile, insensitive, dishonest, and cruel. "Infantile," however, is the adjective that recurs most often. The director of the "Museum of Sexual Science" (74) diagnosed Stephen with "infantilism" (75), and though the assessment is humorous (because Stephen doesn't have specialized sexual tastes), images of infantilism are so numerous as to be almost overkill. Stephen runs back to his nanny after finding Jane with Roy, and his psychosomatically caused accident leaves him helpless in bed, with women feeding him and checking his bedpan. Gerta tells him that "this kid I can see in you I like, very much. Only Stephen, you know, children can be cruel sometimes, by not thinking" (59). Elizabeth, when she first meets Stephen, "smiled and looked indulgent and abstracted, like a mother who listens to her child telling her about the dog having puppies" (83). That infantile relationship continues; Michael tells him that "in another year, you'll be afraid to cross the road without Elizabeth holding your hand" (190). Stephen sulks and throws tantrums to get his way. The equation of infantile narcissism and homosexuality was standard in the 1950s, and Stephen seems a textbook case. He even knows how to use the language of pathology to his own advantage. After seducing Michael, he berates him in fifties Freudian jargon: "I'm not that way, and I won't ever be. If you are, I'm sorry for you. I'm sorry for anybody who's twisted and warped. But I'm not going to let you spoil my life. You don't understand the kind of life I have with Elizabeth. You don't understand any kind of real happiness. You know that, inside; and all this talk about being sorry for me is just a defense. You're the one who's pitiful" (190–91).

Stephen is the consistent problem in all these relationships. Both Elizabeth and Michael are devastated by Stephen's heartlessness, his inability to love. Indeed, both the "normal" heterosexual relationship and the "perverse" homosexual relationship end in hurt and betrayal, thus emphasizing that unhappiness isn't endemic to homosexual relationships but a constant risk in any relationship. His second wife, Jane, has an abortion after he accuses her of infidelity—an accusation he invents because he is horrified by the thought of fatherhood. Jane tells him, with despair, "I just don't know if you're a human being, or what" (249). Stephen is a down-low monster, manipulative and destructive.

Isherwood based his bisexual character on several models: Stephen Spender,[9] Dell book editor and film producer Frank Taylor, and Gore Vidal. Taylor's "dishonest, tricky bisexual posture" angered him because "Frank bragged about his homosexual affairs and even sometimes demanded that they should be respected as serious love dramas. At the same time, he became maudlin over his marriage and his responsibilities as a father."[10] Spender, Isherwood continued, "is deeply false in the same way, but ... he is too shrewd to parade his sentimentality in public."[11] Spender married twice, but continued to have affairs with men, and Isherwood took the side of Spender's jilted lover Tony Hyndman in the 1930s.[12] Gore Vidal, with whom Isherwood had a complicated relationship, claimed publicly that all people were innately bisexual, and that therefore homosexuality did not exist. Isherwood's indictment of bisexuality through the character of Stephen may have been a direct rebuke to Vidal. By placing Stephen at the center of his novel, Isherwood questions many cultural assumptions about the immaturity and narcissism of homosexuality. Stephen is loathsome because he is immature, heartless, and bisexual. Had he been gay—had he the character and the courage to embrace an oppositional identity—he would have been a better man. This conclusion is made explicit at the end *The World in the Evening*, when Jane tells Stephen, "maybe you should have tried being one. You might have been a whole lot happier, that way" (282). He replies, "I doubt it. It takes so much character—much more than I've got—to be a good one. And I can't stand the other kind" (282). Being gay requires superior integrity in the novel, a reversal of Cold War assumptions. No fiction of the era exposes more clearly the devastating effects of the closet.

Those better gay men exist in abundance in *The World in the Evening*. Isherwood offers the homosexual as hero, in Paul Piazza's memorable phrase.[13] Michael, Stephen's first male lover, is forthright, brave, an antifascist warrior, and openly gay. In fact, Michael first articulates a vision of integrity that Stephen will not match, insisting that their sexual encounter was more than a simple pickup: "When two men stick together, they can do anything. And I'd stick by you all my life. With a woman, you're never really free. They always tie you down, in one way or another. ... You ought to be with me. I deserve you" (192). Michael exemplifies the life Stephen should have had, if he had had enough character. His sincerity and devotion make Stephen's rejection of him all the most loathsome. Michael's discovery of a true "friend" in Spain, who dies in his arms, is a clear rebuke to Stephen's aimless life at the time.

Michael's fight against fascism—first symbolically, by removing a Nazi flag from the top of a mountain, and then literally, in his fight in Spain—marks him, post–World War II, as a member of the "greatest generation." Bob Wood also ends the novel as a soldier, both of the United States and of the queer nation; part of his desire to serve is to prove that gay men are as manly and patriotic as their straight compatriots. That, too, is a key revision of the gay war novel. As brave soldiers, both Bob and Michael are, in Cold War ideology, patriotic Americans. Bob explains the political import of his enlistment: "All you have to do is to tell them you're queer, and you're out. I couldn't do that, though. Because what they're claiming is that us queers are unfit for their beautiful pure Army and Navy—when they ought to be glad to have us. The girly ones make wonderful pharmacist's mates, and the rest are just as good fighting men as anybody else. My God, look at all the big heroes in history who—sorry, Steve! I'm starting that lecture again" (266). Isherwood's soldier-heroes push the gay war novel to a more explicit embrace of the patriotic gay man.

The novel also features a gay couple, introduced as a positive role model. We are first introduced to Charles Kennedy and Bob Wood without the labels of "homosexual." Sarah exclaims, "Those two boys! They're so comical when they are together" (59). Charles is "wonderfully kind and helpful," and Bob is "such a fine, clean boy. So thoroughly wholesome" (59). Sarah describes their relationship in safe, adolescent terms, but unlike most gay protest novels, in *The World in the Evening*, this relationship is allowed to continue happily into adulthood.

Charles and Bob are all-American boys who just happen to be gay, and the Americanness of the setting, just outside Philadelphia, birthplace of the nation, is blatant. Isherwood's descriptions of the landscape owe a considerable debt to D. H. Lawrence's image of the Puritan frontier: "the woods," Stephen explains, "reminded you that this country . . . used to be an outpost of a world, a front line of fanatically humorless, drably heroic men and women, entrenched behind their Bibles and prejudices, their dark stuffy clothes and their stone farmhouse walls, grimly confronting the pagan wilderness" (33). Isherwood signals a queer genealogy from these "drably heroic men and women" to the two American Adams they generated, with subtle Whitmanesque touches.

Bob Wood is a consistent advocate for homosexuality in the novel, arguing against prejudice and antigay laws. Isherwood sometimes attempts to mitigate the earnest appeals with deprecating asides like "Sorry Steve! I'm starting that lecture again," but Bob's outbursts are clearly embedded arguments meant to persuade. One early speech tackles sodomy laws (the subject of Isherwood's famous letter to Gore Vidal) directly:

> "Maybe we ought to put people against us. Maybe we're too damned tactful. People just ignore us, most of the time, and we let them. We encourage them to. So this whole business never gets discussed, and the laws never get changed. There's a few people right here in the village who really know what the score is with Charles and me, but they won't admit it, not even to themselves. We're such *nice* boys, they say. So wholesome. They just refuse to imagine how nice boys like us could be arrested and locked up as crooks. They're afraid to think about it, for fear it'd trouble their tender consciences. Next thing you know, they might get a *concern*"—Bob's mouth was twitching ferociously—"and then they'd have to *do* something. Jesus, I'd like to take them and rub their noses in it!" (101–2)

Isherwood's "nice, wholesome boys" rebuke the law's construction of them as criminals. Isherwood advocates through Bob while still keeping him safe by having other characters comment affectionately on his stridency. Readers are guided in their own reactions to such speeches by Sarah, who is clearly persuaded by the human immediacy of Charles and Bob. After seeing Charles forlorn at the departure of his lover, she says to Stephen, "I'm afraid we're all of us apt to be very cruel and stupid, in the presence of what we're not accustomed to. I fear that Charles feels cut

off from us now, and bitterly lonely; and we refuse him any word
of comfort. We refuse to recognize what it was that he and Bob
shared together. Oh dear, we're so dreadfully smug and arrogant,
most of us; so very sure we know what's right and what's wrong.
Sometimes, Stephen, this lack of charity—even among those of
us who call ourselves Friends—it horrifies me!" (273). Such clear
claims for acceptance, not just of adolescent experimentation but
of mature partnering, are unusual in Cold War gay protest novels.
Isherwood pushes the earnest pleas of middlebrow protest novels to their logical conclusion, though he also contains their po-
tency by having Charles respond sympathetically but dismissively,
"He'd like for us to march down the street with a banner, singing
'We're queer because we're queer because we're queer because
we're queer'" (107). Charles's suggestion that this sort of activism
is simply too much would have reassured his mainstream readers
while still building sympathy for Bob's perspective.

Isherwood may have included the strategies of gay protest
novels, but he was aware of their unappealing aspects, and Quakers, long associated with abolition, stand in for the genre of protest in *The World in the Evening*. Charles Kennedy bemoans the
Quakers' "lack of style. They don't know how to do things with an
air. They're hopelessly tacky. They've no notion of elegance" (210).
Stephen finds the style of the Quakers similarly dreary:

> Their women are energetic and bright. They comb their
> hair back and twist it into a knot. They use no make-up.
> They wear flat heels, cheap sensible dresses, and, in sum-
> mer, straw hats which somehow resemble sunbonnets.
> Everybody knows everybody. Everybody is married. If war
> has a smell, the Quakers remind you of a taste; the taste of
> plain homemade bread. . . . Sometimes, after a long illness,
> when the tired stomach recoils from every kind of sauce,
> spice or sweetness, you ask for that bread and you munch
> it humbly and gratefully, admitting sadly to yourself that
> this is your sane and proper diet, that all those fancy dishes
> were unwholesome. . . . It was certainly wholesome. It was
> so wonderfully horribly drearily wholesome that the mere
> prospect of it made me want to weep. (24–25)

Stephen's description of Quaker style as "plain bread" provides Isherwood with the opportunity to distance himself from the earnest aesthetics of protest as "wonderfully horribly drearily wholesome." Like Stephen, Isherwood was also oppressed by Quaker tackiness when he volunteered in Haverford, Pennsylvania, at a European hostel during World War II, the original source of what would eventually become *The World in the Evening*. One gay couple, John Judkyn and Dallas Part, became the models for the characters who would eventually become Charles Kennedy and Bob Wood. "Judkyn," he wrote, "interests me because he has become a Quaker without giving up his urban chic, upper-middle-class tastes: he is still the kind of elegant, well-tailored youngish man you meet at New York Cocktail parties."[14] Isherwood's description of their dining room—"decorated with early nineteenth-century French wallpaper, bought for a stiff price at a New York auction: John and Dallas have a standing argument, because Dallas insisted on papering the room with the pineapple frieze upside down. Their court cupboard. Their Crown Derby. Their pseudo-Chinese chairs from the Royal Pavilion at Brighton"[15]—grants a vision of the habitus of New York gay men, New York camp inserted into Quaker protest.

When Isherwood was in Haverford, he had an even more blatant emissary of New York gay culture. Pete Martinez, a "friend" of Lincoln Kirstein's, was a ballet dancer who moved into the refugee house. He embarked on a sexual relationship with Isherwood and camped unashamedly: "At five o'clock, I happened to meet him in the hall and asked him what kind of a day he'd had. 'Darling,' he exclaimed, for the benefit of several people who were listening, 'if you don't kiss me I shall *scream!*' Pete is certainly an unusual figure for Haverford—with his fluttering black eyelashes, flashing white teeth, ballet gestures, and the scarf which he winds around his mouth like a yashmak—but Haverford takes him very well."[16] Pete, as such, doesn't make an appearance in *The World in the Evening*, except as the much-derided emblem of low camp, "a swishy little boy with peroxide hair." Although, as I discuss later, Isherwood played it safe with his incorporation of New York gay culture, the New York camp Martinez embodied remained central to his vision of the novel.

Camp, then, is Isherwood's solution to protest's lack of style, and Charles Kennedy (modeled on Lincoln Kirstein) becomes camp's spokesman in the novel: "What I'm talking about is High Camp. High Camp is the whole motional basis of the ballet, for example, and of course of baroque art. You see, true High Camp always has an underlying seriousness. You can't camp about something you don't take seriously. You're not making fun of it; you're making fun out of it. You're expressing what's basically serious to you in terms of fun and artifice and elegance" (106). Isherwood's insistence that the exaggerated artificiality of camp can have a serious purpose was a direct rebuke to the earnest, high moral tone of American literary criticism during the 1950s. Both the New Critics and the New York intellectuals sought out great American novels with somber, universal themes and self-consciously literary prose. Even Saul Bellow, long a favorite of the *Partisan Review* and touted as the most talented novelist of the 1950s, provoked ambivalent responses when he abandoned the more controlled prose of *Dangling Man* and *The Victim* for the exuberant, bawdy, and funny *The Adventures of Augie March,* published in 1953.[17] Bellow mocked the attitude in a letter to Alfred Kazin: "Comedy is illegal—it isn't even seen—it *isn't*. In low-seriousness no one laughs until the cue is given and then asks grandly, 'Now, why was it appropriate to laugh.'"[18] If the most celebrated novelist of the 1950s, safely American and heterosexual (though uncomfortably Jewish for some), ran afoul of the literary establishment, Isherwood's own struggles to mainstream camp are unsurprising. Auden summed up the problem succinctly in a letter to Isherwood: "Art is like queerness. You may defend it or you may attack it. But people never forgive you if you like it and laugh at it at the same time."[19] To claim that the literary, like "queerness," can be serious and laughable was anathema to the literary establishment in the 1950s.

When Isherwood began *The World in the Evening,* he wrote Lincoln Kirstein that he had "started a novel secretly entitled Too Queer to be Quaker."[20] That title suggests the merger of the earnest middlebrow strategies of the gay protest (Quaker) with the camp qualities of artifice, elegance, and humor (queer). His challenge in writing paralleled Bob Wood's challenge in his painting: "I thought I could see in them the conflict between Bob's birthright Quakerism and Charles's 'High Camp.' Perhaps the creation of 'Quaker Camp' would be the only possible solution to Bob's problems, both as a human being and a painter."[21] Similarly, Isherwood's middlebrow camp would solve his own problems with American authorial identity.

High culture—ballet, the symphony, opera, abstract expressionist art, experimental writing—was central to the New York milieu that Lincoln Kirstein embodied, and Isherwood's mention of the ballet in his definition of camp gestures toward this emphasis on high culture. Interwar modernism was another fetish of both New York culture and Cold War aesthetics. Stephen Spender was dining out on his reminisces of the Bloomsbury crowd to assert his own cultural capital, particularly in his 1951 autobiography *World within World.* Isherwood embeds his own modernist credentials in *The World in the Evening* through Elizabeth Rydal, based on the writer Katherine Mansfield, and cameos by T. S. Eliot (68), Virginia Woolf (84), and E. M. Forster (86). This narrative of modernist brilliance frames an appropriate backdrop for Isherwood's camp.

Modern architecture also appears as a queer aesthetic. The house of Charles and Bob is described as an idyllic domestic space, "a dramatically angled modern building of redwood and glass. The living room was cantilevered out from the hillside so that the end of it looked like the bridge of a ship, with an outside gallery that was at least thirty feet above the ground. Bob used to do hand stands on the rail of this gallery when he had had a few drinks" (259). Isherwood claims a domestic space for gay characters, but he remakes it as well. Their sleek modern home, reminiscent of Jim Charlton's architectural style, rejects the fussy knickknacks of Sarah's domain. The home is like the prow of a ship, suggesting the navy, another all-male environment.

Isherwood also camps in dialogue between Charles and Bob, which he described as a "boys-will-be-girls facetiousness."[22] An early exchange between Charles and Bob epitomizes the camp tone:

"A surrealist, indeed! Doesn't he know a primitive when he sees one? Bob's a dog primitive."

"I paint with my paw," said Bob, "in various styles. I'm the canine Cezanne, the pooch Picasso, the mongrel Matisse. . . ."

"Sure you are." Charles patted Bob's shoulder, as though he were trying to soothe an hysterical patient. "*And* the tyke Toulouse-Lautrec. Don't be scared of him, Stephen. He gets these attacks quite often, especially when he's in company. I see I shall have to take him home now, and muzzle him. Then he'll sleep it off in his kennel. He's really perfectly harmless."

"Don't worry, Steve." Bob had started to laugh idiotically. "Want to know something? My Braque's worse than my bite."

Charles rolled his eyes upward in mock despair. "I'm terribly sorry, Sarah. I do apologize for this painful scene." (58–59)

This passage marks Isherwood's attempts to capture the inflections of New York camp. The highbrow allusions to modern art (Braque, Cézanne, Picasso, Matisse, Toulouse-Lautrec) are mixed in with puns and wordplay; Bob and Charles love high culture and make fun of it at the same time.

In a deleted scene, Isherwood connects that sense of style to the Cold War bogeyman, "the Homintern":

"Of course it's a banana leaf," Charles said. "The emblem of the Homintern. A fig leaf would be too small. A leaf of grass is too obvious. So we chose the banana, because it isn't straight."

"This is all double-talk to me," I said. "What's the Homintern?" . . .

"The Homintern," Charles continued, "is the Homosexual International. The real menace to bourgeois society; the communists' private dread. As a matter of fact, Hitler, Stalin, Churchill and F.D.R. have just had a deadly secret meeting in the Azores, to decide what's to be done about it."[23]

Charles's facetious discussion—with phallic images of bananas and oblique references to Whitman ("leaf of grass")—embeds serious critique under a ridiculous exterior. Since Charles, elsewhere, rejects "we're queer because we're queer" militancy, his discussion of the Homintern is clearly a rebuke of Cold War homosexual panic. Style has internationally significant consequences in this camp fantasy.

Isherwood's reviewers, unfortunately, were not particularly impressed with his style. The novel's structure, readability, and earnestness led many reviewers to dismiss it as a women's novel. Edward Weeks claimed that "Mr. Isherwood has sagged to a level not greatly above that of the more earnest-minded best sellers serialized in the women's mass magazines," and he suggested that "the movie makers should find here a perfectly dreamy scenario for one of the hollow and pretentious dramas of psychological regeneration with which Hollywood self-righteously pays its due to Freud and Mammon."[24] British reviewers agreed. Kingsley Amis termed *The World in the Evening* "a perfectly acceptable second-grade American novel, tops for readability, okay on human-interest-quotient, a bit paunchy in regard to conflict and selling short on humour; general rating *Fairly Good Entertainment*."[25]

Richard Hayes, in *Commonweal,* even cited Cyril Connolly's famous dismissal of Isherwood in his panning of the novel: "In *Enemies of Promise* . . . Mr. Cyril Connolly anticipated this damaging possibility, foresaw how Isherwood's colloquial brilliance might betray him into a 'fatal readability.' And *The World in the Evening* is never less than readable: indeed, a bland cinematic wash of *expertise* overlays all its smooth and unexceptionable surfaces. Precisely this gloss, however, dilutes the impact of incident, blurs the individual coloring of character."[26] This rejection of the novel because of its sentimentality and slickness suggests that Isherwood's connection to the gay protest novel, and the larger middlebrow culture of letters it represented, would hurt his cultural capital.

The World in the Evening's merger of camp and middlebrow offended something deep at the core of Cold War aesthetics. Writing in Stephen Spender's magazine, *Encounter,* British gay writer Angus Wilson denounced Isherwood's combining of camp and protest in terms that suggest the cultural moment for main-streaming camp had not yet come. Wilson began with the final sentence of the novel—"I really do forgive myself, from the bottom of my heart" (284)—to critique the mix of seriousness and facetiousness that characterizes *The World in the Evening:*

> Forgiveness of oneself is, of course, a spiritual state highly to be desired; but for those who accept the idea of personal guilt—and Mr. Isherwood belongs firmly to the generation of the guilt-acceptors—the deliberate statement of self-forgiving is an act of high seriousness. The slightest hint of triviality either in the conviction of sin or in the belief in its atonement is liable to produce an inelegant impression upon those who are asked to witness the confession.... It is exactly some such chasm between high intention and in-adequate capacity that will, I am afraid, disturb Mr. Isher-wood's admirers who have waited so long for this novel.... A great deal of the novel is highly entertaining, much of it is percipient, some of it very moving, but it is not impor-tant at the level to which it aspires. This does not seem to me in the least degree surprising. Nothing in Mr. Isher-wood's earlier work suggested that either his intellectual powers or his emotional strength would sustain a novel of the kind that could satisfy Dr. Leavis' criteria.[27]

Wilson's utter lack of a sense of humor marks his own literary su-periority and his alliance with the high seriousness of Cold War literary criticism. Indeed, the review applies F. R. Leavis's prescrip-tion for art in the 1948 *The Great Tradition,* which insisted that great novelists were guided by seriousness and moral complexity in their judicious use of form.[28] Obviously, such a formula would read Isherwood's style as trivial and inane. The "self-deprecating facetiousness in which his 'good' characters talk" is a particular default, and Wilson uses the "Dog People" passage quoted earlier in this chapter to suggest that the "two 'queers'" (Bob and Charles) are common and inferior.[29] He even cites the famous passage de-fining "camp" as "arrant nonsense [that] should never be treated seriously, but I fear it is not only Charles and Stephen who do so, but Isherwood himself. It is a nice, cosy substitute for thought."[30] Camp, culturally, was a sign of frivolity in the earnest Fifties. Angus Wilson was a gay writer whose 1953 *Hemlock and After* probably led to his review of *The World in the Evening,* but his rejection of camp—both in this review and in his own writing—suggests how far his own aesthetic was from Isherwood's emerging camp middlebrow.

It wasn't just earnest Cold Warriors who objected to Isherwood's use of camp, however. Lincoln Kirstein didn't think it worked either. He delivered one of the most devastating critiques of the camp dialogue: "I think the queerity is rather ambiguous; happy but not sharp. Somehow if it is as important as it is as tone and atmosphere, the difference between Kennedy (Kirschstein) and Bob,—and Michael should somehow be underlined; I feel Michael much more as a leftist than as a queen. None of them camp; there is the big aria about camp, but they certainly don't do it. Janey is a big camp and very good, and the book ends well, except for a rather perfunctory salute to the American Field Service."[31] "None of them camp": there couldn't be a more thorough criticism of the initial failure of Isherwood's camp middlebrow experiment. But why didn't they camp? What Kirstein suggests is that Isherwood's characters didn't camp because, in the end, he was afraid to make the "queerity" too sharp.

Evolution of *The World in the Evening:* Gay, Interrupted

The World in the Evening went through a number of changes over its long germination. Isherwood first got the idea for a novel in 1943, when he was volunteering at a Quaker home for German refugees. He didn't publish a final, much-changed version until 1954. His "struggle with this horrible bitch of a book,"[32] documented in letters, in his journal, and in his writing notebook, is unsurprising; he was trying to write, simultaneously, an American novel, a "real" novel (by which he meant one with an elaborate plot), and a gay novel. These goals were often at cross-purposes.

Isherwood wanted the book to have a complex structure and multiple characters. His early plans for it encompassed a large cast of refugees, dramatic events, including arson, euthanasia (administered by the doctor), an affair and culminating wedding of the octogenarian Aunt Sarah, a conversion to pacifism and Quakerism, and the dramatic death of Bob—at which point the doctor and Stephen would run away together. This elaborate plotting suggests Isherwood's love of Dickens, but it also reflects the plots of Hollywood movies, in which he had immersed himself since his immigration. The plotting and characterization were scaled back in the final draft, but sometimes this resulted in a lack of clarity. He struggled with the voice of the novel, which reflected his own problem with authorial identity during this time. He wanted to create some distance from the "I" of the Berlin stories and *Prater Violet,* and although he originally planned to write in the third person, he ended up writing the novel from Stephen's point of view. Letters provide us with some of Elizabeth's perspective, but that is the only reprieve from Stephen's narration, told in a manner suspiciously similar to the "Christopher Isherwood" of his previous three novels. He wrote in 1950: "Let me admit: I'm caught in a cleft between my 'Christopher Isherwood' reportage manner—reporting for the sake of reporting—and the new manner I'm trying for in this book. I've got to be bold, and not get scared of having a plot. Reportage is a bog in which I'll stick."[33] In the end, Isherwood felt that his attempt to write a first-person narrative as someone other than himself, and someone he didn't like, was an insurmountable problem in *The World in the Evening.*

Isherwood's biggest challenge, however, was to write about homosexuality explicitly and positively, without sacrificing his own cultural capital by being identified as a gay writer. In 1950, he conceived of a gay novel that used bisexuality to extol coming out: "I now see that Stephen is a bisexual. (The degree to which this notion scares me only proves that I'm on the right track.)"[34] Isherwood sought to bring Stephen to an understanding of his homosexuality: at first, "he has become aware of his homosexual urges and has indulged them in various affairs—but always in a dirty because irresponsible way. He has always felt that what he was doing was wrong. He has refused to fall in love with any boy or man and has treated his homosexual exploits as childish naughtiness." His marriage to Elizabeth failed because "He just didn't find her very attractive in that way," and she was "ghastly jealous, and eternally on the watch for the attractive boys, and girls, who menaced the relationship." His rage over Jane's affair in the doll's house came because "he liked the boy Jane was with. And that she'd made the boy because she knew Stephen liked him." Finally, in Isherwood's 1950 vision of the novel, "He falls in love with Dr. Kennedy."[35]

In this version of *The World in the Evening*, Stephen's homophobic loathing for Roy Griffin (so incongruent with his later casual acceptance of Charles and Bob) stems from his own attraction to Roy. Jane picks up Roy, in fact, precisely because she knows that Stephen wants him—and Stephen's inability to admit this fact leads to his vitriol against the "poor miserable pansy bastard." Isherwood makes this attraction explicit in a scene he later deleted; Stephen has a dream in which the "doll's house" becomes an emblem of the closet. In the dream, Stephen decides that "he was going to disgrace Jane and himself. He was going to do the thing which could never be pardoned. He would open the doll's house. It was right there, in the midst of the crowd; but the guests were disregarding it deliberately. They knew that Jane was inside it, but they wouldn't admit that they knew. There was some contemptible social convention involved. As long as they pretended the doll's house wasn't there, it wasn't."[36] Stephen's destruction of the doll's house reveals not Roy but Bob Wood, a more positive, less loathsome version of gay life. Although the dream ends ambiguously, with Bob's anger, Jane's lies, and a dog licking his ear, it also suggests Stephen's necessary transformation in the novel, and his acceptance of himself. He must open the doll's house and reveal his sexuality to move beyond self-loathing to self-acceptance.

Isherwood, in other words, envisioned a novel much like James Baldwin's *Giovanni's Room*, but without the tragic ending. This fact explains the remaining architecture of the novel: Michael is referenced repeatedly in the novel, before the reader has been introduced to him, and the full details of their relationship are saved until near the end of the novel. The opening sequence—Jane's affair with a "pansy"—and the closing, symmetrical scene—the revelation that Roy had made a pass at Stephen—provide a perfect coming-out symmetry. Bob and Charles serve as role models and mentors for the coming-out process. Unlike Baldwin, Isherwood originally imagined a happy conclusion for the novel, with

Stephen and Charles ending up together. But the crucial epiphany never happens. We see Stephen's affair with Michael, but then he moves on to Jane. He doesn't even admit, in the final scene, that his attraction to men has ever been anything more than "theoretical." This absence accounts for the puzzling aspects of the novel, not the least of which is the character of Stephen himself. During revision, Isherwood backed away from the coming-out narrative, watering it down and making it secondary, so that in the end Stephen's moment of clarity was completely opaque. It isn't an accident that Stephen's destruction of the doll's house didn't make the final cut. *The World in the Evening* is a coming-out story in which the main character never comes out; "its queerity is rather ambiguous," as Lincoln Kirstein astutely noted.

Isherwood suffered a failure of nerve, which partly stemmed from his uncertainty about his new American audience. Once he had his central insight, he allowed his friends to scare him away from his original design. Dodie Smith kept steering him away from writing a queer novel. "I liked all the other people, too," she wrote, "particularly the doctor. And I always liked your idea of treating homosexuality that way—bringing it in as only one facet of the story, instead of blowing trumpets and saying 'Make way for the great daring novel.' "[37] She included a long passage about the "ordinary public" that "may also be a bit set back on its heels by the general attitude to homosexuality, which is brilliant and most true. I do have a slight feeling that you ought to put in a bit more explanation—and, in a way, justification for homosexuals. As it is, you adopt the most sophisticated attitude in the world. It is an attitude which seems right and true to people who either are homosexuals or have many homosexual friends. But it will be very astonishing for the people to whom a homosexual is still something strange and unknown. Again, that ordinary public!"[38] Smith's tolerant facade projects her own discomfort onto the "ordinary public." This was a particularly effective rhetorical move, because Isherwood didn't have a clear sense of his American audience. The gay protest novel seemed to provide an opening, but it still didn't give him an understanding of the "ordinary public," and thus, Smith's invocation of it had a chilling effect on Isherwood's writing. These multiple voices grew increasingly difficult to manage as revisions continued.

Speed Lamkin provided another mitigating voice. Indeed, Smith attributed Isherwood's trouble with *The World in the Evening* to Lamkin, warning, "If he *has* discouraged you, do please remember that, though he is a nice bright child, he is not a reliable critic. He has an ounce of talent only, and that ounce has been nurtured on the demands of the slicks."[39] Given Smith's own negative influence, this warning is ironic, but also accurate. That Isherwood's often-squeamish straight friend Dodie Smith led him away from "the great daring novel" is perhaps to be expected. But Isherwood received similar advice from "flaming pansy" Speed Lamkin. After reading a draft, he wrote, "Also the lesser Michael screwing could go, and you could tone down the Kennedy-Wood affair. You don't want to give the reader the impression that this is The Isherwood Report on Sexology."[40] Lamkin's reference to the Kinsey report did its work. The shadow novel of *The World in the Evening* remained embryonic because Isherwood largely degayed the novel. He omitted the coming-out scene and cut the Homintern sequence quoted earlier.

Whatever gay inflections remained were criticized by Isherwood's editor, Robert Linscott. He wrote in an initial letter that "it's the false (to me) heartiness of Bob Wood that makes me most uneasy,"[41] and gave more extensive criticisms in a subsequent missive:

> In the Bob-Charles scenes, it's the boisterousness of Bob that I query. Yes, I know this excess masculinity is common enough, but it bothers me in real life because it seems essentially false and it bothers me even more spelled out in print. Such phrases, for example, as:
>
> > "Stop talking crap." "You're pretty God damn broad-minded." "Why do you think I stick around this dump?" "It does something for the old curves." "Lap up joy juice." "Jesus, how unworthy of me can you get." "He'll drag your holiest secrets down into the gutter and mash them with his hooves." And the whole episode of their meeting (pages 288–290).

> I must confess that I sound a little foolish even to myself
> in quoting them because, one by one, they sound strictly
> natural, but somehow the cumulative effect is distasteful.[42]

Linscott's aversion to the tone of these exchanges is somewhat surprising. His correspondence with Truman Capote is just as campy, if not more so, and Linscott showed no such squeamishness; indeed, his delight in Capote's description of the International Daisy Chain was unbridled. Of course, frank private talk in letters is one thing; public literary embrace of that same tone is another. (Capote, at this point in his career, kept an almost mockserious "literary" tone in his novels.) Even in his objections Linscott is closeted; he criticized the "excess masculinity" of Isherwood's phrases, not their gayness. Isherwood agreed to "rewrite everything about Charles and Bob,"[43] and though a number of these passages remained unchanged, his confidence was shaken.

Isherwood came to agree with Kirstein's assessment of the novel's failure to camp. The last line of the novel was, for Isherwood, where the omission of camp was most glaring: "At the very end of the book, Stephen says, 'I . . . forgive myself from the bottom of my heart,' but his tone rings false. The words were actually Christopher's; he had once said them to Iris Tree, but in a quite different, campy playacting tone, with a deep comic sigh, when they were talking about sin: 'God knows, Iris, *I* forgive myself— from the *bottom* of my heart.' After which they had both roared with laughter. When Stephen speaks the line one doesn't laugh. One is embarrassed."[44] Isherwood's admission of failure in *The World in the Evening* became a reflexive gesture in his later years, but I think he is right about the end of the novel. And the reason was that, as he wrote later in *Lost Years,* the novel was "half-assed" (182). In the end, it didn't have the courage of his convictions.

Isherwood struggled for years to merge camp with American earnestness. His first foray, through the gay protest novel, led to a bruised reputation with the highbrow literary establishment. Things were about to improve dramatically, however. The publication of *The World in the Evening* brought Isherwood two unexpected boons: paperback reprints and through them, gay American readers.

❖ 3 ❖

"Fagtrash": Pulp Paperbacks and Cold War Queer Readers

THE PUBLICATION OF *THE WORLD IN THE EVENING* DIDN'T bring Christopher Isherwood the accolades he wanted, despite his careful cultivation of a prestige press, Random House, which published W. H. Auden, William Faulkner, Truman Capote, and Stephen Spender, and the well-regarded literary agency Curtis Brown. *The World in the Evening* led to an enthusiastic American gay readership, not through the original hardback edition but through the paperback reprint. Isherwood was thus enmeshed in one of the most lucrative and debated movements in Cold War print culture: the "paperback revolution."

The rise of paperback books in the United States[1] began with Robert de Graff's Pocket Books in 1939, but the Armed Services Editions created a large market for paperback books during World War II.[2] Other competitors hoped to build on this success: Avon Books formed in 1941, and Popular Library and Dell Books were issuing paperbacks by 1943; the New American Library published Signet Books, which was another important player, as were Ballantine and Fawcett books. Avon won a key court case against Pocket Books in 1944, and postwar paperback publishing became a free-for-all, with high royalties and extensive competition for lucrative paperback titles.

Historians rightly note that this "revolution" was an innovation not of technology but of marketing, because paperback book publishers used magazine distributors, not bookstores, and so were available through drugstores and newsstands. The salacious covers of these paperbacks were the most visible aspect of the paperback explosion in Cold War America. Women in various stages of undress dominated the cover art; "even the most casual

observer of cover designs," Bonn suggests wryly, "must have wondered why the shoulder straps of women's dresses and brassieres
were always loose, slipping, or undone."[3] These covers, Bonn suggests, "instilled in the American popular mind a sleazy image of
paperback books."[4] Much of the content of Cold War paperback
books was equally transgressive. Sex was a recurring theme across
genres—gangster, detective, western, romance, science fiction.
Michael Bronski notes that pulp paperbacks featured "illegal or
taboo sex—adultery, prostitution, rape, interracial relationships,
lesbianism, male homosexuality—topics that were, in the words
of the cover-copy writers, 'controversial,' 'explosive,' shocking,' and
ready to 'reveal the sordid truth in a way you have never read before.'"[5] Cold Warrior Malcolm Cowley identified three categories
of contemporary fiction: "the Tobacco Road category," "Deviant
or Off-Beat Sex (or well-of-loneliness)," and "Proletarian Sex."[6]
These salacious covers and narratives prompted police raids, in-
vestigations, and congressional hearings.

The Cold War's larger homosexual panic fueled much of this
official concern about "deviant" sex, particularly the widespread
distribution of "well-of-loneliness" fiction, or what Susan Stryker
calls queer pulp, which included paperback originals and hardback reprints. Lesbian pulp has received most of the critical attention, and while paperback originals predominated, some—
including Jo Sinclair's *Wasteland* and Patricia Highsmith's *The
Price of Salt*—were originally published in hardback. The gay
protest novels I discussed in chapter 1, reviewed in literary magazines and published by prestige presses, had another (and often
much more lucrative) life in paperback reprints, where they were
just as trashy as their lesbian sisters. Susan Stryker's collection
of gay pulp covers makes this translation clear: pulp versions of
Hall's *The Well of Loneliness, The Kinsey Report,* Vidal's *The City
and the Pillar,* and Capote's *Other Voices, Other Rooms* made no
distinction, in presentation, at least, between literary writers and
hacks. This is true even of writers like Gore Vidal, Christopher
Isherwood, and James Baldwin, whose literary reputations have
survived beyond the 1950s.

To consider queer pulp as part of a larger cultural trend of pulp
paperbacks reframes many assumptions about gay life and gay lit-

erary production during the Cold War. Queer pulp may have marketed gay life as "shadowy" and marginal, but the books were marketed openly and widely available. Cold War gay print culture was visible, lucrative, and influential, even if it wasn't celebratory. It also contributed to a larger breakdown of cultural hierarchy in its leveling of literary reprints and paperback originals. It was the threat this lack of distinction posed to Cold War cultural hierarchies that worried Cold Warriors like Malcolm Cowley, much more so than deviant sex. Cowley's description of a paperback bookstore highlights his concern about discrimination in brow level: "It was rich, random, gaudy, vital, corrupt, and at the same time innocent; it put culture at the disposal of the plain man, even the poorest, for less than the price of a bar whisky; it was impersonal, friendly, egalitarian, and it proclaimed as dogmas its lack of discrimination. 'Here we are,' the books in the big racks seemed to be saying, 'the mud and sapphires of our time, and for one or two pieces of silver you can take your pick of us.'"[7] Cowley's concern about cultural hierarchy echoes those of Cold War intellectuals: democratic access equals an utter "lack of discrimination," one that cultural critics saw as the biggest threat to American cultural life. As David Earle astutely notes, "What Cowley is doing in these pages is policing the cultural borders between elite literature and popular literature. He is, as it were, protecting his own intellectual and professional stake in American culture and letters."[8]

Many writers felt a similar need to protect their turf. While Cold Warriors were creating cults of appreciation around a few writers, paperback publishers treated authors like other wage laborers. In their reprint business, paperback publishers paid a flat fee in royalties to hardback publishers, who split the money with their authors; once paperback companies bought the book, they did what they wanted with it, often giving the author no say about the cover of the book or abridgment. Highbrow authors were indistinguishable from writers of paperback originals such as Mickey Spillane; Jean-Paul Sartre and Spillane were on the same rack, available for the same twenty-five cents. A remarkable number of writers being canonized during the Cold War appeared in paperback reprints, including James Joyce, William Faulkner, and Ernest Hemingway.

Isherwood, a self-proclaimed "literary snob,"[9] was just as brow conscious as hypermasculine Cold Warriors like Cowley; he held a long-standing grudge against the paperback industry for slighting his own carefully constructed literary persona. His struggles to control his own authorial brand came to a head when it was time for Random House to assign the reprint rights for *The World in the Evening.* Isherwood weighed in on the decision with his agent, Alan Collins, dismissing Avon: "I will never again have anything to do with the unspeakable Avon people after their disgraceful behavior."[10] Avon Press reissued his novella *The Last of Mr. Norris* in 1952 as a spy/adventure story; Avon was positioned culturally as a publisher of detective stories, which explains how the company marketed his novel. Avon also had a habit of abridging novels without permission. Two paperback publishers did interest Isherwood, however: Frank Taylor of Dell Books (and a model for Stephen Monk) and Victor Weybright, who worked for the New American Library, publisher of Signet Books.[11]

Weybright was particularly appealing to Isherwood. A well-known and powerful figure in New York publishing, Weybright liked to play the part of gentleman farmer; his memoir *The Making of a Publisher* begins with a romantic portrait of his small-town roots and underscores his interest in farming and his weekend trips to his childhood farm in Maryland. That emphasis on agrarianism and conservation, he claimed, helped him value the intelligence of the general public and dedicate himself to publishing quality books. After stints at the Butterick Publishing Company (which published pulp magazines and books) and the *Survey Graphic* magazine in the 1920s and 1930s, Weybright worked for the Office for Strategic Services (the forerunner of the CIA) in London during World War II. His numerous contacts with publishers and writers paid off handsomely; Allen Lane, director of Penguin Books, wanted him to take over the New York branch after Ian Ballantine left to start his own rival company.[12] Editorial differences parted Weybright and Lane, and by 1949, Weybright had formed the New American Library, which published its fiction as Signet Books.

Signet Books was known as the "most literary of the mass market publishers," and its writers included William Faulkner, George

Orwell, D. H. Lawrence, Truman Capote, James Baldwin, Boris Pasternak, and Flannery O'Connor.[13] Certainly, this was how Weybright liked to portray himself—a visionary whose commitment to quality writing earned him a well-deserved literary reputation. As he wrote at the end of his score-settling memoir, "I had run the gauntlet and emerged with proof, widely acknowledged, that widespread cultivation of new and habitual readers of inexpensive books does not lead to vulgarization and the lowest denominator of quality."[14] There is no question that Weybright's reprinting of modernist classics made a crucial cultural intervention; he published Faulkner before Malcolm Cowley's *The Portable Faulkner* appeared in 1948, and he went to court to defend Lawrence's *Lady Chatterley's Lover* from an obscenity charge, making these books available outside urban areas.

It's not entirely clear when Isherwood first met Victor Weybright. Weybright made frequent trips to Hollywood and could easily have met Isherwood after World War II. But he clearly knew him by 1952 through *New World Writing,* which billed itself as a contemporary little magazine, publishing the most promising, high-quality writers.[15] The opening chapter of *The World in the Evening* appeared in the inaugural 1952 edition of *New World Writing.* This may be why Isherwood wanted to give Weybright the rights to the novel, despite that fact that Weybright's bid was three thousand dollars lower than the bid from Popular Library. Isherwood explained his reasons in a letter to Robert Linscott at Random House: "Victor Weybright has always been anxious to establish a publisher-author relationship with his writers, similar to those which exist between hard-cover publishers and their authors. Of course, this relationship is not legalized by contract; but, still, it seems to me a good idea in principle—since I firmly believe that publisher and author should stick together as a team and feel themselves responsible to each other and bound together by ties of friendship as well as business interest."[16] Isherwood wanted monogamy, of a sort, with his paperback publisher, even though this relationship could not be formalized by contract. Such fidelity would help him maintain cultural capital even in his paperback reprints, through a faux marriage.

Weybright's New American Library, however, was a strange

place to look for either literary prestige or noncommercial relationships. Signet's book covers were among the most lurid on the market, which may have contributed to Weybright's break with Allen Lane; Weybright recounts in *The Making of a Publisher* that Allen Lane was "fussy about cover designs in the United States which . . . were sometimes revelatory of female anatomy and amatory desire" (13). Indeed, Weybright's fiction was often similarly revelatory, emphasizing "off-beat sex." Signet's best-selling authors were Erskine Caldwell, Mickey Spillane, and Ian Fleming, all of whom featured transgressive sexuality. In fact, it may well have been sex that created the Signet modern canon, uniting Spillane and Caldwell with Faulkner and Lawrence. So important was sexuality to Signet's financial success that Weybright asked authors to sex up their titles. He proudly describes persuading Ludwig Lewisohn to change the title of *The Case of Mr. Crump* to *The Tyranny of Sex* (204); "the book," he concludes, "was a tremendous success, selling over a million copies" (205).

But it wasn't just the interest in sex that complicated Weybright's gentleman publisher facade. Read between the lines of Weybright's memoir, and you discover that his "high-quality fiction" was not the developing modernist canon of Lionel Trilling. Weybright published Faulkner, but he spent just as much time in his memoir discussing James Farrell and Erskine Caldwell, both of whose literary reputations were in decline during the Cold War; Farrell, particularly, was dismissed in the *Partisan Review* for his naturalism. Weybright published Mickey Spillane and he defended the literary merit of Spillane's work, planting an article in *New World Writing* that noted "the resemblance of Spillane's themes to folklore and to the fairy tales of the Brothers Grimm. His cruel justice served as a catharsis, and dispelled aggressive tendencies by vicarious means."[17] It is remarkable how many Signet writers have fallen off the literary map since 1966, when *The Making of a Publisher* came out. Weybright considered his acquisition of Ian Fleming as compelling a piece of evidence about his discerning literary genius as his republication of William Faulkner.

Weybright's wandering brow suggests the fragility of the Cold War attempt to police cultural hierarchy, and complicates Cowley's assumptions about discernment and quality. Pulp paperbacks rebuked the Cold War modernist canon, replacing it with an egalitarian marketplace that made the assessment of literary merit more difficult. It isn't, as Cowley claimed, that paperbacks erased distinction, but that readers, not authors, insisted on the right to make their own distinctions and to read for different purposes. Quality cuts across genre and brow level, and publishers, Weybright believed, shouldn't decide for readers. He made this point when discussing which books to publish in Africa; a "promising and well-educated young African" argued that "Africans had as much right to read Mickey Spillane as the Europeans did. He suggested that we make available every sort of book for which we had selling rights in East Africa to all readers."[18] Weybright's claim suggests that the labels highbrow, middlebrow, and lowbrow ultimately tell us less about the texts themselves than about a particular reading community's anxieties and assertions of hegemony.

That concern with the bottom line prevented Isherwood from working with Signet. Weybright refused to match Popular Library's higher offer and instead released Isherwood from their verbal agreement. His letter about this to Isherwood provides an incisive, if self-serving, commentary on the status of paperback publishing in 1954:

> Even though New American Library is probably the most flourishing enterprise in the paperbound field, we are experiencing great difficulty with fiction except those books which have momentum, promotional handles such as film tie-ins, overwhelming critical acclaim, or that intangible "vibration" which reaches beyond the normal book audience to the everyday folks in Main Street and the Bronx, which are without book shops. . . . "Chris hasn't yet reached the position where, like Willie Maugham, his name would attract hundreds of thousands of Signet readers" . . . That was so brutally frank that I didn't have the heart to paraphrase it in a letter to you. . . .
>
> Now comes THE WORLD IN THE EVENING. It is a fine book, with the most terrifyingly suspenseful first chapter in any modern novel that I have read—and yet I

am afraid of its fate in the *mass market,* because of the de-
tached subtlety which distinguishes most of the book.[19]

It is interesting that for most "literary" reviewers, Isherwood's
novel was too slick, too pulp, yet for Weybright, it was too subtle,
too literary. Of course, he could well have been using this praise to
justify his low offer for the novel. Weybright complains that "the
newsstand apparatus had become glutted with paper products of
every description in book form," hurting his ability to promote
"books of quality." He ends his letter to Isherwood with a vision of
himself as a kind of cultural missionary that must have appealed
to Isherwood's own Anglo-American crusade: "When the small
book revolution and its claim on the new reading public shakes
down—and shakes out the marginal producers—we shall be a
dominant instrument between creative and scholarly imagination
and the missions of readers beyond the conventional book shops."
Weybright's insidious "we" obscures his refusal to match Popular
Library's offer, suggesting just where cultural capital and profit
making were in his list of priorities.

Isherwood's attempts to control his literary persona in pulp
paperbacks continued to be thwarted during the Cold War. Despite his desire for a close, consistent relationship with one paperback publisher, Isherwood was pressured into accepting the larger
royalty from Popular Library. Robert Linscott assured Isherwood
that "we have been fortunate enough to secure the definite assur-
ance of Popular that they will in no way cut or alter the text and
that they will submit to us for okay the cover and the description.
This is an unusual concession for a reprint house and, in view of
it, I hope you will let us take advantage of this larger offer."[20] Of
course, Isherwood received a request for cuts almost immediately
and had to fight to keep the novel unabridged.

Popular Library's marketing of Isherwood's novels *The World
in the Evening* and *Down There on a Visit* emphasized love triangles and the "decadent" lifestyles of the very rich. A brooding
man, hemmed in on two sides by buxom women, graces the cover
of *World. Down There on a Visit* even adds a moralistic blurb: "A
journey through the private hells of those who try to make a life
of sex, alcohol and drugs." Isherwood was even more unhappy

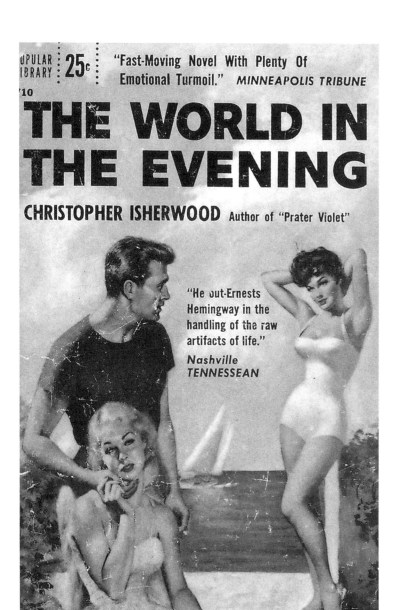

"Fast-Moving Novel With Plenty Of Emotional Turmoil." *MINNEAPOLIS TRIBUNE*

THE WORLD IN THE EVENING

CHRISTOPHER ISHERWOOD Author of "Prater Violet"

"He out-Ernests Hemingway in the handling of the raw artifacts of life."

Nashville TENNESSEAN

Complete and Unabridged

The cover of the Popular Library paperback edition of *The World in the Evening* emphasized love triangles and decadence.

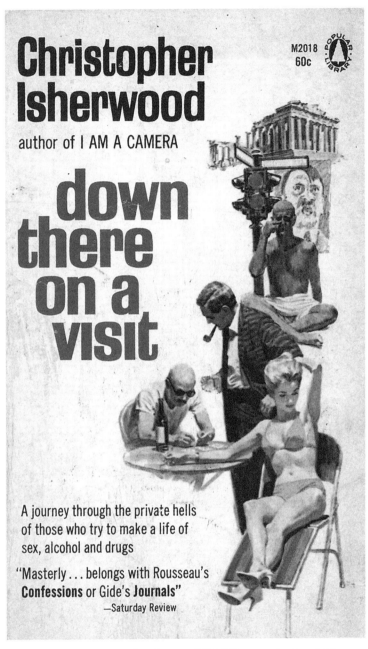

Christopher Isherwood

author of I AM A CAMERA

M2018
60c

POPULAR LIBRARY

down there on a visit

A journey through the private hells
of those who try to make a life of
sex, alcohol and drugs

"Masterly... belongs with Rousseau's
Confessions or Gide's **Journals**"
—Saturday Review

The moralistic blurb was a key feature of Cold War paperbacks, which promised lurid descriptions of "sin" and disapproved of them simultaneously. The implied denunciation of "those who try to make a life of sex, alcohol and drugs" on the paperback cover of *Down There on a Visit* belies the book's content.

with the reprints of *A Single Man* and *A Meeting by the River.*
Only new publisher Lancer books wanted them—a firm known
mainly for science fiction and explicit sexuality (as I discuss in
chapter 7). Isherwood wrote to Perry Knowlton, who had become
his agent in 1959, "I am deeply dissatisfied with the paperback history of my recent books. The last two novels went to Lancer, who
pushed them as semi-pornography, with captions which caused
them to be sold in the hard-core sections of bookstores here, to
vast disappointment of the customers, I should think."[21] Oddly,
the covers of these two paperback reprints strike me as much
more respectable than any of his reprints in the 1950s. They are
primarily black-and-white covers; *A Single Man* has a splash of
lavender in its illustration, but most of the focus is on a review
from *One* (the Mattachine Society's magazine): "The most honest book ever written about a homosexual." Both covers do mention homosexuality explicitly, which may have been part of Isherwood's complaint.

Isherwood's horror at his paperback book persona stemmed
from his authorial dilemma during the Cold War. One particularly telling moment in his memoir *Lost Years* epitomizes his
double bind. Discussing James Barr's *Quatrefoil* (a late 1940s gay
protest novel he declined to review), Isherwood wrote that he
preferred it, in the end, to the quasi-literary pretensions of other
gay protest novels, because at least *Quatrefoil* was "honest fagtrash."[22] "Fagtrash": a host of assumptions underpin this irreverent
coinage. Isherwood assumes that the line between literature and
trash is clear: cultural phenomena that don't claim cultural capital
are harmless diversions, whereas texts that blur these boundaries are the true danger. Isherwood may have consumed fagtrash
enthusiastically, and he may have written fagtrash himself, both
intentionally (in his privately circulated short story "Afterwards,"
which I discuss in chapter 7) and unintentionally (in *The World in
the Evening*), but he still wanted to distinguish "fagtrash" from his
own literary practice. Such differentiation became almost impossible in the paperback book industry, which, as Stephanie Foote
notes, "recalibrated the ways that presses imagined the relationships among 'literary quality,' readership, and profitability."[23] Despite Isherwood's best efforts, simply by including gay content, he
aligned himself with "fagtrash."

"THIS IS THE ISHERWOOD WE HAVE BEEN WAITING FOR.
IT SEEMS TO ME HIS BEST NOVEL."—GRAHAM GREENE

CHRISTOPHER ISHERWOOD

LANCER BOOKS 72-969 **50¢**

A Single Man

"The most honest book ever
written about a homosexual...
about life, death, love, sex...
it would be difficult to
overpraise it." —JAMES COLTON IN ONE

The paperback cover of *A Single Man* was conservative, but its publisher
(Lancer Books, an adult publishing house) and the blurb from *One* magazine (a Mattachine Society publication) marked it as adult entertainment.

Isherwood wanted to incorporate increasingly explicit descriptions of gay characters and a gay ethos in his writing while avoiding the cultural and literary consequences of this decision. The problem of representation in a mainstream environment was fraught for all writers of "sexual deviance." "Homosexual" equaled "perverse" and "pornographic" in the popular imagination; any book that discussed gay issues was, by definition, explicit, even when sex was not openly described. One might conclude, in fact, that to write about homosexuality at all was to write "fagtrash" in Cold War America. This fear of being associated with "fagtrash" continued for Isherwood and led to a convoluted public persona in the 1960s. Isherwood never embraced his paperback identity, but he should have, because it gave him a community of American gay readers.

Cold War Queer Readers and Isherwood

In 1954, after the publication of *The World in the Evening*, Christopher Isherwood wrote to Stephen Spender, "I have lots and lots of fan-mail of the type you can guess. I believe if I gave the word, right now, I could start a queer revolution; they are just longing for a Hitler, poor dears."[24] To compare a scattered group of queer readers to Nazis was a particularly unsympathetic rhetorical move in 1954, but Isherwood quickly made it clear that he didn't quite mean it; indeed, the existence of American gay readers both surprised and moved him: "I don't mean that nastily, and I don't really mean a Hitler. Actually, it's heart-breaking, the sense you get of all these island existences, dotted about like stars and nebulae, all over the great black middle west."[25]

"The great black middle west" was no longer a blank for Isherwood, thanks to gay readers in both rural and urban settings, who shaped Isherwood's American authorial incarnation. Evidence of this relationship comes primarily from preserved letters from readers, which are scattered throughout his correspondence at the Huntington Library. The letters he kept are (with two exceptions) all from men, and of those, a great majority are gay. *The World in the Evening* began what would be an evolving and ongoing correspondence with his readers, a relationship that would affect Isherwood's formal choices in the 1960s.

The comparison to Gore Vidal's campy *Myra Breckinridge* framed *A Meeting by the River* as a salacious paperback novel, as did its alliterative promise of "Hinduism, Hollywood and homosexuality."

A Philadelphia bookseller epitomizes the intensity readers brought to their reading in a 1954 letter:

Dear Mr. Isherwood,

It is very early morning and I have just finished reading *The World in the Evening* for the second time. I've been crying like a baby. . . . I want to write feverishly and unashamedly. But I remember Elizabeth being embarrassed by her "fan" mail . . . and I feel an almost belligerent resentment rising at the thought that authors and readers should be cut off from each other by these artificial walls . . . as though we were somehow enemies instead of partners in the act of creation. But dammitall, I can't sleep for talking to you. So here it is! . . .

I have felt your love as though it were directed personally to me. If you had sat down for all the painful, wonderful hours of your creation with only one thought in mind: What [do I] need more than anything else in the world at this time? . . . if this had been your spur and your goal, as perhaps—in a sense—it was, you could not have fulfilled yourself more completely. To fail to return that love with all its overwhelming gratitude would be a most unworthy denial on my part. . . .

If I could think of a word less abused and more beautiful, I would use it . . . but the word *is* Love. Whether you know it or intended it or want it or even understand it, you have drawn together all things I've known and forgotten (including the pain . . . a great deal of the pain) and made them useful to me . . . because I don't think I can ever really hate again—not even myself. . . .

Thank you forever for *The World in the Evening.*[26]

This bookseller reads *The World in the Evening* in ways that have been defined as middlebrow: he emphasizes his emotional experience reading the novel ("I've been crying like a baby"); he identifies with the narrator explicitly, and personalizes the story ("I have felt your love as though it were directed personally to me"); he talks about the novel as a model for living, a therapeutic transformation ("you have drawn together all things I've known and forgotten . . . and made them useful to me"); and he emphasizes the symbiotic relationship between reader and writer ("I feel an almost belligerent resentment rising at the thought that authors and readers should be cut off from each other by these artificial walls . . . as though we were somehow enemies instead of partners in the act of creation"). Critics of *The World in the Evening* found it slick, trite, and crass, but many readers found it moving and profound, and they told him so directly.

While most letters aren't as detailed, many reflect similar sentiments. The emotion the bookseller experienced is evident in another letter:

> My Dear Mr. Isherwood,
> I Love You. Period.
> I should like to write a much longer exposition, but frankly I do not feel up to meeting the degree of effort or caution needed to properly justify my "worthiness."
> Be it sufficient to note I shall always have a deep and intense personal rapport with your work, your life and, above all, you.
> I should like to think one day I might chance to meet you. For now, then, just another "silly boy."[27]

This reader's desire to prove his "worthiness" suggests a nervous suitor, as does his simple, opening declarative statement: "I Love You." The intense emotion Isherwood inspires in his American readers runs directly counter to many critics' dismissal of Isherwood's formal failures. Whatever these critics found wanting in Isherwood's Cold War novels, readers found exactly what they wanted.

This reader not only "loves" Isherwood, but has "a deep and intense personal rapport with your work, your life and, above all, you," and this identification runs across letters from readers. The Philadelphia bookseller had written, "To say that I *am* Stephen would, I suppose, be absurd and presumptuous. At best, I'm Stephen in the first day of the case . . . or perhaps your book is the truck just running me down in the street. I'm certainly not Sarah, or Elizabeth or

Gerda or Bob and Charles or Michael . . . or even Jane. They are way beyond me. You have helped make them very real to me. But I have such a very long way to go."[28] Identification marks readers' intense emotional experience with Isherwood's novels.

His readers identified not only with his characters but with Isherwood himself, believing that they knew him through his novels. One wrote of a later novel, "With most authors I have great difficulty, either because they are so ceaselessly serious and pretentious as to suffocate lesser souls and make us feel guilty, if we don't like them, of bad taste, even bad faith (Mann and Sartre, in particular—I hope I didn't name your favorite writers), or their novels are so trivial and commercial as to qualify as sophisticated comic books without any pictures. Your books are an exception to the general rule. I have never felt any didacticism in them, but always unvindictive truthfulness."[29] This reader constructs Isherwood as frank and unpretentious, equating his narrative persona with himself. Isherwood encouraged such identification by making himself unusually available to his readers. He tried to respond to every letter he received, and if he didn't succeed, he responded to a remarkable number, which encouraged additional correspondence. He invited them to his house; Don Bachardy explained that readers came to the house often, sometimes making long pilgrimages for that purpose.[30] Christopher Isherwood and Don Bachardy were always listed in the phone book, and sometimes his readers would call him up late on a Saturday night, after fortifying themselves with alcohol for courage. He would sometimes talk to them for an hour.[31] His readers appreciated his openness; one wrote, "Your card was in its tone much more honest and straightforward than I had imagined I should expect. . . . When I proudly displayed your card to my 'colleagues' in one of our local taverns they were impressed with the informality and they suggested that I write in hopes of getting an answer to something that has been a problem to us concerning an experience which we haven't and you probably would understand."[32] Isherwood's accessibility invited his readers to consider him a trusted friend.

That sense of accessibility inspired letters that went beyond hero worship to casual encounters, and the taking of considerable liberties. A teenager pushed this cheeky tone to the limit:

But don't be hard on Trevor, be hard on me . . . please
be hard on me . . . pretty please, (UP BONDAGE!!) Well
cheeky I got a whole lot of answerin' to do after what I've
done . . . all over the Atlantic. But cutie-pie I'm sure you'll
forgive me (wont you just?)

Am I an utter fool, who calls me so? No. No I'm not, I'm
nice and not in the least bit boring (so there.) No I'm not
a pretentious poet, I write good earthy trash-stuff. But let
me tell you sonny, I *respect* them having just read Vedanta
for the Western World, The Song of God and Paddington
Bear. You see I'm a sado-intellectuall [sic].

It's terry firing to think these words are having themselves read by the *greatest* Author (grovel grovel.) It's
amazing these words don't just fade away into the paper in
shame. But no, these are manly words (Never say die if you
can use a lie (KILL KILL) These li'le ol' words *wont* be put
down. No I say. Women of England say Go-Go. We wont
be sat upon. Well O.K. we will. . . .

P.S. JOKE (make you laugh)[33]

Far from offending Isherwood, the teenager's facetious tone rec-
ommended him because of a shared camp sensibility. He veers
from flirting, pandering, and criticizing Isherwood, even making fun of himself for being too praising. This reader was entirely successful in his ploy; he visited Isherwood in California
and corresponded with him for years. That joking tone earned
Isherwood's interest, though many of the letters are much more
earnest.

There are also remarkable offerings in the Isherwood archive.
One interspersed his eight-page letter, complete with lists of likes
and dislikes, with beautiful watercolor drawings.[34] Another from
North Carolina sent him eight portraits of young men who identified as straight and with whom he was having sex. He added
helpfully, "The photos I'm enclosing are 'introductions' to these
boys—for some of them I have naked shots I'd be happy to send.
(Sometimes when I'm knocked over by a guy's looks, I'd really like
to know what his body was like; don't hesitate to ask me for more
photos of any of these guys, or for a different dozen 'samples.')"[35]

Dear Christopher Isherwood

I am fumbling around trying to begin this letter. You see, just a few hours ago - on the advice of Gerard Malanga I met John Halliwell for a drink One drink lengthened into four...

John and I talked about various people we've known in common in New York and California among other places. He firmly suggested that I contact you.

Now that you have an idea of what's coming, may I tell you a little bit about myself?

I am Craig Makler.
My symbol is
♡ the green heart.
I am a poet unknown, unpublished.

People who admire me say the same things as people who mistrust me. They say I'm honest, physically beautiful and smart. I don't know who to believe.

This illustrated letter to Christopher Isherwood from a reader in Philadelphia is an example of the devotion expressed by Isherwood's fans. Reproduced by permission of The Huntington Library, San Marino, California.

The back of each photograph has extensive descriptions of the young man and the sexual acts he enjoys. Here's a sample:

Rick, Eddie, Terry—Three baseball players, friends of one another and good to me. Rick is now married. (photo was taken 10 months ago) but even when engaged couldn't

A reader from North Carolina included several photographs of young men, with explicit descriptions and offers of additional photographs. Reproduced by permission of The Huntington Library, San Marino, California.

get enough blow jobs—would even want me to go into the bathroom with him for a minute if his roommate was here. Ideal trade. Terry is called T-Bone by his friends, and is our best pitcher. Pitches it to me more often than I can count, and enjoys being appreciated for his fine body, dick. Very aloof to people (inc. me) at first, but is a hell raiser.

In the middle is Eddie, Terry's roommate when this was taken. A heart stopper in person. A good buddy to me, but not ready for sex. Yet, anyway. Rick knew about Terry, Terry doesn't know about Rick (I don't think) and Eddie doesn't know about either, which is good. By the way, Rick should be in color, because his eyes are startlingly light blue.[36]

This reader's frank discussion of his "trade" with a famous writer he does not know is surprising, particularly since he tells Isherwood details that even his own lovers don't know about each other. But Isherwood's writerly persona during the Cold War was influenced as much by paperback reprints as by more reputable cloth editions. It is impossible to know how many of his readers encountered him in cheap paperbacks, but considering the small print run of his cloth editions and the extensive range of paperbacks, it is likely that those gay readers in "island existences, dotted about like stars and nebulae, all over the great black middle west" read his books in paperback. David Bergman notes that these books "reached a wide spectrum of readers, as well-educated writers were as interested in them as sweaty teenage boys. . . . Both better-educated and less-educated gay readers came together in the reading of pulp."[37] It well may have been the medium as well as the message of Isherwood's novels that encouraged such intimacies. The reader from North Carolina provides another, less salacious reason:

Your writings let me know you by being so personal and by having so many places where a perceptive reader can read into a situation (by your permission, actually by your willing it) more than what you say. . . .The communication I try for in my photos is what I've gotten from you through your books—that is, I think of you as a hero because you celebrate life the way I see it, too, so that I am your distant relation, brother, son, comrade. I can never repay you with words or gifts for all you've given me, without knowing me. And I want you to know *me* a little, not for my ego, but because I do share with you a kind of love, a kind of mutual feeling. An object from you to me (a book, a photo) or an

object from me to you (personal photos) is an important
sign, a token of shared feeling.[38]

This reader views the photographs as part of a mutual exchange
between reader and writer. In these and other cases, readers pay
respect but demand equality, and insist that they have something
to give back to Isherwood.

Nowhere is this insistence on equality clearer than in the literary offerings in readers' letters. One titled his poem "Love Letter
to Christopher Isherwood":

YOU ARE TOO FOND OF THE EXCLAMATION MARK.
You have never made a sufficient act of contrition
For your sins (who does?). Several of your books are dreadful.
I love you. . . .
Because of your eyes, and because you are hellishly readable:
You draw me on, even at your worst. It won't damn you:
God's not a critic, thank God.
Because you are mistaken and mortal.
Because I loved you before I knew we were both
Homosexual. Because of Sally Bowles. . . .
Yes, because of *Exhumations,* for something
About it has led me to write to you—
Some tone in your voice. Yes, in spite of,
In spite of, in spite of, in spite of—I love you.[39]

He writes a poem in praise of Isherwood but includes a number
of criticisms. Indeed, "in spite of" is the final refrain. Yet far from
being offended, Isherwood kept this letter and continued to cor-
respond with its author.

This reader wasn't asking for feedback on this poem, but a
number of Isherwood readers did want feedback on their writing.
This embedded writing community is one of the most interesting
things about readers' letters to Isherwood. Of course, Isherwood
met would-be writers through his teaching at California universi-
ties, but many readers sent him their literary offerings, particularly poetry and short stories. Isherwood read and responded to
a number of these efforts, quite patiently. Some of Isherwood's

correspondents eventually went on to become published authors. Sailor Leo Madigan's book, the immortal *Jackarandy,* took advantage of loosened markets for gay fiction in the 1970s. Even Isherwood's former lover, architect Jim Charlton, sent him a novel he had written. Isherwood read it carefully, gave feedback, and used his publishing connections to help Charlton get the novel, *St. Nick,* published in 1981 under the pseudonym Jack Challenge.

Not all of Isherwood's would-be writers were so fortunate, especially those writing before gay liberation. The author of the self-published *Kala with Poetic Therapy* wrote Isherwood in 1954, claiming discrimination and pleading for his intervention because the post office had declared his book obscene. The author objected strongly to this designation, claiming that "books which really are obscene, e.g., THE NAKED AND THE DEAD, FROM HERE TO ETERNITY (with its frequent use of the word *fuck*), THIS IS MY BELOVED (with its graphic description of an orgasm during intercourse), and other books ad infinitum (some ad nauseum) go thru the mails freely with the Post Office's awareness and blessing."[40] He included a copy of the flyer that attracted the censors' attention, and this complicated his claim of racial and economic discrimination. Isherwood, of course, could see how the writer made some of his own trouble; the advertisement for the novel began with a bold promise: "My dear Friend: THIS [arrow pointing to text below] is the *FIRST PAGE* of the WORLD'S MOST PUISSANT LOVE STORY! ITS KARACHING LOVING SCENES WILL STIMULATE YOU INTO UNLIMITED BLISS."[41] Its subsequent description included numerous typos and often-incomprehensible details. Isherwood likely believed this novel to be another kind of trash, but he took the time to discuss the work with the letter writer quite seriously: "I agree with you that there is nothing in the novel which could fairly be called obscene, according to current standards and the precedents set up by a number of best-selling books in the recent past. . . . But the presentation of the book is another matter. . . . It reads like an advertisement for some kind of aphrodisiac."[42] Isherwood consistently provided this sort of detailed feedback to his correspondents.

Isherwood's patience would seem remarkable, except that readers were treating him as an equal and a friend, and he, in response,

treated them the same way, reading their literary efforts as seriously as he read his English friends, or his students. He didn't always like his readers' literary offerings, but he responded much as
he did to Stephen Spender, Edward Upward, and W. H. Auden. In
his correspondence with his readers about their writing—much of
it gay themed—Isherwood seems to embrace his readers as fellow
connoisseurs of good writing.

In other words, Isherwood's readers behave like fans, as fan
studies define them. Henry Jenkins's germinal work *Textual
Poachers* argues that fans insist on their right to construct and
invent characters, and they resist attempts by the creators of the
medium to fix meaning.[43] They identify with characters, invest
emotion in them, and very often create their own tributes to these
media through fan fiction and discussion boards. Jenkins emphasized the oppositional nature of such fan identity; they reject a
subordinate status and impose their own meaning and values.
Subsequent fan studies have been more suspicious of this ideal-
ization of fans, finding their interests to be consistent with larger
cultural hierarchies. But in the 1950s and 1960s, when Isherwood
was first discovering his gay audience, gay and lesbian readers
used a variety of print media, popular culture, and fiction to construct oppositional identities. Marilyn Schuster's argument about
Jane Rule's readership is typical, I believe, of this larger focus on
the resisting reader: "The negotiation between writer and reader,
the bond of reading," she argues, "is always in process, always in-
flected by the time of place of both writer and reader."[44]

That identity was grounded in an emotional connection that
exceeds the acceptable boundaries of highbrow aesthetic appreciation. Indeed, recent fan scholarship emphasizes the role of
aesthetics, and the differing understanding of aesthetics, in fan
communities. Jenkins discussed the role of emotion in fandom
in an online interview, contrasting fan engagement with Pierre
Bourdieu's notion of aesthetic appreciation: "Fandom is not about
Bourdieu's notion of holding art at a distance, it's not that high art
discourse at all; it's about having control and mastery over art by
pulling it close and integrating it into your sense of self. And that
is an aesthetic transformation, but it's not the way that discourses
of high art usually operate, although it is a way individuals talk

about their relationship to high art. But you never really see an art critic talk about that moment of passionate transcendence in which they couldn't articulate why they were responding to the music or the painting."[45] More recent fan scholarship has questioned the deferral of aesthetic issues in fan studies, insisting that connoisseurs of highbrow culture could be considered, profitably, as fans. Jenkins's notion of identification and emotional resonance is also true of middlebrow print culture. Both middlebrow and fan studies emphasize the symbiotic relationship between reader and writer. For gay readers of Isherwood, that relationship was grounded in desire, both its satisfaction and its deferral.

Indeed, what Isherwood gained from his readers was, from his perspective, as valuable as what they gained from him. Although Barbara Hochmann argues that twentieth-century writers resisted readers' desires to equate narrator and author,[46] Isherwood apparently never got the memo. His secure place in the literary establishment makes this accessibility even more remarkable. Despite often-vicious reviews, Isherwood's books were always reviewed broadly, and his associations with Auden, Spender, and Forster meant that he could not be simply ignored. That such a writer, accepted (however reluctantly) by a mainstream literary establishment, should be constructing "passionate communities" similar to those of gay pulp writers suggests that our notions of "mainstream" and "oppositional" aren't adequate to account for the complex layering and encoding of gay identity during this period.

Don Bachardy explained Isherwood's remarkable availability to fans this way:

> He was always interested to meet people who were interested in what he'd written, and especially if they were young people and especially if they were young men. He identified with young people and to see what their experience meant to them to see if he could identify with it. He was feeding himself as well as being helpful to them. . . . He really was curious about them, especially if they were interested in him, and especially, as I say, if they were young men, then he could really relate to them on the basis of his own experiences as a young man.[47]

Isherwood imagined his relationship with Cold War gay readers as truly symbiotic: he identified with them as much as they with him.

These extensive encounters with readers had a profound effect on Isherwood's subsequent authorial identity. Isherwood expanded his small group of gay writers to include a transnational cast of gay readers, similarly allied against the Enemy. His sixties novels *can* pass but can also be decoded. He turned his own consumption of popular texts, his own fandom, into a source of his literary production. All that, however, could only flower with the literary and cultural movements of the 1960s.

❖ 4 ❖

Sixties Literature and the Ascension of Camp Middlebrow

THE SIXTIES MARKED CHRISTOPHER ISHERWOOD'S MOST productive decade as an American novelist; after publishing one novel per decade from 1940 to 1960, he published three novels between 1960 and 1967. Certainly an important factor in Isherwood's productivity was the emerging ethos of experimentation and rebellion during the 1960s. While most discussions of the sixties emphasize the Civil Rights movement, SDS, the antiwar movement, and Black Power, Isherwood avoided political protests and mass movements.[1] Even his relations with the emerging gay rights movement in California were measured. Rather than radical politics, the cultural and aesthetic expression of the 1960s fostered Isherwood's literary production. What had been understood as Isherwood's flaws, like his focus on individual experience, his humor, and his embrace of cultural outsiders, became virtues in the emerging sixties ethos. The aesthetic style of the decade prompted Isherwood to experiment with composition, style, and subject matter.

In the sixties, the outsider took a central place in literary culture. Mark McGurl notes "the ironic centrality of the figure of the outsider, both as a threat to social order and as a source of spiritual purity and violent renewal of that order."[2] Isherwood's own self-perception as an outsider had always been central to his writing, and in his lectures to college students in California during the 1960s, he writes himself within that tradition: "From the sublime to the ridiculous, or to the minor, I can say that I myself am more than usually an outsider in certain respects, temperamentally speaking, because I really enjoy being a foreigner. I am a foreigner by temperament, and I've always liked to live in countries other than the one I was born in, because I find that a slight edge of foreignness prevents me somehow from taking life too much for granted."[3] Isherwood's description of himself as "a foreigner by temperament" shows his evolving sense of American authorship. No longer were nice middle-class boys from the Midwest the epitome of the American experience. Now, the quintessential American might be a Native American schizophrenic, or a black queen from Harlem, or a stoned Hells Angel enthusiast on a bender in Las Vegas. A typical American might just be a queer, middle-aged foreigner living in Los Angeles. Isherwood no longer felt the need to construct a fictional "real" American from Philadelphia to write himself into the national imaginary. His own hybrid experience was American enough for the 1960s.

An interview from 1959 shows Isherwood's shift in terms of authorial identity. Asked by interviewer Robert Robinson, "Are you part English now in your idiom, or are you completely American or do you think you have retained your Englishness totally?," Isherwood responded, "I think I am all mixed up. But after all why not be a mixed-up character? Why not be an Anglo/American?"[4] This public embrace of his hybrid status was something new for Isherwood. When asked as a follow-up, "Is it your aim to become American in every respect?," Isherwood retreated from his Americanization mania: "Oh, certainly not. How could it be? . . . California at any rate is a very very mixed place. Los Angeles is full of immigrants from other parts of the States, quite aside from thousand and thousands of foreigners. One feels one has just as much right to be there as anybody else."[5] Strategically positioned in California, Isherwood was no more foreign to American sensibility than the rest of California.

The role of the outsider was expressed through plot and subject matter, but it was also expressed linguistically as a matter of "voice." From avant-garde innovators like Thomas Pynchon, Donald Barthelme, Kurt Vonnegut, Ishmael Reed, and John Barth, to more mainstream literary writers like John Updike, sixties writers created a distinctive style liberated from blind convention. The inspiration for many of these writers was the Beats, particularly Jack Kerouac and Allen Ginsberg. Gore Vidal was horrified by this new generation of writers, and he wrote bitchy letters to Isherwood

about their undisciplined rantings.[6] Isherwood had similarly un-
settling encounters with Ginsberg in the 1960s, calling him and
Peter Orlovsky "demon guests, harpies who descend and wreck
the homes of the fat bourgeoisie with self-righteous malice,"[7] but
he also considered them an important part of his larger network
of American gay writers. Ginsberg's ethos of liberated experimentation and experiential free association began to inspire Isherwood's own composition style in the late 1950s.

Isherwood spent the second half of the 1950s writing an homage to Dante's *Inferno,* featuring an updated Homer and Virgil
traveling through Mexico. Isherwood eventually abandoned this
novel, which he imagined as an elaborate fantasy, but he drew on
its drafts in the composition of *Down There on a Visit* and *A Single
Man.* As interesting as what he wrote, however, is *how* he wrote
that original novel. He explained in his writing journal: "I realize
that this is an experiment—quite a new one for me. I'm trying
to poke my way down to the underground river of subconscious
creation, instead of making plans. . . . And it almost seems I'm
succeeding. Because, as I continue to write this nonsense, some
impatient voice is beginning to tell me how I *ought* to write. The
only thing is, I know I must go on with the intuitive nonsense-
work until the rational brain has been blackmailed into giving up
all its secrets."[8] Isherwood's account of his writing process dis-
avows the careful plotting of *The World in the Evening* and allies
him with the loose experimentation of Jack Kerouac.

This experimentation with voice was intensely personal. Both
reading and writing became a means not only to discover the individual self but to invent or create one; McGurl notes "the period's increasing commitment (even within the avant-garde of
psychotherapy) to the idea that each person should be the creator
of the autonomous 'fiction' of his or her own life."[9] First-person
narration became an explicit literary and ethical value. New Journalism even embraced the centrality of self, rejecting claims of
objectivity and putting the author's subjective experience front
and center. Writing by Tom Wolfe, Truman Capote, Hunter S.
Thompson, Norman Mailer, and Joan Didion emphasized the role
that "I" plays in shaping supposedly objective accounts of facts
and events. By the late sixties, both New Journalists and sixties

experimental writers had abandoned the earnest universalism of Cold Warriors.

Finding one's voice was about breaking taboos, and sex was one of the great taboos of the Cold War; consequently, a new sexual explicitness suddenly became an acceptable vogue in the sixties, fueled by a series of publicized obscenity court cases. In the late fifties, Allen Ginsberg, *One* magazine (a publication of the Mattachine Society), and *Physique* magazine avoided obscenity prosecutions, suggesting a changing legal climate.[10] *Lady Chatterley's Lover* was accused of obscenity in Britain when it was published in 1960, and Isherwood followed this trial with great interest, through letters from Stephen Spender (who attended the trial) and a book about the proceedings.[11] The novel was deemed not obscene. By 1966, even the longest-banned book in U.S. history, *Fanny Hill; or, Memoirs of a Woman of Pleasure,* had escaped censure. The results of these court cases were uneven—sex publishers, for example, were still subject to harassment and lost cases later in the sixties—but the tide had clearly turned. The notion of "community standard" broadened considerably in the 1960s, and this led to the boom in gay pulp, as I discuss in chapter 7, and greater freedom for all writers.

It should be clear from this brief overview how much sixties literary style suited Christopher Isherwood. Isherwood was always famous for his distinctive style—his voice—and his tendency, through first-person narration, to insert himself, or versions of himself, into his fiction. Both his voice and first-person narration led to critical disapproval, and Isherwood himself believed in the late 1940s that his reliance on first-person narration showed a lack of serious purpose and artistic capability. Much of his attempt to write, as he put it, a "real" novel with *The World in the Evening* came from this emerging modernist/New Critical emphasis on conscious structure and impersonal control. Suddenly, what had been considered artistic flaws became positive virtues. Isherwood was similarly invigorated by changes in obscenity laws. He even agreed to testify in a Los Angeles trial about *Tropic of Cancer* because Henry Miller had become a friend. He ended up not being called, which he felt was just as well, since "it's not just Miller's book which I don't find pornographic; I don't believe that there is any such thing as pornography. And I don't believe, for the matter of that, that the young can be corrupted by talk about sex."[12] Isherwood took advantage of greater freedom in the 1960s, writing about sex in all of his sixties novels.

Despite the emphasis in the 1960s on individuality and personal freedom, however, the decade also witnessed the valuing of marginal group identities. Oppressed cultural minorities became potent symbols of the outsider, particularly African Americans; Marianne DeKoven notes that "the most important force underlying the political and cultural phenomena of the sixties in the United States" was "the Civil Rights movement, and its inheritor, sibling, and (to some extent) rival, the Black Power movement."[13] African American culture was important because it became a model for cultural otherness, including the white counterculture.[14] Collective marginal identity animated 1960s literary culture. The outsider could be defined not just by an individual but by a group identity—a collective outsiderness.

This emerging focus on cultural minorities was particularly important for Isherwood because gay political movements in the 1950s and 1960s based their activism on this model. Harry Hay, a Communist and activist, formed the Mattachine Society in 1952 as an underground Communist cell structure that strenuously protected members' privacy; in its original incarnation, it was, quite literally, a Homintern. Hay's definition of gay identity was his most important legacy. As C. Todd White explains, "Chuck Rowland once announced to his cohorts that he would willingly devote his life to the organization, provided they develop some 'sound theory or philosophy' from which they could unify and proceed. Hay replied instantly, 'We are an oppressed cultural minority.'"[15] Harry Hay's innovation was to imagine gay people as a kind of ethnic group, with the same concerns and cultural continuity. This notion took a long time to evolve into a broad-based political and cultural movement, but it was germinating throughout the fifties and sixties.

Isherwood had reservations about this emerging notion of gay identity in the 1960s, as his relationship to the Mattachine Society illustrates. He was invited to submit pieces to early issues of *One*, along with a number of other published writers, but declined.[16]

He wasn't an early gay activist, despite his proximity. Yet by the 1960s, he was clearly aware of the group, especially because Gerald Heard became involved with One, Inc. Heard arranged for Isherwood to speak on February 7, 1965, to a group of activists at the offices of One, Inc.[17] Isherwood's public stance toward homosexuality, however, was not what those activists wanted. A letter from one of them highlights Isherwood's complicated relationship to gay activists and provides a useful corrective to his later rebirth as grandfather of the gay rights movement. Isherwood refused to consider gay rights as at all analogous to "the Civil Rights" battle, and earned a sharp rebuke from one activist present:

> Of course, Mr. Isherwood, there's always Public Assistance and Mental Hygiene Rehab for referral for the poor son-of-a-bitch who has been ruined and can't ever hold a decent job again, who has been branded for the rest of his life. . . . The poor slob who must register every time he breathes and bear endless roustings, be hounded as long as he lives as a registered sex criminal. This ain't the same "Civil Rights"? Not the same, at all, at all, of the second class citizenship of the negro? You are so right! If you believe, at best, the homophile is a sick psychopath who must suffer for his own good and that of the community. . . . This is a war of minorities outside the society of the community.[18]

For the letter writer, the homophile/Negro analogy was so self-evident that to question it was to be ignorant, insensitive, or prejudiced. His impassioned list of outrages, particularly regarding false arrests and imprisonment, made the analogy indisputable for him. Note his language: "a war of minorities outside the society of the community." His minorities are defiant, attacking not just individual wrongs but respectability itself.

And for the activist, Isherwood was the epitome of that suspect respectability. This became clear as the letter writer moved from his impassioned claims about mistreatment and group demonization (something, as a matter of fact, Isherwood knew about, having been arrested in a gay bar in the 1950s and gotten out of it by playing dumb)[19] to a more direct assault on Isherwood:

Mr. Isherwood, I don't know whether you are one of us or not. I never presume on that score. If you aren't, I hope you got whatever you were after from us. A nice, new book, maybe? May it be a great financial success! . . . But, if you are one of us, you are getting yourself into one filthy rotten mess, I warn you. . . . It is later than you think. Fence-sitters might be in for one hell of a surprise! Freedom will tolerate no side-sitters. It is no spectator sport. Freedom is freedom. . . . You are either for it or against it. Tyranny is tyranny. . . .

We, the homophile, are not fighting for "our rights." We are fighting "their" oppression and persecution. The dignity of the human estate is all that matters, Mr. Isherwood; whether it's his skin or expression of his glands and mind that is being used to strip him of it, is quite beside the point. . . . If nothing else, let us take at least one lesson from our black brother. If he had carried a big stick, showed it, and made no bones as to his intention to use it, maybe himself, his women, and his children wouldn't be subjected to beatings and murder today, maybe he would have saved a lot of lives on both sides. . . . No, I don't want to bear arms. . . . But resist I will! And show for all to see, who have eyes to see, that the time is *now,* not tomorrow.[20]

The activist was clearly outraged by Isherwood's refusal to declare himself, even when talking to a group of gay men. The letter writer's implied threats about the coming violence of the gay revolution must have seemed unrealistic and dramatic to Isherwood, who gently satirized such attitudes. Given how open Isherwood was in other areas of his life about his homosexuality, notably, at Hollywood parties, his reticence at One, Inc. suggests a mistrust of the particular strategies of the group, and a careful delineation of public and private declarations.

There isn't any evidence of Isherwood's reply in his archive. He did respond in his diary: "He more or less takes the 'fire next time' Jimmy Baldwin tone of voice. And all because I cautiously said that I didn't think the Negro problem was quite the same as the homosexual problem, and that I didn't think the measures taken by the Negroes were necessarily those which we should take to solve it. So I am accused of fence-sitting. I can't say that I feel guilty of this, because I do stick my neck out quite far, in my own way. But of course a man like [that] (who, incidentally, is on the police force and claims that he has told them he is homosexual) sees 'the struggle' in terms of group action."[21] Isherwood did, of course, "stick my neck out quite far, in my own way"; his Cold War novels mainstreamed gay content in unprecedented ways. In the seventies, he would embrace his "tribe," but in the sixties he resisted the minority argument, even as he quoted the activist's statement about minorities in his diary as "interesting."[22]

Isherwood sometimes tried out similar arguments without implicating himself. An interview from 1965 (the same year he received his letter from the Mattachine activist) highlights the paradox of his public stance in the sixties. He talked about the idea of homosexuals as a minority, which led to a spirited exchange:

> ISHERWOOD. For instance, this book, insofar as it is about homosexuality, is really about a minority. . . .
>
> INTERVIEWER. Now, must we accept the proposition that the homosexual is part of a minority group which has its own rights and privileges?
>
> ISHERWOOD. Whether it has rights and privileges is quite another matter, but it sure as hell is a minority. A persecuted minority. No question of that.
>
> INTERVIEWER. But increasingly one gets the feeling that an organized attempt is being made to gain for homosexuals an official status with rights and privileges.
>
> ISHERWOOD. Well, I don't really know exactly how far this organized attempt would go. There's one very simple objective concerned and that, of course, is to get the law changed. . . . I think most homosexuals would say that once that happened, then they would be very happy to retire into the privacy of their lives and not be heard from as a minority. . . . When they are fighting for equality, which is after all what it amounts to, they are always bound to

overcompensate. I mean that while one is conducting any kind of a campaign, it always goes further than one's objective, and certainly homosexuals are no exception to this rule.[23]

Isherwood is a maddening mix of disingenuousness and defiance. He is both aggressive and accommodating in this exchange—insisting on homosexuals' persecuted status, pointing out the injustice of antisodomy laws, and validating the fight for equality. In this, he seems to have accepted the Mattachine activist's argument about civil rights. Yet Isherwood won't make a direct claim that the minority has inherent "rights and privileges," he frames some activism as overcompensation, and he accepts the interviewer's distaste. He even suggests that homosexuals will go away quietly once sodomy laws are lifted; equality lay in the right to privacy, not public recognition. Isherwood discussed "those" homosexuals, as if "their" fight for rights were not his as well. Add to that his vexing insistence, in this same interview, that "I have never written 'about' homosexuality. . . . I really have never written about homosexual love, for instance, or homosexual relationships, or anything of the kind as the theme of a book or story."[24] Part of that claim was to avoid the interviewer's bullying, who did everything but ask, "Are you homosexual?" Talking about homosexuality is exactly what Isherwood does in his Cold War American writing. He wants to claim these stories as universal, not just homosexual, but he can't quite bring himself to claim them as both at the same time. In the 1960s, Isherwood couldn't accept the idea of homosexuals as an "oppressed cultural minority" as he would during the 1970s. Instead, he understood gay culture through the prism of camp—a cultural and aesthetic concept that, during the 1960s, would have a public coming out.

The sixties embraced a new aesthetic ethos, visible in the visual arts, literature, television, and film, that emphasized irony and the transgression of cultural boundaries. A number of names for it circulated in sixties literary and cultural criticism: under Andy Warhol and other visual artists, it earned the moniker "pop art," but by the mid-1960s, it was most likely to be identified publicly as "camp," thanks to Susan Sontag's famous 1964 essay "Notes on

Camp," published in the self-consciously highbrow *Partisan Review*. Fabio Cleto argues that Sontag's essay marked an explosion of the term "camp" in the mid-1960s; it became "part of the mainstream cultural economy of the 1960s," he claims, ubiquitous in U.S. periodicals as a description of the "new taste."[25] "Isherwood's disconcertion at its absence from public discourse," Cleto concludes, "had been fully satisfied" (302). Suddenly, what had been a private term of New York gay culture became national "camp mania" (303). Camp's investment in popular culture was particularly important for Isherwood's authorial identity.

For Cold War intellectuals, camp's alliance with popular culture demonstrated a dangerous assault on taste and hierarchy. Sontag notes this shift in "Notes on Camp": "Camp taste," she claimed, "turns its back on the good-bad axis of ordinary aesthetic judgment. Camp doesn't reverse things. It doesn't argue that the good is bad, or the bad is good. What it does is to offer for art (and life) a different—a supplementary—set of standards" (525). Oscar Wilde epitomized this "democratic *esprit* of Camp" for Sontag, "the equivalence of all objects—when he announced his intention of 'living up' to his blue-and-white china, or declared that a doorknob could be as admirable as a painting" (528). She concludes, "The old-style dandy hated vulgarity. The new-style dandy, the lover of Camp, appreciates vulgarity. Where the dandy would be continually offended or bored, the connoisseur of Camp is continually amused, delighted. The dandy held a perfumed handkerchief to his nostrils and was liable to swoon; the connoisseur of Camp sniffs the stink and prides himself on his strong nerves" (528). Camp embraces both the delight in vulgarity and the playfulness of this new structure of feeling, evident in the performances of the Merry Pranksters, in the androgynous gender performance of rock stars like Mick Jagger and Jimi Hendrix, and in the hybrid artistic creations of both pop art and what we call the postmodern novel. Camp, in other words, embraced the cultural insubordination of pulp fiction. Marianne DeKoven claims that sixties letters featured "the open-ended, free mixing of previously distinct modes of cultural practice and form . . . so that a 'literary' novel, for example, can be comprised, in varying degrees and mixtures, of modernist, traditional, subgeneric, and graphic fictional forms, and a 'genre' novel can contain many 'literary' or 'high literary' elements. Popular culture, vehicle and expression of postmodern egalitarianism, is no longer meaningfully distinct either from high culture or from consumer culture."[26] The mixing of cultural forms was nothing new, but the celebration of this cultural mixing as a liberatory force was. Mark McGurl notes that writers embrace "what must be called meta-genre fiction," including "romance, western, science fiction, fantasy and detective fiction."[27] "Popular culture," he concludes, "would now be understood as a force of liberation from the strait-jacket proprieties of 'official' high culture" (217). A number of novelists in the late sixties incorporated radio, movies, genre fiction, fairy tales, commodity goods, and other staples of Cold War consumer culture.

Isherwood doesn't seem to have been familiar with experimental sixties novelists like Donald Barthelme and Ishmael Reed. He did read *Esquire* in the early 1960s, which introduced him to the writing of Tom Wolfe, but his library, aside from William Burroughs, has only one book by a sixties experimental writer, Richard Brautigan's *Trout Fishing in America*. But he was more familiar with another manifestation of sixties camp, pop art. Artists such as Roy Lichtenstein and, perhaps most famously, Andy Warhol incorporated the detritus of consumer capitalism—cartoons, advertisements, news articles—into their pieces. Cécile Whiting describes pop art's "principal object of interest" as "the popular, which seemed to dominate everywhere," particularly in "the homes managed by, and supermarkets patronized by, efficient homemakers in the vast plains of American suburbia."[28] Mario Amaya's 1965 study *Pop as Art* defined that relationship to the popular through humor:

> They rely to a large degree on humour for startling effect— but is a mid-twentieth century brand of twisted or ironic humour called "Camp." Camp is expressed by a love of things being what they are not; by a fascination with the androgynous, particularly in over-exaggerated sexual forms which themselves become parodies; by ambiguity, irony, paradox and inverse humour; and by a feeling for artifice, for surface appeal, for thrilling, timely, sensational, stylish

anti-conventions. Both the Low Camp of transvestism and the High Camp of exaggerated impersonation have a place here. Furthermore, the confusion of male and female, of reality with make-believe, of seriousness with fun, dignity with irreverence, etc. are important hallmarks of the new art, which appears to aim at being what Miss Sontag calls "a solvent of morality," through a sponsorship of playfulness. (20–21)

Amaya demonstrates the ubiquity of "camp" as a mode of cultural analysis and Isherwood's role in this mode: Amaya draws on Isherwood's *World in the Evening* distinction between High Camp and Low Camp.[29] He also emphasizes the role of humor, artifice, and surfaces. Indeed, the Cold War critiques of gay artists that Michael Sherry catalogs—superficial, sterile, artificial—for Amaya become accolades.

Pop art was centered in New York, but Whiting argues persuasively in *Pop L.A.* that Los Angeles played an important role in the movement, both as "the undisputed world capital of middlebrow purchase and pleasure"(3) and as a center of pop artists. David Hockney, one of those L.A. artists, was a friend of both Christopher Isherwood and Don Bachardy and painted one of the most famous portraits of Isherwood and Barchardy in 1968. In addition, Barchardy knew a number of other artists associated with pop art in Los Angeles, including Ed Moses, Bill Al Bengston, and Ed Ruscha (68, 70), whose artwork decorated Isherwood and Bachardy's home.[30]

David Hockney provides a visual counterpoint to Isherwood's middlebrow camp of the sixties. Hockney's paintings emphasize sleek surfaces, bright colors, and suburban settings. They have been read as commentaries on "the superficiality of the city's architecture and the empty lives of all its residents";[31] when critics suspected that Hockney was celebrating Los Angeles, they accused him of inanity. What few acknowledged, Whiting notes, was Hockney's "homoeroticsm" (110), despite the fact that in his paintings, "Nude men lounge by the pool, float in the water, and place their buttocks on view, right there, on the surface of the canvas. Hockney depicted a homoerotic fantasy of Los Angeles that functioned . . . as an alternative to the booster's claims about California" (124). That fantasy both participated in and subverted the middlebrow images of the California as epitome of the good life. According to Whiting, "Hockney's nudes do not simply colonize the most visible symbols of Los Angeles—the suburban house and backyard pool—and rest on the surface of the canvas; they themselves are materially about surface. Male bodies, their torsos flattened and their surfaces composed of visible swatches of paint, draw attention to the two-dimensional flat surface of the surface of the picture. As such these nude bodies allegorize a process of painting that is all about surface: that of the canvas, of sexuality, and of the city" (129). There is no better analysis of how a camp middlebrow aesthetic functions. Whiting articulates an aesthetic that claims, aggressively, to be only about surface, while through multiple layers, it subverts conventional images and ideologies. This aesthetic isn't closeted, nor does it embody Eve Sedgwick's notion of the open secret. Painting men's naked asses is open, but it isn't secret. Hockney's provocation can always be ironically disavowed at the last second. Susan Sontag pointed to this layered notion of meaning when she explained in "Notes on Camp" that "the Camp sensibility is one that is alive to a double sense in which some things can be taken. But this is not the familiar split-level construction of a literal meaning, on the one hand, and a symbolic meaning, on the other. It is the difference, rather, between the thing as meaning something, anything, and the thing as pure artifice" (520). Sixties camp is a queer encoding that hides in plain sight.

Isherwood appreciated the playful queer camp of pop art. I offer exhibit A: the portrait he had made with Don Bachardy in 1954. Isherwood scandalized even his close friends when he got involved with Bachardy, thirty years his junior. Bachardy was eighteen when they met, but looked much younger—so much so that Evelyn Hooker, a psychologist who had long championed equal rights for homosexuals, asked Isherwood and Bachardy to leave her property because she was afraid that the apparent pedophilia would hurt her academic reputation.[32] Rumors ran through New York that Isherwood had taken up with a twelve-year-old.[33]

Perhaps in response to this criticism, Isherwood had a photographic portrait made that flaunted images of predatory homosexuals. The two are posed in a formal studio portrait, beaming broadly. As if to emphasize his youth, Bachardy wears khaki pants and a white T-shirt. In other photographs and home movies from the time (for example, their first trip to Europe), Bachardy wore suits, so this casual, young look seems deliberate. Isherwood is dressed in a plaid wool sports jacket with a shirt open at the collar, and he has a crew cut. Though he cut his hair short, he rarely, if ever, wore a crew cut, except in this photograph. The photograph poses the two as if they are father and son.

There is nothing closeted about this photograph. It appears, on the surface, to meet every Cold War stereotype about white picket fences and happy families. Yet the reality of this photograph—an intergenerational gay relationship—makes the ironic posing deeply transgressive. I have shown it to a number of undergraduate classes, and it never fails to elicit gasps and nervous laughter. No wonder Isherwood is grinning so devilishly. Isherwood's sixties writing, as I discuss in the next three chapters, embodies this same layered gesture of camp middlebrow, one that epitomizes the rise of popular culture and gay presence. Isherwood's discovery of a gay readership and the decade's inspired disregard for cultural capital transformed him into an innovator of camp gay middlebrow.

Isherwood's literary snobbery was mitigated by his love of camp in the 1960s; he seemed less anxious about his reputation. At the start of the 1960s, the clearest sign of his shift in priorities was his change in book publishers, from highbrow to popular. Isherwood had been unhappy with Random House for a long time; he originally signed with them for the coauthored *Journey to a War,* and it is very likely that Auden, not Isherwood, was seen as the real prize. Random House disliked *The World in the Evening,* and word of editor Robert Linscott's disparagement reached Isherwood back in Santa Monica. He insisted that Curtis Brown release him from the contract and find another, more supportive publisher. Despite Random House's reservations about Isherwood, however, they were surprisingly fussy about letting him go. Alan Collins, his Curtis Brown agent, consulted with Random House in 1957 and reported to Isherwood that they were "most anxious to keep you and think that you are an author of outstanding talent"; they blamed the "deterioration of a good relationship" on editor

This portrait of Don Bachardy and Christopher Isherwood taken in 1954 flaunted stereotypes about predatory homosexuals yet also posed as a wholesome father and son image. Reproduced by permission of The Huntington Library, San Marino, California.

Robert Linscott.[34] (Of course, the fact that Random House was also "quite frank" about its assessment of *The World in the Evening* as neither "a good novel, nor a saleable one"[35] must have irritated Isherwood anew.) He was unimpressed, and remained firm in his desire to leave Random House.

The press he wanted to join was Simon and Schuster. Alan Collins was horrified, writing him that "you should stay with Random

House and, as I said, despite Jack Goodman's personal enthusiasm, Simon & Schuster is definitely about as wrong a publisher for you as you could pick."[36] Collins's hostility suggested that in the sixties, Simon and Schuster still had not shed the crass, nouveau riche reputation that its founders had richly earned in its inception in the interwar period. Founded by Richard Simon and Max Schuster in 1924, Simon and Schuster was an upstart whose first publication was a book of crossword puzzles.[37] The company solicited books it wanted to publish (including Will Durant's *The Story of Philosophy*), spent freely on advertising, and published very few novels. In 1944, it was acquired by the Chicago-based businessman Marshall Field, who owned the firm and Pocket Books for the next thirteen years. Jack Goodman, an enthusiastic editor known for "set[ting] the chatty, conversational, sophisticated tone of the firm's advertising,"[38] embraced the firm's interest in commercialism. Not primarily known as a literary press, Simon and Schuster had none of the literary reputation that Random House enjoyed, despite Goodman's charm and publishing acumen. An old-school literary agency like Curtis Brown could not have been pleased.

Isherwood's reply is worth quoting at length because it suggests Isherwood's concerns on the eve of the 1960s and how personal relationships with publishers trumped economic or even strictly literary concerns:

> I want to go to Simon and Schuster. I do not want under
> any circumstances to remain with Random House. This
> is contrary to your advice and you will probably think me
> unreasonable and reckless. Admittedly I am acting on feeling and instinct rather than on commonsense business
> calculations. Rightly or wrongly, I believe that Simon and
> Schuster and I will get along. . . . I earn, most years, at least
> three quarters of my money from movie-work. What quality, then, do I most want in my book publisher? Enthusiasm. And who has shown the most enthusiasm? Paradoxically, Jack Goodman. S & S may be, as you say, "about as
> wrong a publisher for you as you could pick" but how can
> they possibly be any wronger than Random House? How

could I possibly do any worse with any publisher than I have done with them?[39]

Isherwood's admission that "three quarters" of his income is from "movie-work" suggests both a serious commitment to and enjoyment of moviemaking, and a tacit admission of his ambiguous cultural status in his American sojourn. It's not that Isherwood hadn't been made aware of the culturally compromising position movies put him in. English critics, even his friends, had attacked him in the press for his movie work and dismissed his postwar work as fundamentally unserious. The artistic styles of the 1960s made Isherwood's cultural hybridization more palatable. It may be claiming too much to suggest that Isherwood's sudden lack of concern with brow level came in part from the cultural transgressions of pop art. But by embracing the literary equivalent of Campbell's Soup, Isherwood placed himself on the side of the decade's challenges to highbrow aesthetic taste. Simon and Schuster paved the way for the full flowering of middlebrow camp in Isherwood's sixties novels.

❖ 5 ❖

"A Delicious Purgatory":
Sex and "Salvation"

T HE NEW SIXTIES ETHOS WAS APPARENT EVEN EARLY IN the decade. Homosexuals began to emerge in literary culture as a particular kind of antihero, often as hustlers, quite different from the American boys next door in postwar gay protest novels. These gay men were social outcasts, symbols of the larger despair in American culture. These novels featured sordid sexual encounters, and in many ways confirmed stereotypes of the "homosexual lifestyle." They also universalized gay experience for a wide range of readers, insisting that the gay underworld was emblematic of a human experience, not solely a gay one. If gay characters were isolated and lonely and even doomed, so too were the straight ones. Indeed, some novels even suggested that the respectable mainstream might be worse off.

This cultural interest in outsiders provided a sympathetic context for Christopher Isherwood's 1962 *Down There on a Visit,* an autobiographical novel with four self-reflexive episodes in the author's life that construct him as an antihero, clinging to the margins of both Europe and Hollywood. The novel also participated in a subset of early sixties gay novels, which circulated images of a gay underworld, including James Baldwin's 1962 *Another Country,* John Rechy's 1963 *City of Night,* and Jane Rule's 1964 *Desert of the Heart.* These novels critiqued mainstream society and argued for a queer reimagination of American culture. Isherwood both built on and camped this tradition of a queer underworld, resulting in a novel that exemplified his emerging ethos of camp middlebrow.

"Hell Is Queer": Sixties Gay Novels

In May 1962, Gore Vidal shared with Isherwood his misgivings about *Down There on a Visit:*

> You are visiting hell and hell is queer (not queerness is hell) and within the frame of what you set yourself to accomplish you have given some true ammunition to the enemy. . . . I only question that, in detail, you tend to celebrate a kind of cozy homosexual domesticity while simultaneously unfolding four hell dramas in which all the actors are homosexual, undermining the argument that one is neither more wretched, nor more happy, hetero or homo. I seem *not* to be putting this plainly but you know what I mean. I have had to go through a bit of the same thing: on the one hand declaring that homosexual relationships are as meaningful as any kind, while on the other hand recording hell, and not meaning to link the two in any causal way.[1]

Vidal's identification of the novel as a visit to hell was primed by the jacket copy, "which, according to Bachardy, Isherwood wrote himself":[2] "The words *Down There* refer to a netherworld within the individual, a place of loneliness, alienation, and hatred. Here are people shut up inside private hells of their own making, self-dedicated to a lifelong feud with the Others. The Author is often amused by them, for even a private hell can be funny; but he cannot sneer at them, knowing how much they and he have in common. His visits to them are also visits to the Down There inside himself." Isherwood began writing this novel as a modern version of Dante's *Inferno;* the suggestion that Isherwood's hell is queer is provocative, if oversimplistic.

Isherwood was not alone in his linkage of gay life and hell. The notion of a decadent gay underworld had circulated for quite some time, most notably in Proust. In the early sixties, a small group of gay writers framed a queer hell as a metaphor for the human condition and insisted that the suffering of homosexuals was the suffering of all men. Baldwin's *Another Country,* Rechy's

City of Night, Rule's *Desert of the Heart,* and Isherwood's *Down There on a Visit* take the hell-is-queer trope and transform it into a critique of mainstream society. The intertextuality of Isherwood, Baldwin, Rechy, and Rule reveals a queer early-sixties zeitgeist. Isherwood was publishing excerpts from *Down There on a Visit* in 1959, before its publication in 1962. Baldwin's 1962 novel grew, like Isherwood's, out of interests from the 1950s that could suddenly be appreciated in a more open sixties landscape. Rechy published his novel in 1963, but excerpts like "Mardi Gras" and "The Fabulous Wedding of Miss Destiny" were published in 1961 and 1962. Jane Rule's novel was written in 1961 but was not published until 1964.

Publishers mediated this intertextual conversation. Simon and Schuster's first Isherwood novel was *Down There on a Visit,* thus placing Isherwood's queer hell on the edge of literary respectability. James Baldwin existed in a similarly liminal state. He was able to get the 1954 *Giovanni's Room* published in the United States only by signing with paperback publisher Dell Press for a three-book contract.[3] *Another Country* was part of that commitment, and it became a huge best seller, Baldwin's most successful book to date, largely because of Dell's distribution potential and its ability to cross over as a pulp exposé. Although Dell was trying to up its brow level in the early 1960s, not only through Baldwin but also by signing literary bad boy Norman Mailer, it still was identified as a pulp publisher—so much so that Baldwin complained in the early 1960s about being represented by a paperback book company.[4]

Baldwin and Isherwood both published with presses whose cultural capital was suspect. John Rechy's Grove Press, by contrast, was firmly in the highbrow avant-garde; its Greenwich Village location aligned it with political and cultural rebellion. Grove Press quickly gained a reputation as a press that would challenge obscenity laws in the cause of art, reprinting banned books like Henry Miller's *Tropic of Cancer* and D. H. Lawrence's *Lady Chatterley's Lover.* Barney Rosset acquired the firm in 1952, at the age of twenty-nine, and used his banker father's deep pockets to sustain the firm and build its literary reputation. John Tebbel notes that "Rosset was thus in the vanguard of the struggle to remove works of literary merit from the grip of the censors who had so long pursued them, and in fact he played a substantial role in freeing serious writers in America from the suppressive influence of censors of every variety. The court battles he fought were for all publishers. He 'loosened up' trade publishing in America, as even his competitors had to admit."[5] Grove Press was a key player in the sixties assault on obscenity laws, using the claim of "literary merit" to undermine decades of precedent. *City of Night* epitomizes the alliance of pulp and the avant-garde in the 1960s; the pulp market created an audience that turned both *Another Country* and *City of Night* into best sellers, and avant-garde presses' successful invention of the "literary merit" argument provided a successful legal strategy for the pulps in the 1960s.

Jane Rule's position in American pulp was more fraught. She had significant difficulty finding a American publisher; she was, by her own estimate, rejected by "about twenty five publishers,"[6] and she recalled fifteen years later that "one reaction was 'If this book isn't pornographic, what's the point of printing it . . . if you can write in the dirty parts we'll take it but otherwise no.'"[7] The rejections preserved in her archive aren't quite as salacious, but they do confirm the double bind she found herself in—both criticized for not being explicit and dismissed for constructing another melodramatic lesbian pulp. A representative from W. W. Norton and Company explained that the book "put me off on a couple of counts: chiefly the theme, of course, which is pretty familiar stuff in paper books of a certain sort."[8] Rule's treatment of a lesbian theme was praised by Harcourt Brace because she "managed a candor about what, in some quarters, could be considered extremely objectionable, but she has not allowed it to become distasteful"; yet her reserve seems to have worked against her, because "we find the subject matter, of itself, of insufficient interest."[9] Houghton Mifflin summed up the problem: "Despite the author's competence and taste, the novel's appeal necessarily rests on its sensational theme, and we feel we are not the house to capitalize on the kind of exploitation the book would need in making it a commercial success."[10] Rule's failure to find a hardback publisher—because of the association of lesbian themes with "paper books" and a contradictory lack of interest in undistasteful candor—marks the continued difficulties in mainstreaming gay content, despite periodic gay publishing trends.

Rule found an English publisher and had *Desert of the Heart* published by Macmillan in Canada. The New American Library eventually obtained the rights to publish the novel, and NAL editor David Brown (or "Mr. Helen Gurley Brown, the husband of Helen Gurley Brown")[11] was prepared "to capitalize on the exploitation the book would need." As Jane Rule recalled, "I went to call on Mr. Helen Gurley Brown in New York City and he gave me a pitch that was just unbelievable: 'This book is sensational! You want to know why it's sensational?! Because it's not sensational! Now we're gonna put you on the Johnnie Carson show and we're gonna do this and we're gonna do that . . . ' I said: 'it's no good; I'd throw up.' And he said: 'You must do something more sincere than that to attract attention.'"[12] Brown, an import from Hollywood, sought to capitalize on the novel in ways that both built on and distinguished the sensationalism of *Another Country* and *City of Night.* Rule's resistance to her pulp incarnation—she did no publicity for the novel—may have contributed to its erasure from this larger mainstream gay publishing trend.

There are some personal links that make this intertextual conversation intriguing. Rechy's story "The Fabulous Wedding of Miss Destiny," published in the *Evergreen Review,* earned him a fan letter from James Baldwin,[13] and Baldwin later wrote a blurb for *City of Night.* Isherwood and John Rechy were introduced in Los Angeles in 1960, and the two corresponded as Rechy worked on *City of Night:* "Is it Immodest of me to come on so strong and say that I think it's coming along just great? Im actually flipping over the sections that Im working on now. I'll be anxious for you to see them and the whole book. . . . And thank you for reading the 'Shawn' section and giving me your fine opinions."[14] Isherwood, apparently, warned Rechy about being "dogmatic," and Rechy's response shows deference to him: "*And believe me, 'dogma' is the last thing I want to emerge from this book.* The narrator must *not* be dogmatic. If this is how it appeared, I would consider the book a fantastic failure."[15] Rechy explains that "my letter to Christopher about his reactions to 'City of Night' as I was writing it was—I confess—intended only to show my appreciation for his responsiveness. Truly, I was not seeking writerly suggestions."[16] Rechy was interested in Isherwood as a fellow writer, but Isherwood seemed to respond to him primarily as a hustler; Rechy describes Isherwood's seduction attempt while Don Bachardy was out of town—and his boorish behavior when Rechy, eager to keep his writing and his hustling separate, refused. (Isherwood declined to drive him home and made him hitchhike back to Los Angeles from Santa Monica at 2 a.m.)[17] However Rechy may have felt at the time, he continued the professional association well after this incident. In fact, it was Bachardy and Isherwood who broke with Rechy, dramatically—sending a telegram to uninvite him from a dinner party in 1967. The offense? Rechy's novel about cruising, *Numbers,* which included characters clearly based on Bachardy and Isherwood. Bachardy seemed angrier than Isherwood, insisting that Rechy take his drawing off the cover of the novel.[18]

These novels are quite different in terms of plot. *Another Country* tells the story of five New Yorkers—Vivaldo, Ida, Eric, Cass, and Richard—who are haunted by the suicide of Rufus Scott, which opens the novel. The characters' emotional and sexual interactions with each other form the core of the novel's action. *City of Night* follows an unnamed narrator, a hustler, through queer underworlds in New York, Los Angeles, and New Orleans, introducing the reader to multiple characters on the margins. *Desert of the Heart* sends Evelyn to Reno for a divorce, where she falls in love with Anne, a casino dealer and cartoonist. Despite significant differences between these novels, the intertextual resonances suggest an early-sixties reimagination of queer hell in the national imaginary. The novels share recuperated images of the doomed/damned, explicit descriptions of sex, critiques of a hypocritical mainstream, and gay characters as saints or transformative agents. *Another Country* talks about "the doomed" rather than "the damned," but it is clear throughout the course of the novel that New York City functions as a kind of urban hell that imprisons all its characters. And that hell is, in fact, largely, if not solely, queer. From the first section, where Baldwin tells us that "in any of the world's cities, on a winter night, a boy can be bought for the price of a beer and the promise of warm blankets" (41), *Another*

Country immerses the reader in a world of queer sexuality. Yves, who has worked as a hustler in Paris, as Rufus did in New York, explains that "you do not meet many women in the places I have been; you do not meet many human persons at all. They are all dead. Dead" (209). Eric explains that his isolation as a young man in Alabama stemmed from "the instinct which compels people to move away from the doomed" (200). Cass's final pronouncement—"This isn't a country at all, it's a collection of football players and Eagle Scouts. Cowards. We think we're happy. We're not. We're doomed" (406)—sums up Baldwin's vision.

City of Night evokes the damned in its sympathetic portraits of hustlers, queens, and trade. Miss Destiny sets the stage for a theological reading, describing an angel who would appear and say, "This is it, the world is ending, and Heaven or Hell will be to spend eternity just as you are now, in the same place among the same people—*Forever!*" (115). Exiles trapped in hell circulate throughout Rechy's novel. In the final section, *City of Night* merges religious imagery with sexual anarchy:

> Then I had the feeling that I was in hell. To be swallowed by those monstrous apparitions; but before I can be swallowed, is it possible that this nightmare city will suddenly flare into flames—set off from one of the torches carried by the contorted dancing snaking bodies? I imagine the floats devoured by flames, the clowns-turned-angels, the clowns-turned-devils sprouting wings to join that vast exodus to heaven . . . or hell . . . or nowhere; and seeing the costumed people determinedly laughing—and the skeletons, the jesters, the cannibals, the vampires, the ragdolls, the witches, the leopard-people—I imagined the razing fire sweeping this rotten city. . . . Vengefully, I cling to the vision of that terrible apocalyptic fire. (370–71)

The fusion of a gay urban underworld with the "apocalyptic fire" marks the heavy symbolism of *City of Night.*

In *Desert of the Heart,* Rule uses the physical presence of the desert to evoke literary visions of hell. Evelyn's lesbian awakening coincides with her entry into a landscape of damnation: "Evelyn had nevertheless felt, at the sight of that Nevada desert, a Catholic desolation. 'It was as if I saw, in fact, what I do not believe,' she wrote" (41). Ann Childs calls herself "one of the damned," explaining, "It's hard not to believe in an Old Testament sort of world. Fire and brimstone have weathered some four hundred towns into dust already. Everyplace is a Sodom or Gomorrah: it's only a matter of time, and very little time at that" (103). The emerging love story takes place against a backdrop of damnation inspired by the *Inferno* and *Pilgrim's Progress.*

Like these other hell-is-queer novels, *Down There on a Visit* is structured as portraits of the damned, a clear homage to the *Inferno.* All four sections explore human despair—Mr. Lancaster, Ambrose, the narrator himself (during the Munich crisis), and Paul, who turns to religion as an alternative to suicide. The second section, "Ambrose," incorporates explicit references to the boys on the island as devils: "I always suspected those two weren't human. Now I'm sure of it! Did you see how those obscene jelly-fish positively fawned on them? *They* knew! You don't believe me? All right, I'll bloody well prove it to you. . . . I suppose you'll admit that this place is unmitigated and utter hell, as far as normal human beings are concerned? Well—what sort of creatures are at home in hell? Devils, obviously! Devils don't mind the heat—they fairly revel in it" (97–98). Ambrose refers to himself as dead (75), and Paul's early demise is read by many as a result of his willful entry into the underworld of addiction.

Isherwood cut his most explicit discussion of hell—the narrator's hashish-inspired vision—though he included a version of it in *Exhumations* ("A Visit to Anselm Oakes"). The scene is nightmarish—the dealer explicitly represented as a devil, and the trip a nightmare of damnation. Here, the hellish creatures are his own multiple unrealized potentialities:

> As above, so below. As without, so within. The shifting sliding planes of potentiality weren't only outside and around me. They were also inside myself. *I* was potential. *I* was shifting. . . . I no longer existed in any comprehensible way. I didn't make sense. I was a sum that didn't add up anymore. . . . I had made an act of choice—long ago—at

birth or before birth, and chosen one of my million million potentialities and arbitrarily declared it to be myself. But now I could see *all* the potentialities again. I was infinitely disintegrated. . . . It would take no more than the tiniest further touch of the thumb-screw to refract and blur the planes beyond all semblance of re-inter-relation. Then I should be utterly nothing. I dreaded this, as one dreads the tearing apart of all one's members. I almost held my breath, lest the desperately delicate balance should be jarred and destroyed. . . . If I were to make one incautious move, the whole pack of screaming bellowing neighing squeaking trumpeting roaring hissing crowing barking growling beasts would sweep me headlong away with them.[19]

The narrator's view of the demons of hell as his own "million million potentialities" suggests that Isherwood's rejection of identity was fraught. While he often dismissed the relevance of any identity categories, like "homosexual" or "woman," he also viewed that dissolution of identity with horror, and clung to essentialist notions of identity, including homosexual identity. The "pack of screaming bellowing neighing squeaking trumpeting roaring hissing crowing barking growling beasts" is hardly a postmodern celebration of the demise of identity politics.

Paul's terrifying proclamation about hell, in this omitted version, suggests Isherwood's original intention for the novel: "'You see my point?' said Paul pleasantly. 'Hell can be *anywhere*. None of the ordinary people, as you call them, would notice it. They couldn't, possibly. It takes time to notice something—a fraction of a second at the very least. *But hell doesn't take any time at all.*'"[20] Hell as a psychic state—a potentially universal human condition—becomes explicit in this hashish scene.

Isherwood, however, omitted that final scene for a reason: he abandoned a serious theological investigation for something infinitely more playful and subversive. As he explained in response to a fan, "The allusions to Hell which are to be found in the published version are really just leftovers from the original. Furthermore, I regret the blurb on the jacket; which was an unsuccessful attempt to tie the original conception of the novel on to the late version."[21] Isherwood isn't writing an *Inferno* but a *Purgatorio,* and that distinction is crucial to parsing out the key difference between *Down There on a Visit* and the other early sixties gay texts discussed here. The suffering one endures in purgatory is essential to one's ultimate salvation, a suffering that is merciful because it allows one to atone. Isherwood explained:

> The basic idea is of a conducted tour, similar to Dante's tour of the inferno. But this inferno is more of a purgatory, because nobody in it is permanently damned—only indefinitely self-detained. It is a place of self-exile, which you *could* leave at any time if you became aware of your exile as exile, and if you then wanted to leave. There is no God presiding over this purgatory; it isn't ordered by divine law. It is a situation that you get yourself into. Being there isn't necessarily unpleasant. In fact, if you start to dislike being there and then begin to question the necessity of your remaining there, you are on the way to getting out of it.[22]

Isherwood's notion of purgatory as self-detention complicates more traditional tropes of the "hell" of homosexuality. His characters are in limbo, not suffering eternal damnation, and their lot isn't unpleasant. Many seem to be having a delightful time. Indeed, Isherwood's notions of purgatory seem closer to cruising, as he wrote in his diaries: "It has always seemed to me that there is in fact only one Turkish bath—an enormous subterranean world, a delicious purgatory, a naked democracy in which the only class distinctions are anatomical. And that this underworld merely has a number of different entrances and vestibules in all the cities of the earth. You could enter it in Sydney and emerge from it to find yourself in Jermyn Street."[23] The pairing of "delicious" with "purgatory" both queers it and reclaims it from Christian punishment.

Heavy-handed pronouncements about hell in the novel—by himself, friends, and critics—don't seem to match the text itself. Isherwood describes the novel in a letter to Edward Upward as a "serious farce,"[24] and indeed, *Down There on a Visit* is funny, irreverent, and joyfully profane. If hell is queer, then hell isn't particularly hellish. Isherwood constructs a layered purgatory in which queer characters suffer, not for their sins, but from the machinations of the "others," and he constructs, as well, queer agents of salvation within the modern wasteland. Hell is a mad camp, Mary, and it isn't really hell at all.

As Isherwood's paean to the baths suggests, sex is a key characteristic of this "delicious purgatory." In all four of these novels, of course, sex figures prominently. Baldwin's *Another Country* was notorious for its explicit descriptions of both heterosexual and homosexual sex. Indeed, sex is the primary way he shows shifting relationships between the characters; traditional notions of fidelity to people or fixed sexual identities are absent, as gay men sleep with straight men and straight women. Rechy structured *City of Night* as a series of fragmented sketches to simulate the rhythm of the hustler's trade. Even Rule's *Desert of the Heart,* far less explicit than the rest, portrays nonnormative sexuality undramatically. Silver is a former madam who sleeps with both women and men; Ann combines one-night stands with strangers with longer-term liaisons with men and women; Evelyn, divorcing and in love with Ann, had a kind of Boston marriage during the war with a woman.

Isherwood's own novel was permeated with sex. A group of homosexual men, in the section titled "Mr. Lancaster," frames Isherwood's embrace of sensuality, then Waldemar initiates Christopher in an "unforgettable, happy, shameless afternoon—an afternoon of closed Venetian blinds, of gramophone music and the slippery sounds of nakedness, of Turkish cigarettes, cushion dust, crude perfume and healthy sweat, of abruptly exploding laughter and wheezing sofa springs" (54). The explicitly queer Ambrose is in charge of a colony of boys, whose sexual tastes cross not only gender but also species. One of the boys suggests that "the chicken we had just eaten for lunch had been raped by Petro before he had killed it" (108). Maria celebrates the "passion for the young boys," claiming ironically, " 'I adore the pederast. They are so sensitive. So *fine*' " (117, 119). The narrator has sex obsessively in "Waldemar," juggling multiple partners during the Munich crisis. Section four's protagonist, Paul, is a notorious kept man. In addition to talking about his multiple conquests, he is sexually attracted to a twelve-year-old girl, and a public accusation of sexual abuse forms a dramatic sequence in section four. All this adds up to the most transgressively sexual novel of Isherwood's career to that point.

In his writing notebook, Isherwood makes it clear that the sexuality is intentional. He discussed the first section, "Mr. Lancaster":

> The final scene with Waldemar should be made much more physical—not only about the braut but the swimming, the wrestling, the putting on of the bathing-slip. You must feel that Chris is horny. *All through* the story. Don't forget the sex-shocker which the Captain gives him to read. It makes Chris hot, and he's glad that he doesn't have to apologize for the hotness, as he wd if he were with his literary friends. Same thing with the attempted seduction by parrot-shark: it must be shown that a man like parrot-shark takes entirely the wrong tone with a boy like Chris. Oh yes, he could have had Chris if he'd amazed him, taken him by storm, mastered him. Chris wd have quite liked that. But Parrot-shark doesn't know how to be shameless enough. (Waldemar *does* know.)[25]

That obsessive horniness feeds into what Jamie Carr argues is the heteronormative disciplining of sexual identity, one inspired, she suggests, by the actor John Gielgud's arrest in 1953 for solicitation in a public bathroom.[26] Although Gielgud's fine was small, the press coverage led to public denunciations, prevented travel to the United States, and threatened the opening of his play.

That critique of sexual disciplining extends to larger societal denunciations in all four novels from the early 1960s. *Another Country* uses Ida to discuss the sick society American culture has constructed around race. Eric critiques the binary sexual economy that depends upon the marginalization of gay men for straight men's sense of superiority:

> He remembered that army of lonely men who had used him, who had wrestled with him, caressed him and submitted to him, in a darkness deeper than the darkest night. It was not merely his body they had used, but something else;

his infirmity had made him the receptacle of an anguish which he could scarcely believe was in the world. This anguish rendered him helpless, though it also lent him his weird, doomed grace and power, and it baffled him and set the dimensions of his trap. Perhaps he had sometimes dreamed of walking out of the drama in which he was entangled and playing some other role. But all the exits were barred—were barred by avid men; the role he played was necessary, and not only to himself. (210–11)

Baldwin's critique of the regimes of "normalcy," and the key role gay men play in those regimes, resonates in work by both Foucault and Sedgwick. Those who stray outside the mainstream, Baldwin argues, are more likely to find knowledge, if not happiness.

City of Night portrays its doomed sexual exiles sympathetically, saving its venom for the hypocritical "law" that harasses them and the establishment that patronizes them, in both senses of the word. Miss Destiny fantasizes that "one day, in the most lavish drag youve evuh seen—heels! and gown! and beads! and spangled earrings!—Im going to storm heaven and protest! *Here I am!!!!!* I'll yell—and I'll shake my beads at Him. . . . And God will cringe!" (116). This theological protest extends into other indictments, both large and small. Police harassment is commonplace, and the straight world humiliates this queer underworld, though many come for sex when the lights go down. During Mardi Gras, one queen, Chi-Chi, is mocked by a heterosexual couple: "I wanna show everyone back home what a real big fairy looks like. . . . You go ahead and give us a real big fairy pose!" (331). Chi-Chi suddenly breaks, yelling, "Father-fuckers! I'll take you on together or alone! Prove to *Me* what big men *you* are!" and punches the man in the face (331). His rebellion becomes, for the narrator, a moment when "Miss Destiny's evil angel . . . relented—was perhaps even smiling graciously, if only for a few moments, over Chi-Chi" (332). Rechy's sexual exiles may be trapped, but their fate, he insists, is unjust.

Desert of the Heart critiques mainstream society in much broader terms. Convention itself comes under assault in its famous opening paragraph, one that places Evelyn and Ann's story in a larger context of rebellion: "Conventions, like clichés, have a way of surviving their own usefulness. They are then excused or defended as the idioms of living. For everyone, foreign by birth or by nature, convention is the mark of fluency. That is why, for any woman, marriage is the idiom of life. And she does not give it up out of scorn or indifference but only when she is forced to admit that she has never been able to pronounce it properly and has committed continually its grossest grammatical errors. For such a woman marriage remains a foreign tongue, an alien landscape, and since she cannot become naturalized, she finally chooses voluntary exile" (5). This notion of convention as an oppressive force hovers over the novel. Rule builds on this notion, using the casino as the logical outcome of capitalist America. Signs in the casino explain, "Remember, if you play long enough you'll lose," and Ann appreciates the lack of hypocrisy: "No university published the odds against learning, no hospital the odds against surviving, no church the odds against salvation. Here, anyway, people weren't being fooled. They were told that no one was intelligent enough or strong enough or blessed enough to be saved. Still, they played" (22). Mainstream society is little more than a card game, rigged from the start.

Isherwood's own larger critiques are similarly explicit. In "Mr. Lancaster," the narrator details his youth rebellion—one sure to resonate with the emerging youth rebellion of the 1960s: "As far as I was concerned, everyone over forty belonged, with a mere handful of honorable exceptions, to an alien tribe, hostile by definition but in practice ridiculous rather than formidable. The majority of them I saw as utter grotesques, sententious and gaga, to be regarded with indifference. It was only people of my own age who seemed to me better than half-alive. I was accustomed to say that when we started getting old—a situation which I could theoretically foresee but never quite believe in—I just hoped we would die quickly and without pain."[27] Isherwood's description of himself shows D. H. Lawrence's influence; he sees a tired older generation squelching the essential "westering spirit." Certainly, the older narrator is somewhat bemused by the younger "Christopher's" resentments, but this sense of "the enemy" continues throughout the novel: the "hearties" who wrecked Ambrose's rooms, the establishment of England during the Munich crisis, the pious who condemn Paul.

Jamie Carr argues that *Down There on a Visit* is "about the discursive power that makes of 'homosexuality' an object of classification, of condemnation, of persecution."[28] Despite this larger critique, however, Isherwood still maintains an interest in homosexual identity, and this interest comes out in both explicit and encoded gay characters. The evocative details leave out exactly what happened, and with whom—the sex in *Down There on a Visit* carefully avoids being specifically homosexual. And yet, its encodings are anything but subtle. Ambrose is clearly marked as gay; his oft-cited vision of a homosexual dictatorship, told to a disgusted Geoffrey, identifies him as such, as does his group of boys. But he is also marked aesthetically as queer. As a student at Cambridge, Ambrose established a camp haven, an emerald green room with "green china," "green apples," "Venetian glass," and "a lovely old carpet which came from the Turkish Embassy in Paris" (111). This room codes him as an Oscar Wilde devotee. When the "hearties" trash his rooms, smash his dishes, and "smear filth on the walls and over the pictures" (112), Ambrose breaks from his ordinary life: "I felt as if everything—all my past life—had been smeared with their dirt. They'd put their filthy hands on it. And now I never, never wanted to have anything to do with it again. . . . What I couldn't stop being amazed at was that these people—whom one had imagined never thought about one, or were even aware of one's existence—that they'd actually loathed one, without one's dreaming of it" (112). This rejection, a specifically homophobic one, leads to Ambrose's death and rebirth. As he tells Christopher in concluding this story, "The day you arrived, I told you I was dead. You didn't understand what I meant, did you? I meant, I'm dead as far as England and everybody in it is concerned" (114). If England was dead, the new world he sought to build was a gay millennium, one in which the hearties were marginalized and fey Ronald Firbank devotees were empowered.

In section four, Paul is introduced as the most famous male prostitute in the world, and his lovers are all women (though the model for Paul, Denny Green, was primarily homosexual). Yet Paul is also coded as gay in the text. He refers himself as "auntie," refers to Augustus as "Miss Parr" (263), and once, disapproving of a self-righteous passage, exclaims, "How she dare!" (254). A kind of camp humor marks his speech. In one encounter, Christopher points out the car that is to take him to his volunteer work. "'Look,' I said, 'that must be her, parked over by the wall. They said it was a blue pickup truck, didn't they?' 'Auntie's last pickup,' Paul murmured" (286). Paul is accused of having sex with an adolescent girl—another queer sexual encounter, though this time unconsummated. Paul explains why he doesn't want the truth to be told in a truly Oscar Wilde-esque aphorism: "There's something so shaming about having your name cleared. Let's leave it dirty for a while" (287). Much of this posturing is intended to provoke, as Christopher notes: "After this remark, I braced myself for some kind of demonstration. And sure enough—when May had returned and they were ready to leave—'Au revoir, mon amour,' Paul exclaimed, taking me in his arms and kissing me passionately on the lips, '*tu sais que je t'adore!*' I kissed him right back, lest I should see to put myself on the side of the enemy" (287). That public kiss marks both Paul and Christopher, the narrator, in a rebellion encoded clearly as queer. Unlike *The World in the Evening,* Isherwood's characters camp in *Down There on a Visit,* particularly his "dear auntie" Paul.

Gay characters in *Down There on a Visit,* however, are not simply visible; they are exemplary. The hell-is-queer cadre does something similar, setting up gay characters as guides or mentors. Eric in *Another Country* uses his queer sexuality to help other characters face their own identities, strikingly in the most positive depiction of sex in the novel, the sexual encounter between Eric and Vivaldo. Jeremy, at the end of *City of Night,* forces the narrator to face his own identity and desires, and their sexual encounter brings a self-knowledge from which the narrator flees. Ann, in *Desert of the Heart,* becomes a guide for Evelyn to shed "guilt and goodness" and accept the alternative morality and beauty of the desert.

Down There on a Visit, I want to argue, takes this preference for gay mentors further. Gore Vidal found the argument so explicit that he chided Isherwood for his "homosexual chauvinism":

I know you don't do it in the sense that there is a world elsewhere, and a better one where boys lie with boys as opposed to the corrupt world of boy-girl-baby. But it does keep coming out that way. I shouldn't in the least mind a work which said bluntly that homosexual relations can be more pleasurable, more honest, less compromising than heterosexual relations.[29]

Gore's characterization is somewhat surprising, since the encoded gay characters end in exile or death and Isherwood's most successful gay domestic relationship—his thirty-year partnership with Don Bachardy—doesn't enter this novel at all. Yet I think Vidal is right about the "homosexual chauvinism" of *Down There on a Visit*. Isherwood embraces Ambrose and Paul as mentors of cultural rebellion and spiritual enlightenment. His encoded gay characters are gay saints, and their rejection of conventional life has a deeper spiritual consequence. Isherwood merges sex and spirituality in his depiction of two gay saints—with potentially a third in training, himself.

Gay Saints and the Counterculture Hero

Isherwood proposes the saint as the appropriate model for a religious writer in two essays, "The Writer and Vedanta" and "The Problem of the Religious Novel." In the first essay, written in 1961, just before the publication of *Down There on a Visit*, he claims that "contact with Vedanta has made me see that of all characters, the saint is the most interesting. He is the most interesting because he is the most flexible and he is the most flexible because he is not driven by hate, fear, greed, and all the other limiting motives" (161). In an earlier essay, "The Problem of the Religious Novel" (1946), Isherwood had addressed the possibilities of the saint: "Because his motives are not dictated by fear, vanity, or desire—because his every action is a genuine act of free will—you never can predict what he will do next. He accepts life more fully, more creatively, than any of his neighbors. And therefore he is the most interesting person to write about. The most interesting and the most difficult. . . . The saint, considered as an end product, resembles Mr. Jones as little as he resembles a giraffe. And yet Mr. Jones and Mr. Smith and Mr. Brown are all potentially saints" (164). Isherwood connects the saint with freedom, a recurring sixties theme, thus rejecting the traditional notion of the saint— "The public has its preconceived notion of a saint—a figure with a lean face and an air of weary patience, who alternates between moods of forbidding austerity and heartbroken sweetness"—as "the dreariest of bores" (164–65). The saint becomes a new kind of antihero in Isherwood's sixties lexicon.

His claim that "Mr. Jones and Mr. Smith and Mr. Brown are all potentially saints" is what makes Isherwood's interest more than an arcane religious obsession. The "struggles toward sainthood" are available to everyone, and Isherwood thinks of such suffering like "the hardships of a boxer's training" (167). In fact, the journey toward sainthood *is* the novel, because "the portrait of the perfected saint" is impossible: "Here, I am sure, I should give up in despair. Nothing short of genius could succeed in such a task. For the mystical experience itself can never be described. It can only be written around, hinted at, dimly reflected in word and deed. . . . Perhaps the truly comprehensive religious novel could only be written by a saint—and saints, unfortunately, are not in the habit of writing novels" (167–68). Isherwood claims that "if I ever write a religious novel, I shall begin by trying to prove that my saint-to-be really *is* Mr. Jones" (165). In his case, the saint is Miss Thing, for the saints in *Down There on a Visit* are marked as gay. Ambrose and Paul portray the development of gay saints.

Even in their names, Isherwood marks these characters as part of his larger religious project. Ambrose suggests Saint Ambrose, known for his gifts to the poor, his universalism, and his belief that all people would eventually gain salvation. Ambrose is trying to buy an island he names St. Gregory for a famous recluse who withdraws from the world and creates a monastery with brother monks. Ambrose's absolute acceptance of all behavior on his island may correlate with Saint Ambrose's universalism. Paul has even more provocative Christian connotations. The persecutor Saul, struck dumb on the road and given a vision of the truth, becomes Paul, father of the New Testament and the organized church. In both cases, it is Saul/Paul's utter commitment to persecution or defense of the faith that marks him as a saint, and this same utter commitment of purpose marks Isherwood's Paul, whether he is chasing underage tail or pursuing the depths of his psyche.

Isherwood marks these characters as saints in his descriptions. His initial description of Ambrose is a case in point: "Ambrose was about my age, I supposed. . . . His figure was slim and erect and there was a boyishness in his quick movements. But his dark-skinned face was quite shockingly lined, as though life had mauled him with its claws. His hair fell picturesquely about his face in wavy black locks which were already streaked with gray. There was a gentle surprise in the expression of his dark brown eyes. . . . And yet there was a kind of inner contemplative repose in the midst of him. It made him touchingly beautiful. He could have posed for the portrait of a saint" (71). Posing for the portrait of a saint is explicit, of course, but the "contemplative repose" is also suggestive, as is the boyishness. Ambrose is, simply, unlike the people around him.

Boyishness also marks Paul, from his initial description on. The final portrait we get of Paul, however, is particularly evocative: "Paul was sitting propped up by pillows in a huge Empire bed, which was littered with books and magazines. He was corpse-white, and his face looked as though it had the firmness of hard wax and was semitransparent. There was an air about him of being somehow preserved and, at the same time, purified; his skin seemed to be absolutely without blemish. Indeed, he was marvelously, uncannily beautiful" (312). Paul, in the end, looks as if he has been transfigured into an icon. The beauty of both Ambrose and Paul marks their religious wisdom.

Ambrose is notable for his utter serenity and disregard for ordinary conventions of politeness and morality. Christopher notes this lack on his first meeting: "I was a little surprised he took it so casually for granted that I was coming to his island, even for a short visit. . . . What I found disconcerting was that Ambrose shows so little curiosity about me; that he didn't even ask questions about our journey or what was going on in Berlin. I felt that he was absolutely self-sufficient within his own world. If you cared to enter it—well, good; that was your affair" (72). Ambrose's total acceptance of actions and circumstance is marked on a number of occasions. In a stormy passage, drenched, Ambrose is "languid . . . he seemed perfectly relaxed." Christopher tells him, "I can quite imagine you getting out and walking on the water" (68), and, as always, Ambrose smiles. "Ambrose has the sort of indifference to discomfort and hardship which you would expect to find in a great hero or saint. And as he is quite unaware of this, he keeps expecting us to have it, too" (100). That indifference to hardship and discomfort isn't simply for himself, however. Anyone on his island has to accept this as well. When Aleko assaults another boy on the island, Ambrose refuses to get the police involved, because "as an anarchist, he couldn't recognize the authority of the police and the law under any circumstances" (104). This principle holds even when Aleko's murderous impulses lead to the destruction of Ambrose's house in a spectacular dynamite blast.

We meet Ambrose once his arduous journey toward sainthood is complete, but we do get a glimpse of what leads him on this journey. Ambrose's fall from grace—sinful outsiders destroying his aesthetic green Eden—causes him to reject the world. Paul's journey, by contrast, stems from an absolute intolerance of sham. He was devastating in his critiques of Augustus Parr's play at sainthood, down to Parr's wearing of a Christlike beard. "Without even a polite show of hesitations, he would blandly take and gobble up the best food that Augustus had to offer. 'I utterly refuse,' he told me, 'to play Miss Parr's humbler-than-thou game.' . . . On one occasion when Augustus received us in a crudely patched shirt and a pair of jeans with the cuffs cut off and their edges left ragged, Paul remarked, in his slowest drawl, 'Let's face it, Augustus, that Robinson Crusoe thing isn't really you.' Augustus laughed, but I think he was slightly hurt" (263). The camp humor punctures pretension; Paul refuses pretense. He even highlights white racism by referring to his friend at camp, "a plump, bespectacled Negro named Wilson," as "Nigger" (293), much to the discomfort of his white employers.

What Paul wants is an authentic spiritual experience. He shows an unexpected interest in Christopher's somewhat shamefaced religious quest. Augustus Parr describes him as having a "dynamic despair. The kind that makes dangerous criminals, and, very occasionally, saints" (237). Paul has come to his own knowledge of the "sheer beastliness of the world," and he is ready for the spiritual awakening Augustus promises. When Paul meditates, Augustus notices "the completeness with which he gave himself to the experience. Self-knowledge is impossible for most of us because we can't push aside this thing that stands in the way of it; but here one felt that the entire ego-sheath had been sloughed off" (239). Paul's absolute commitment contrasts with Christopher's more inconsistent interest. Paul later decides to get hooked on opium to "see if I was *really* changed by any of what happened to me in California—meeting Augustus, and meditating, and all of that. I didn't know any other way to find out" (315). His fearlessness, even self-destructiveness, is a mark of his potential sainthood. Christopher's halfhearted offer to try a pipe provokes Paul's final devastating assessment of Christopher:

> Oh, darling Chrissikins! If you only knew how funny you are! So you want to try it? *Once! One pipe!* Or a dozen pipes for that matter! You're exactly like a tourist who thinks he can take in the whole of Rome in one day. You know, you really are a tourist, to your bones. I bet you're always sending post cards with 'Down here on a visit' on them. That's the story of your life. . . . I'll tell you what'd happen if you smoked one pipe: nothing! Nothing would happen! It's absolutely no use fooling around with this, unless you really want to know what's *inside* of it, what it's all *about.* And to do that, you have to let yourself get hooked. Deliberately. Not fighting it. Not being scared. Not setting any time limits. (315–16)

Paul ends up dying young, but we receive news of the ultimate success of his spiritual journey from an impartial observer—a friend who never believed in Paul's spiritual quest. When he hears *"young intellectuals . . . arguing with each other about the impossibility of life after death,"* Paul dismisses them with a simple rejoinder: "'You little fools!' *My dear, you ought to have heard him! It was positively shattering. And he said it with such an air of authority; it was as if he actually knew something"* (317; emphasis in the original). Paul claims authority and personal experience; despite, or perhaps because of, his unlikely sainthood, he succeeds in attaining true knowledge. Isherwood redeems Paul, although the real-life model Denny Green died while still an opium addict.[30] His gay saints triumph over the "enemy," combining sixties antiheroes and spiritual gurus.

Early in "Ambrose," Christopher has a sudden realization about his host: "Perhaps it was a slight gesture he made with his cigarette; perhaps it was the odd way he smilingly lowered his eyelids and looked away as if avoiding the glare of a strong light. (I realized, a few moments later, when he looked directly at me, that he had never done so before; never, at least, while I was looking at *him.*) Anyhow, whatever the clue may have been that I subconsciously picked up, the recognition came to me in a flash. 'Why, Ambrose,' I exclaimed, '*I know you!*' Ambrose said nothing. He kept his eyes averted, still smiling" (74). Of course, this is a literal recognition—Christopher knew Ambrose at Cambridge—but it is also another "Listen, baby, I know you" moment, one in which the essential humanity of each is affirmed. In *The World in the Evening,* Stephen has a similar recognition looking at Aunt Sarah, when he sees an eternal presence behind her eyes (276). Here, the recognition is more personal. When Christopher says that he knows Ambrose, he is also saying that he recognizes himself in Ambrose—just as later, he identifies with Paul. Each of these gay saints becomes a powerful kind of role model for the narrator Christopher. *Down There on a Visit* details the training of a potential saint, Christopher, whose own spiritual strivings are modeled on these two gay saints. Gay saints push the hell-is-queer trope as far from Vidal's damning assessment as one might imagine. Isherwood's *Down There on a Visit* constructs an innovatively new kind of sixties countercultural heroism, one in which queer writers and characters can claim a central place.

◈ 6 ◈

Secret Agents and Gay Identity: Cold War Queerness

A *SINGLE MAN* HAS BECOME ONE OF ISHERWOOD'S MOST-lauded and well-known novels; Edmund White, for example, embraced *A Single Man* as "one of the first and best novels of the modern gay liberation movement."[1] The novel has been read as prophetic, anticipating the gay liberation movement of the 1970s and queer theory of the 1990s and later. Tom Ford's beautifully filmed movie of the novel in 2009 introduced it to a new generation of readers. These subsequent critical appreciations of *A Single Man* don't indicate how Isherwood created and framed the novel within and against the cultural mores of the 1960s. Joseph Bristow warns against reading the novel "within post-Stonewall debates about the need to come out and declare one's gayness in the public sphere," because "Isherwood's homosexuality was not exactly located either inside or outside the doors of the closet: the emblem that would become one of the most powerful means of thinking about gay oppression and gay liberation in the 1960s and beyond. His fictions . . . make same-sex desire legible in a rather different set of terms."[2] Isherwood's "set of terms" for same-sex desire involve a complexly layered fictional persona intimately tied up with camp. *A Single Man* reread popular culture tropes of the secret agent, embodying an emerging sixties queer ethos as a secret fraternity that would develop into an unambiguous sense of minority status by the 1970s.

Cold War culture was obsessed with spies: movies, pulp fiction, and magazines circulated images of nefarious interlopers and brave agents of good battling in the midst of an unsuspecting public. Early Cold War narratives, Michael Kackman argues, "construct[ed] an idealized masculine figure on whom rest the hopes and fears of the nation" and "contain[ed] any expressions of cultural, racial, or gender difference within those narratives."[3] By the 1960s, however, "a growing incredulity toward political institutions and practices . . . made the neat ideological package that was the 1950s spy drama an untenable proposition."[4] The simple dichotomy of "good spies" and "bad spies" becomes ambivalent; the spy is more transgressive and less easily assimilated into simple moral binaries.

The innate queerness of the spy may explain Isherwood's long fascination. *Mr. Norris Changes Trains* frames Mr. Norris as a double agent for the Nazis and the Communists who involves the narrator, William Bradshaw, in his schemes. Isherwood's first job for MGM was to adapt the novel into a spy screenplay, though he objected to their simple construction of Norris as a loathsome enemy agent.[5] *The World in the Evening* ends with the narrator, Stephen, imagining the upcoming "war on the queers," and when Bob Wood jokingly warns him, "Don't think I wouldn't shoot you down with the rest of them," Stephen proclaims, "You would not! *I'd* be a C.O then. Or else one of your spies" (266).

In the early 1960s, Isherwood had a new focus for his spy fixation: James Bond. Fleming started writing Bond novels in the mid-1950s, but it was the James Bond movies, starting with *Dr. No* in 1962, that brought them into sixties popular culture, with key reprints of the James Bond novels in New American Library editions. Isherwood's library boasts sixteen James Bond novels, almost all NAL paperback reprints from the early 1960s. He also owned Kingsley Amis's 1965 celebration of the Bond phenomenon, *The James Bond Dossier;* Amis, a respected British writer who was often discussed as one of Britain's "angry young men," treats the series as a serious object of cultural criticism. In a letter to Cyril Connolly, Isherwood confessed, "I am a second-to-none Fleming fan & have read all his books twice."[6]

Isherwood's interest in Bond may have centered on Bond's transgressive refusal of monogamy and state-sanctioned sexuality. Bond's seductions transgress nation and ideology, and while he often can convert foreign spies through his virility, in *From Russia with Love,* he is also fooled, quite shamefully, by double agents such as Vesper in *Casino Royale.* Whatever Bond's ultimate loyalty to Cold War ideology, he destabilizes the simple binaries on which it relies. Fabio Cleto suggests that "there's something queer in what a spy *is*," since spies are "ethically ambiguous," "break taboos," and have divided loyalties.[7]

But if there is something queer in what the spy is, James Bond aggressively disavowed any such association. Isherwood confided to Connolly that "I have several times resented his attitude to the Minority to which I belong."[8] Cold War homophobia recurred in the Bond novels. From the gay assassins in *Diamonds Are Forever* to the bisexual seducer and head of the abhorrent Russian group SMERSH in *From Russia with Love,* gay figures are described with relish. The only positive gay character—Pussy Galore from *Goldfinger*—is redeemed by Bond's virilty at the end of the novel, diminished from her magnificent self-possession into a lost lamb begging to be ravaged. Fleming's homophobia reflected Cold War culture's homosexual panic. As John D'Emilio details in *Sexual Politics, Sexual Communities,* Cold War policies targeted homosexuals (41). D'Emilio quotes from a Senate report: "Immature, unstable, and morally enfeebled by the gratification of their perverted desires, homosexuals lacked the character to resist the blandishments of the spy" (43). Homosexuals, like spies, blended in with the "normal" population and hid their nefarious purposes. This obsession with the "homosexual menace" led to explicit discrimination, numerous firings, and untold suffering (45). In the public imagination, to be gay was to be a member of a fifth column.

In response, some gay artists embraced this fantasy. W. H. Auden's idea of the Homintern, of course, imagined gay culture as an effective international secret society, and Harry Hay's Mattachine Society was established explicitly on the model of the Communist secret cell. As the 1960s progressed, Cold War images of spies themselves became fair game for camp satire, an explicit queering of the spy that had gay culture embracing its designation as a security risk. One of the earliest gay spoofs of James Bond was published by Cyril Connolly in *London* magazine in 1963, a year before the publication of *A Single Man.* M sends Bond undercover to a gay club in drag as "Gerda," to ensnare a Russian general. Bond's transformation into a drag queen gives Connolly delicious material for satire:

Bond was wearing one of his many pheasant's eye alpacas which exaggerated the new vertical line—single-breasted, narrow lapels, ton-up trousers with no turn-ups, peccary suede shoes. A short covert-coat in cavalry twill, a black sting-ray of a tie, an unexpected width of shoulder above the tapering waist and the casual arrogance of his comma of dark hair low over the forehead under his little green piglet of a hat completed the picture of mid-century masculinity. The young man seemed unimpressed. "Well, well, how butch can you get? You've left it rather late. But we'll see what we can do."

He turned Bond towards the lighted north window and studied him carefully, then he gave the comma a tweak. "I like the spit-curl, Gerda, we'll build up round that. Now go in there and strip."[9]

Connolly's spoof highlights Bond's obsession with clothes. Although such attention to clothes also marks interwar hard-boiled detective fiction like *The Maltese Falcon* and *The Big Sleep*,[10] Bond's clothes obsession was markedly fey, and Connolly's wicked satire undermines Bond's hypermasculine swagger. The scene also features a sassy queen who deflates Bond's manly persona as an obvious form of drag by calling the obsessive "comma" of hair falling over his forehead a "spit-curl." Even naming Bond's gender identity as "butch" satirizes his supposedly unassailable masculinity. Like the narrator in John Rechy's *City of Night*, Bond becomes "trade," implicated in a queer sexual system. Isherwood wrote Connolly to praise this satire, saying, "I think he had this coming to him."[11] Although the piece concludes with M declaring his undying love for Bond, M is punished for making their homosocial relationship explicit; Connolly may have been gay friendly, but he was not writing from a gay perspective.

Gay writers went much further in their textual poaching. Victor Banis's *The Man from C.A.M.P.* (an example of gay pulp, which I discuss in the next chapter) epitomizes an oppositional sixties queer consciousness. The novel spoofs the television series *The Man from U.N.C.L.E.*, which, as Michael Kackman explains in *Citizen Spy*, was an homage to, and then a parody of, the James

Bond movies (81). The television series was central to the "new Pop aesthetic": "Not only were the sets of these shows decorated with icons of Pop Art, the narratives themselves increasingly reflected Pop themes. Indeed, these programs increasingly explored the play of surfaces and fixated upon consumer goods and everyday objects" (88). After 1966, the show became explicitly campy: it "embraced the heightened intertextuality, consumerism, and slapstick comedy of Pop" (91).

The Man from U.N.C.L.E., then, was already enmeshed in the encoded world of gay popular culture in the mid-1960s. It was a short hop into explicitly gay parody. Banis's *The Man from C.A.M.P.* features secret agent Jackie Holmes, who acts like an ineffectual queen as a cover for his clandestine work. Our first view of Jackie comes from the homophobic FBI agent Ted Summers, who is contacted in the men's bathroom:

> He had just stood up to the urinal when the door opened behind him and an effeminate blond stepped up beside him. For a moment Summers ignored the newcomer, thinking instead about the mysterious Jackie whom they should have met an hour ago.
>
> He was suddenly aware of the fact that he was being stared at. He glanced angrily sideways. The blond, short and slender, was looking him over brazenly, an irritating smile playing on his lips.
>
> "Nice," he said simply, raising his eyes to wink at Summers.
>
> "Knock it off," Summers snapped angrily, stepping back quietly. . . .
>
> "Oh, no, you can't be . . ."
>
> The blond nodded. "Umm-hm, I'm Jackie." . . .
>
> "Do we have to stand here like this?" Summers asked. Standing at a urinal with a homosexual beside him was proving to be disquieting. "It's sort of a peculiar way to make contact."
>
> "It's a rather good way, as a matter of fact," Jackie informed him, clearly deriving more enjoyment from the situation than Summers was. (3–4)

"Listen, baby, I know you" takes on a whole new meaning as the gay secret agent sizes up his contact's secret package. Jackie Holmes deliberately provokes homosexual panic, propositioning straight men with brazen delight.

As the title suggests, camp is central to these novels. The entrance to Jackie's secret office is in the men's room of the local gay bar; his miniature poodle is a trained attack dog. Jackie appears weak but can outfight, outthink, and outtalk anyone he encounters. He is irresistible, even to straight men, as the notches on his enormous wooden phallus amply demonstrate. Jackie Holmes is, in other words, a gay fantasy, "a superb subcultural icon" (351). Victor Banis detailed Jackie's wish fulfillment for gay readers:

> Jackie took every cliché leveled at gays and turned them upside down inside out. Gays were supposed to be either tops or bottoms, for instance. Jackie went at it every way including sideways. Yes, he could certainly swish, as all gays were alleged to do in those days, but he could deliver a haymaker that would leave his opponent out cold. He owned that white poodle featured on the cover—the very dog that symbolized gays in so many minds but Sophie had razor-sharp teeth and was trained to kill. . . . And as for that old canard about gays being out to seduce every straight man they meet? In book after book, Jackie always managed to get his man in the end—so to speak. . . . Better yet, it was they who inevitably came, panting and eager, to him. (351)

Certainly, for a community still legally and socially illegitimate, such fantasy satisfied a particularly potent cultural desire. Fabio Cleto calls Jackie a "gay superhero," and certainly his impossible knowledge and talents qualify him. Matthew J. Costello suggests that the superheroes of comic books during the 1960s placed "secret identities" at the heart of the superhero, indicating a "societal identity crisis between public and private identity."[12] Bond was a fantasy figure, but one who excluded gays and lesbians; Banis queered that fantasy.

Much of the blacklisting of gay people in the 1950s stemmed

from the idea that gay people were un-American, criminal, and loyal not to the common good but to their own secret, sordid, hedonistic society. After all, if they cared for the common good, they wouldn't be queer. *The Man from C.A.M.P.* embraces this paranoid cultural projection as its premise. Yes, you're right, straight America—there really *is* an international gay conspiracy, coordinated at High C.A.M.P., the headquarters. The embrace of the homosexual as outlaw by enthusiastic gay readers—and Victor Banis reveals that these novels each sold "in the six figures" (350)—suggests an emerging gay subjectivity in the sixties enamored of the secret double life. A sixties queer ethos embraced a secret network of queers who could and did communicate with each other but were hidden from mainstream society. The double life suggests a superior ethic and aesthetic; the gay secret agent isn't persecuted or frightened but masterful, consciously concealing "the truth" for sake of the larger mission of C.A.M.P.

The Man from C.A.M.P. may be understood as an early form of fan fiction that became a lucrative publishing trend. Although *A Single Man* is less blatant, it participates in the same sixties queering of popular culture. In the pages that follow, I read *A Single Man* as a queer mashup of James Bond, despite the fact that Isherwood would not have identified Bond as an influence. He claimed *Mrs. Dalloway* as his model for the novel; the structure—a life in one day—bears this out, and the modernist influence matched Isherwood's sense of himself as a literary writer. But Isherwood wasn't just reading Virginia Woolf[13] while drafting the novel; he was reading James Bond obsessively.[14] He wrote of Fleming on June 29, 1962, "He's not all that good but he has atmosphere. It's a world. You can enter it and have fun."[15] The intertextual connections between *A Single Man* and Fleming's books are numerous, suggesting that Bond's world was irresistible.

A Single Man: Uncle George and Queer Wish Fulfillment

There are a number of parallels between Fleming's Bond and Isherwood's George that suggest George's inflection as a spy. Despite Bond's defense of England, he is an ambivalent figure—the son of a Scottish father and a Swiss mother, educated in Switzerland,

and disdainful of inherited wealth. His appearance at Blades, one of the oldest gambling establishments of the British elite, marks him as a man out of place: "And what could the casual observer think of him, 'Commander James Bond, C.M.G. . . . Something a bit cold and dangerous in that face. Looks pretty fit. May have been attached to Templer in Malaya. Or Nairobi. Mau Mau work. Tough-looking customer. Doesn't look the sort of chap one usually sees in Blades. Bond knew that there was something alien and un-English about himself. He knew that he was a difficult man to cover up. Particularly in England. He shrugged his shoulders. Abroad was what mattered."[16] Bond's transgressive qualities permit him to fulfill his role superbly outside the mainstream. Similarly, George is a foreigner—an Englishman living abroad—but he is also a foreigner by choice. Standing before his classroom, "he feels brilliant, vital, challenging, slightly mysterious and, above all, *foreign.* His neat dark clothes, his white dress shirt and tie (the only tie in the room) are uncompromisingly alien from the aggressively virile informality of the young male students."[17] While Bond recognizes his foreignness as a potential liability, George delights in the delicious sensibility of "foreignness."

Bond is obsessed with his anonymity (despite the fact that he uses his real name constantly). In *Live and Let Die,* Bond reflects that "anonymity was the chief tool of his trade. Every thread of his real identity that went on record in any file diminished his value and, ultimately, was a threat to his life" (7). Bond's willingness to inhabit a number of facades—diamond smuggler, monied lord in league with the English gentry—makes a malleability of identity an essential, even noble, attribute of the successful secret agent. George's own anonymous facade is reflected in the opening sequence of *A Single Man:* "Sitting on the john, he can look out of the window. (They can see his head and shoulders from across the street, but not what he is doing.)" (17). George appears to be the serious scholar at work, while he is really involved in matters scatological. George continues these subterfuges; rather than give his neighbors knowledge of Jim's death, thus exposing himself as an object of pity, he prefers to tell them that Jim has moved back east (28). This may also explain George's suspicion of the IBM identity card, and his subversive fantasy of its destruction: "This card *is* his identity. Suppose, instead of signing it as requested and returning it to the Personnel office, George were to tear it up? Instantly, that student would cease to exist, as far as San Tomas State was concerned. . . . George dislikes the card, holding it steady with two fingertips. He dislikes even to touch these things, for they are the runes of an idiotic but nevertheless potent and evil magic: the magic of the think-machine gods, whose cult has one dogma, *We cannot make a mistake*" (46–47). George's suspicion of IBM's marking of identity parallels Bond's own: anything that fixes identity inhibits the necessary malleability of the secret agent. George has a primitive horror of IBM's power. But George is an amateur; whereas Bond would undoubtedly have destroyed the card, or perhaps the entire machine of identification, George is content simply to tease the secretaries about impairing the card (47).

Early in *A Single Man,* in a seemingly unimportant aside, Isherwood suggests another aspect of this fantasy of anonymity: "(Like everyone with an acute criminal complex, George is hyperconscious of all the bylaws, city ordinances, rules and petty regulations. Think of how many Public Enemies have been caught just because they neglected to pay a parking ticket! Never once has he seen his passport stamped at a frontier, his driver's license accepted by a post-office clerk as evidence of identity, without whispering gleefully to himself, *Idiots—fooled them again!*)" (33). The fact that this passage is in parentheses is one of its most charming textual features—as if, on the one hand, this information is so top secret that it must be whispered, behind one hand, and yet also so unimportant to the action that it is merely an interesting aside. This "acute criminal complex" is central to George's sense of identity. Secret agents must be hyperconscious of "petty regulations" to maintain their anonymity, but presumably they don't get a thrill every time they fool a mark. George "gleefully" plays at being a gay secret agent; like Sally Bowles, his amateur status is part of both his charm and his ineffectuality. The secret agent trope provides another way to understand George's multiple identities throughout the course of the novel. Secret agents must be talented actors; multiple identities are a tool of the trade, a conscious transformation of the (queer) self to protect and operate undetected in a hostile environment. James Bond often felt set apart in his subversive roles; in the first James Bond novel, *Casino Royale,* he reflected on this double consciousness: "Against the background of this luminous and sparkling stage Bond stood in the sunshine and felt his mission to be congruous and remote and his dark profession as an affront to his fellow actors" (30). Acting, of course, is central to George's identity, most explicitly before his class, when the narrator describes his "entrance" as "quite undramatic according to conventional standard. Nevertheless, this is a subtly contrived, outrageously theatrical effect" (56). George's malleable identity, framed through acting, reads less like a sermon or postmodern anticipation when read through a trope of the secret agent.

Bond's combination of foreignness and anonymity makes him a particularly acute observer of local situations, and this is something else George shares. Fleming has two novels with significant settings in the United States (*Live and Let Die* and *Diamonds Are Forever*), and Bond's observations of New York in *Live and Let Die* show the details a trained foreign operative can provide: "It was no waste of time to start picking up the American idiom again: the advertisements, the new car models, and the prices of second-hand ones in the used-car lots; the exotic pungency of the road signs: SOFT SHOULDERS—SHARP CURVES—SQUEEZE AHEAD—SLIPPERY WHEN WET; . . . the Civil Defense warnings: IN CASE OF ENEMY ATTACK KEEP MOVING—GET OFF BRIDGE; . . . THE MARCH OF DIMES—all the small fleeting impressions that were as important to his trade as are broken bark and bent twigs to the trapper in the jungle" (9). Bond shows his attention for detail here, but also implicit in the description is the survey of Cold War capitalist culture, with its banal slogans, its suppressed sexuality, and its Cold War paranoia. Fleming, through Bond, critiques American culture as inferior to English. Isherwood, of course, embraced the cause of Anglo-American détente, and was less critical of American culture than most of his British peers, yet he shared some of this perspective. An earlier title for *A Single Man* was *The Englishman,* and in his writing journal, he explicitly identified *The Englishman* with himself.[18] He also allowed himself more pointed critiques of American culture in *A Single Man,* all grounded in close observation of a culture from which he holds himself apart.

George's dissension from mainstream society is equally crucial. Isherwood's reservations about American culture had been simmering for years. In an early draft of *Down There on a Visit,* he wrote about his relationship with his adopted country in surprisingly evangelical terms: "The old thing is not hostile to the Americans; when he thinks of himself in relation to them, he thinks of himself as a missionary of a sort, doomed to work with them for the rest of his life and quite resigned to that, and even prepared to enjoy it. He will fight, he says to himself, until his last breath, against television commercials, billboards, presidential messages to the nation, newspapers, gossip columns, books of the month, radio sermons and professional sincerity in all its forms; he will fight, he will never never yield—and they will never never notice."[19] Isherwood's hostility to the banalities of American life is palpable throughout his post–World War II writing. Despite his fervent belief in an Anglo-American merger, he believes in his own moral superiority, much as he did in previous skirmishes with English bourgeois culture. *A Single Man* is filled with offhand dismissals of American life.

Most of these critiques focus on U.S. capitalism. Professors, George observes, "have cut themselves off from the majority— the middlemen, the hucksters, the promoters—by laboriously acquiring all this dry, discredited knowledge. . . . All the middleman wants are its products, its practical applications. These professors are suckers, he says. What's the use of knowing something if you don't make money out of it?" (83). This obsession with productivity marks George's most serious indictment of American culture, leading him to describe his work as a teacher as "selling a real diamond for a nickel." Consumer culture's failures are linked to the larger absurdities of Cold War politics for George. World events keep appearing in George's conversations, in his observations, even in his offhand comments, attached to rampant consumerism. One of the most explicit references is to the Cuban Missile Crisis: "Shoppers crowd the stores and the sidewalks, their faces somewhat bewildered, their eyes reflecting, like polished buttons, the cynical sparkle of the Yuletide. Hardly more than a month ago, before Khrushchev agreed to pull his rockets out of Cuba, they were cramming the markets, buying the shelves bare of beans, rice and other foodstuffs, utterly useless, most of them, because they can't be prepared without pints of water. Well, the shoppers were spared—this time. Do they rejoice? They are too dull for that, poor dears; they never knew what didn't hit them" (103). Serious world events are no more than a spur to conspicuous consumption, a sign of their vacuity and their fear. Isherwood's Cold War commentary is the opposite of Ian Fleming's; while Fleming seeks to make readers more paranoid in their appreciation of a Communist conspiracy, Isherwood notes the inanity of the obsession with difference and secret consortia, even as he plays with the idea in George's psyche.

On the other hand, George defends this same aspect of consumer capitalism in terms that echo the arguments of pop art. In a debate in the lunchroom, he opines, "Motels are deliberately designed to be unreal, if you must use that idiotic jargon, for the very simple reason that an American motel room isn't *a* room in *an* hotel, it's *the* room, definitely, period. There is only one: *The Room.* And it's a symbol—an advertisement in three dimensions, if you like—for our way of life" (91). The notion of consumer culture as a legitimate aesthetic evokes pop art, which enshrined the artifacts of capitalism at the center of artistic creation. George suggests that these commodities are deeply spiritual, symbols of a deeper reality—and that this aesthetic is superior to the European model of "individual differences and romantic inefficiency and objects-for-the-sake-of-objects. All that dead old cult of cathedrals and first editions and Paris models and vintage wines" (90–91). Europeans, with their traditional definitions of art, George suggests (only half-facetiously), are "trying to subvert us, every moment, with their loathsome cult-propaganda. If they ever succeed, we'll be done for. *That's* the kind of subversion the Un-American Activities Committee *ought* to be investigating" (91). George indicts the entire aesthetic agenda of Cold War intellectuals as anti-American.

In general, however, George views Americans' dependence on commodities as a means of managing fear. Americans' Cold War paranoia is personal, directed at George. For example, George details his neighbor's moral failures and fears in oppositional terms: "They are afraid of what they know is somewhere in the darkness around them, of what may at any moment emerge into the undeniable light of their flashlamps, nevermore to be ignored, explained away. The fiend that won't fit into their statistics, the Gorgon that refuses their plastic surgery, the vampire drinking blood with tactless uncultured slurps, the bad-smelling beast that doesn't use their deodorants, the unspeakable that insists, despite all their shushing, on speaking its name. Among many other kinds of monster, George says, they are afraid of little me" (26–27). This passage, one of the most widely quoted from the novel, often is used to establish Isherwood's queer, oppositional credentials, embracing "the love that dare not speak its name." What this reading misses, though, is George's Walter Mitty–like fantasy. His imagined presence in the neighborhood is as a monster, a transgressive outlaw who threatens their sleep and their self-image: "Your exorcism has failed, dear Mrs. Strunk" (29). But we discover, in the only perspective in the novel not filtered through George, Mrs. Strunk's actual attitude toward the queer menace in her midst: "Poor man, she thinks, living there all alone. He has a kind face" (32). Now, we may read this response as patronizing or misguided, but it is difficult to read it as frightened. It is even insightful, for Mrs. Strunk recognizes George's bereavement when no one else does—not his colleagues, his students, his gym friends. Of course, even this is typical of the spy; James Bond misreads a number of situations, and his extreme confidence in his own insight leads to some of the most gruesome scenes of torture in Fleming's novels.

This disjuncture happens often in *A Single Man.* George's interior monologues and his outward behavior rarely match up. Although he embeds critiques of straight culture, Isherwood seems more interested in George's oppositional subjectivity than in making a claim for his actual oppressed status. Take another oft-quoted passage: his "Uncle George" fantasies. "A local newspaper editor has started a campaign against sex deviates (by which he means people like George)," and circulates the common stereotypes: bars, men's rooms, public libraries, and "[homosexuals] all, without exception, have syphilis" (36). George imagines a covert campaign—one that would require the best agents from C.A.M.P.: "Then, that newspaper editor, George thinks, how funny to kidnap him and the staff-writers responsible for the sex-deviate articles . . . and take them all to a secret underground movie studio where, after a little persuasion—no doubt just showing them the red-hot pokers and pincers would be quite sufficient—they would perform every possible sexual act, in pairs and in groups, with a display of the utmost enjoyment. The film would then be developed and prints of it would be rushed to all the movie theaters . . . under the heading of Coming Attractions" (38). The revenge here is clearly tongue in cheek, a camp fantasy not unlike Jackie Holmes's seduction of the most-entrenched homophobes. Indeed, C.A.M.P. has a number of divisions, as Victor Banis explained, groups including "social problems," "legal fields," "research departments," "scientific laboratories," and "the police branch."[20] By the end of the Uncle George fantasy, he has moved beyond covert spies to roaming homosexual death squads, a shift from whimsy to anger. But he is immediately ashamed of this ideological extremism, just as he is ashamed of literally playing the monster when he chases the neighbor children from his house. These fantasies represent not his true self (for he doesn't have one true self) but a fantasy life that enhances his own sense of importance and power.

That fantasy life, however, is written in cipher so that outsiders can't understand. This is a key characteristic of the spy. Bond is constantly talking to headquarters in code. His calls to "Universal Export" convey essential information that is inscrutable to outsiders listening in. A report on an encounter with Mr. Big in *Live and Let Die*, when Bond must report a violent altercation that ends in the death of several of Mr. Big's employees, is a case in point:

"You're connected, caller," said the overseas operator. "Go ahead, please. New York calling London."

Bond heard the calm English voice. "Universal Export. Who's speaking, please?"

"Can I speak to the Managing Director?" said Bond. "This is his nephew James speaking from New York." . . .

"I went uptown to see our chief customer last night," said Bond. "Three of his best men went sick while I was there."

"How sick?" asked the voice.

"As sick as can be, sir," said Bond. "There's a lot of 'flu about."

"Hope you didn't catch any."

"I've got a slight chill, sir," said Bond, "but absolutely nothing to worry about. I'll write to you about it. The trouble is that with all this 'flu about Federated think I will do better out of town." Bond chuckled to himself at the thought of M's grin. "So I'm off right away with Felicia."

"Who?" asked M.

"Felicia," Bond spelled it out. "My new secretary from Washington."

Bond put down the telephone. He grinned. He could imagine M calling in the Chief of Staff. "007's already tangled up with the FBI. Dam' fool went up to Harlem last night and bumped off three of Mr. Big's men. Got hurt himself, apparently, but not much. Got to get out of town with Leiter, the CIA man. (59–60)

Fleming provides an elaborate example of spy code here, carefully translating the true meaning and showing the relish both M and Bond take in getting away with a secret language. The idea that a secret fraternity is operating undetected becomes a thrilling possibility in the sixties. Isherwood, too, talks in code through George to his queer readers, including markers of a secret gay community invisible to outsiders.

In George's classroom performance, for example (before his famous definition of a minority, which "constitutes some kind of a threat to the majority, real or imaginary. And no threat is ever *quite* imaginary"; 70) he directs the speech to his fellow secret agent in the class: "George looks at Wally Bryant with a deep shining look that says, I am with you, little minority-sister. Wally is plump and sallow-faced, and the care he takes to comb his wavy hair and keep his nails filed and polished and his eyebrows discreetly plucked only makes him that much less appetizing. Obviously he has understood George's look. He is embarrassed. Never mind! George is going to teach him a lesson now that he'll never forget. Is going to turn Wally's eyes into his timid soul. Is going to give him courage to throw away his nail file and face the truth of his life" (70). George shares that distaste for queens of Cold War gay protest novels, but he also recognizes his "minority-sister" because of queen markers like nail files and tweezers. Despite George's "profile in courage," however, Wally makes himself much more visible. George argues that minorities are a legitimate threat to the order of things, but he doesn't ever use the word "homosexual" in class, sticking with an innocuous example of "freckles," and shying away from more confrontational discussions of race. His brave tonic is no more than a "deep shining look," one that Wally may well have interpreted as a come-on. Whatever gay identity George embodies, it is not an "out and proud" post–gay liberation ethos but a secret-agent code.

In other words, George's violent fantasies and his strident speeches don't come to fruition in the real world. He makes no "we're queer because we're queer because we're queer" speeches— not to Doris, the "earth bitch mother," whom he kisses rather than cussing out; not to Mrs. Strunk, whom he thanks sincerely for her invitation to dinner; not to Charlotte, whose smothering motheresque love makes him feel that he has betrayed Jim. Indeed, Isherwood goes out of his way to point out that George, unlike his colleagues, has a private income and would risk little in speaking out. Yet he doesn't. Despite an interior outrage about the political circumstances of the Cold War, including the Cuban Missile Crisis and queer baiting, George sticks to theoretical conversations in class and novels, such as *After Many a Summer Dies the Swan,* that can easily be dismissed as esoteric mysticism and melodramatic plot.

That doesn't mean, of course, that Isherwood's careful encoding of Los Angeles gay life wasn't perfectly visible to those in the know. Take, for example, George's visit to the gym. That encounter is described as almost a Greek idyll, men of all ages in a "physical democracy":

> How delightful it is to be here. If only one could spend
> one's entire life in this state of easygoing physical democ-
> racy. Nobody is bitchy here, or ill-tempered, or inquisitive.
> Vanity, including the most outrageous posings in front of

the mirrors, is taken for granted. The godlike young baseball player confides to all his anxiety about the smallness
of his ankles. The plump banker, rubbing his face with skin
cream, says simply, "I can't afford to get old." No one is perfect and no one pretends to be. Even the half-dozen quite
well-known actors put on no airs. The youngest kids sit in-
nocently naked beside sixty- and seventy-year-olds in the
steam room, and they call each other by their first names.
Nobody is too hideous or too handsome to be accepted as
an equal. Surely everyone is nicer in this place than he is
outside it? (109)

Bodybuilding culture in Los Angeles was, of course, notoriously
queer. Isherwood mentions the city's muscle culture in his essay
on Los Angeles; he was also a member of Gold's Gym, one of the
famous centers of that culture. *Physique* magazine epitomized
that queerness of bodybuilding during the Cold War. Christopher Nealon frames the homoerotic/homosocial male images of
Physique as indicative of a "secret public" of queer readers, who
were drawn to the idealized images of a male physicality, similar
to the "naked democracy" that George celebrates in *A Single Man:*
"The physique magazines encourage us to interpret the bodies in
their pages as standing in for the many bodies of their readers—
a move that, as I show, is suspected but never quite provable to
censors and yearned for but never quite confirmed by those readers. This is the 'secret' in the 'secret public' of physique culture:
that the single body might represent desires that are, in fact, more
elusive and more collective than single bodies."[21] That notion of a
"single" body, which symbolizes a collective identity, suggests the
larger ways that *A Single Man* could stand in for the many bodies
of its readers. David Hockney drew on those *Physique* images in
his own queer Los Angeles paintings, further circulating gay images of naked domesticity. George's seemingly innocent description of his gym becomes a message in code to gay readers.

Other secret messages abound. George twice refers to the L.A.
hustling scene that John Rechy made famous in his 1963 *City of
Night.* The first allusion is almost an innocent aside, as George
discusses the Christmas shoppers: "Everyone can afford to spend

at least something, except, maybe, some of the young hustlers (recognizable at once to experienced eyes like George's) who stand scowling on the street corners or staring into shops with the maximum of peripheral vision" (103). Again, note the parentheses; codes are "recognizable" to those with "experience," not just to L.A. johns, but also to gay readers, who know to pay special attention to supposedly unimportant parenthetical remarks. After the gym, however (another encoded gay space), George mentions hustling much more directly: "The scowling youths on the corners see him as a dodderer, no doubt, or at best as a potential score. . . . For a few bucks he could get any one of them to climb into the car, ride back with him to his house, strip off butch leather jacket, skin-tight levis, shirt and cowboy boots and take part, a naked, sullen young athlete, in the wrestling bout of his pleasure. But George doesn't want the bought unwilling bodies of these boys. He wants to rejoice in his own body—the tough triumphant old body of a survivor" (104). George's description of the "butch leather jacket, skin-tight levis, shirt and cowboy boots" matches Rechy's hustler's uniform in *City of Night;* selections from *City of Night* had already been published as Isherwood was drafting *A Single Man.* Whatever else these images were, they represented a recent and public encoding of a gay community that, like physique culture, connected single men to a broader community.

Public cruising is another means of depicting both sex and a larger gay community in *A Single Man.* George's description of the tennis players on campus and at the end of the novel may, in fact, be a coded reference to the tennis scene in Charles Jackson's *The Fall of Valor,* in which John Grandin surreptitiously watches a tennis match, "looking obliquely down through the window at the thrusting lunging arms, the play of muscle across the lean backs, and the almost formless legs that seemed to have been fashioned cleanly and sparely, like pistons or driving rods" (34). George's description is similarly erotic:

> Only one court is occupied, by two young men play-
> ing singles. . . . They have nothing on their bodies but
> gym shoes and thick sweatsocks and knit shorts of the
> kind cyclists wear, very short and close-fitting, molding

themselves to the buttocks and the loins. . . . Their nakedness makes them seem close to each other and directly
opposed, body to body, like fighters. . . . He is Mexican,
maybe, black-haired, handsome, catlike, cruel, compact,
lithe, muscular, quick and graceful on his feet. His body
is a natural dark gold-brown; there is a fuzz of curly black
hair on his chest and belly, and thighs. He plays hard and
fast, with cruel mastery, baring his white teeth, unsmiling,
as he slams back the ball. He is going to win. . . .

This game is cruel; but its cruelty is sensual and stirs
George into hot excitement. He feels a thrill of pleasure
to find the sense so eager in their response. . . . From his
heart, he thanks these young animals for their beauty.
(53–54)

This description of the "Mexican" is similar to the descriptions
of Waldemar in *Down There on a Visit,* and in both cases, it is
the ruthless, animal nature that provides George with vicarious
satisfaction. He is a secret agent deriving erotic pleasure from a
seemingly innocent occupation. This interior "queering" of an os-
tensibly heterosexual scene is another version of camp, only one
that has immediate gratifications.

George's final outing, to the bar on the beach, is another encoded reference to Los Angeles gay culture. He provides a detailed
genealogy of the bar that isn't exclusively gay, but nevertheless embraces a transgressive ethos of gay bars:

The Starboard Side has been here since the earliest days
of the colony. Its bar, formerly a lunch counter, served
the neighbors with their first post-prohibition beers. . . .
But its finest hours came later. That summer of 1945! The
war as good as over. The blackout no more than an ex-
cuse for keeping the lights out at a gangbang. . . . Here, in
the complete privacy of the din and the crowd, you and
your pickup yelled the preliminary sex advances at each
other. You could flirt but you couldn't fight; there wasn't
even room to smack someone's face. For that, you had
to step outside. Oh, the bloody battles and the sidewalk

> vomitings! The punches flying wide, the heads crashing
> backwards against the fenders of parked cars! Huge diesel-
> dikes slugging it out, grimmer far than the men. The siren-
> wailing arrival of the police; the sudden swooping of the
> shore patrol. (147)

The Starboard Side is a kind of bacchanal; its fighting and cruising
reproach the "breeder" neighbors who have since overtaken the
neighborhood. Because, as Allan Bérubé details in *Coming Out
Under Fire,* one of the unintended consequences of WWII was its
creation of gay community in West Coast towns, while soldiers
were waiting to be shipped out, the recurrence of hitchhiking
servicemen would evoke special knowledge in those in the know.
George continues his celebration of chaos when he describes the
bar after the war:

> And then the beach-months of 1946. The magic squalor
> of those hot nights, when the whole shore was alive with
> tongues of flame, the watchfires of a vast naked barbar-
> ian tribe—each group or pair to itself and bothering no
> one, yet all a part of the life of the tribal encampment—
> swimming in the darkness, cooking fish, dancing to the
> radio, coupling without shame on the sand. George and
> Jim (who had just met) were out there among them eve-
> ning after evening, yet not often enough to satisfy the sad
> fierce appetite of memory, as it looks back hungrily on that
> glorious Indian summer of lust. The hitch-hiking service-
> men are few now and mostly domesticated, going back and
> forth between the rocket base and their homes and wives.
> Beach fires are forbidden, except in designated picnic areas
> where you must eat sitting up on benches at communal
> tables, and mustn't screw at all. (147–48)

Unlike the tragic and damned in the California beach bars in *City
of Night,* Isherwood's bar is the embodiment of anarchic freedom,
a "glorious Indian summer of lust," a tribe that resists the horrible conformity of the nuclear family. George's nostalgia for that
"vast naked barbarian tribe" marks his discontent with Cold War

America, but he suggests that this tribe has simply gone underground, anchored by the encoded gay community of the novel.

That "glorious Indian summer of lust" returns, briefly, when Kenny pursues George at that same bar. They swim in the ocean, "refugees from wetness," an encounter that suggests both baptism and wild sex. Both end up at George's house, physically and emotionally naked. George feels that he may "begin to speak with tongues" (173), and holds forth:

> Look—things are quite bad enough anyhow, nowadays . . . without getting ourselves entangled in these dreary categories. I mean, what is this life of ours supposed to be *for?* Are we to spend it identifying each other with catalogues, like tourists in an art gallery? Or are we to try to exchange *some* kind of signal, however garbled, before it's too late? . . . You could know what I'm about. You could. But you can't be bothered to. Look—you're the only boy I ever met on that campus I really believe could. That's what makes it so tragically futile. Instead of trying to know, you commit the inexcusable triviality of saying "he's a dirty old man," and turning the evening, which might be the most precious and unforgettable of your young life, into a *flirtation!* You don't like that word, do you? But it's the word. It's the enormous tragedy of everything nowadays: flirtation. Flirtation instead of fucking, if you'll pardon my coarseness. All any of you ever do is flirt, and wear your blankets off one shoulder, and complain about motels. And miss the one thing that might really—and Kenneth, I do not say this casually—*transform your entire life.* (174, 176–77)

Kenny cannot, or will not, read the codes here. Is George offering spiritual enlightenment, or a first homosexual encounter? Or is it both? "Fucking" serves both physical and spiritual ends here, both symbol and trick. Isherwood, as the writer, also opts for flirtation instead of fucking, having George pass out instead of consummating the classic pulp sex scene. But gestures toward the pulp tradition are another kind of encoded message to his fellow secret agents.

In the final scene, Isherwood revisits the tennis players after his abandonment by Kenny and playfully turns George into a "one-handed reader," who uses a fantasy for his own pleasure. "The play has begun, now, and George isn't about to stop it. Kenny must be provided with a partner. So George turns Lois into the sexy little gold cat, the Mexican tennis player. No trouble about getting *him* upstairs! He and Kenny are together in the front room, now. George hears a belt drop to the floor. They are stripping themselves naked. The blood throbs deep down in George's groin. The flesh stirs and swells up, suddenly hard hot. The pajamas are pulled off, tossed out of bed" (179). George's literal masturbation here, in which he explicitly queers a standard heterosexual scene, is another model for camp transformation, a gesture of solidarity with his gay readers, whose masturbatory use of gay pulp was well known within gay circles. Such coded gay sex scenes in the novel correlate with the larger dreams of a queer utopia embedded in the erotic freedom and chaos of the beach. The truth of this vision is less important than the vision itself, the gay paradise toward which all these gay secret agents are striving. Isherwood's *A Single Man* longs for a queer life made flesh even as it models the powerful role of gay fantasy. This makes the novel a key moment in an evolving queer sixties ethos.

Camp Obfuscation and Secret Agency

The secret agent trope may help to explain Isherwood's puzzling public stance after the publication of *A Single Man*. In many ways, it was his most out novel thus far, about a homosexual man with personal details remarkably similar to those of Isherwood, the author. In an environment in which the two most talked about books of 1962 and 1963 were the gay-themed *Another Country* and *City of Night,* Isherwood could have talked openly about his own investment in the gay themes of *A Single Man*. But he didn't. He spoke up very powerfully for the rights of homosexuals as a persecuted minority when asked, but he refused to call it a gay novel, insisting that it treated "universal" themes. As I discussed earlier, Isherwood insisted that George's homosexuality was simply a potent symbol of man's innate isolation. Furthermore, Isherwood refused to implicate himself as part of this persecuted minority, at least publicly. He talked about "those" homosexuals, in the third person, and refused to come out, despite interviewers' repeated attempts to call him out.

Secret agents, of course, are taught never to blow their covers. Although Isherwood wrote sympathetically about gay characters, he never gave himself away. His resolute denial publicly marked him as a spy to his fellow secret agents, one who demanded the attention of the "others" and advocated for the rights of homosexuals. This suggests Isherwood's connection to the 1960s embrace of camp. Public figures like Andy Warhol and David Hockney celebrated drag queens and naked men, but their public personas were inscrutable and impossible to pin down. And neither, yet, was Isherwood, who operated within a changing but still hostile culture establishing the codes that would allow the survival of the "tribe."

◈ 7 ◈

Spiritual Trash: Hindus, Homos, and Gay Pulp

EARLY IN THE 1967 NOVEL *A MEETING BY THE RIVER*, PATRICK, on his way to India to persuade his brother Oliver not to become a monk, receives a special gift from his lover Tom in Los Angeles:

> That coverless and obviously much thumbed-through paperback novel you suddenly pulled out of your pocket and gave me at the airport—*wow* (as you would say)!! You know, you might at least have warned me what it was about! I suppose I should have guessed, from your wicked grin. Anyhow, I didn't. After we'd taken off, I opened it in all innocence at the first chapter and almost immediately found myself in that sizzling love scene between the character called Lance and that younger boy. Did you think that a hard-boiled publisher couldn't be shocked? I began blushing, yes actually! And then I suspected that my neighbor was reading it too, out of the corner of his eye. So I put the book away for private consumption later—behind a locked door! (38)

The appearance of a dirty book in a novel that has been understood as Isherwood's most religious is surprising. Two years before, Isherwood's biography of the founder of his branch of Hinduism, *Ramakrishna and His Disciples*, publicly claimed his religious identity just as interest in Eastern religions was peaking. Though Hinduism marks all of Isherwood's American novels, *A Meeting by the River* was his most Hindu fictional experiment, incorporating setting (India), terminology, and rituals. The novel's "much thumbed-through paperback," however, connects Isherwood's Hinduism to his deep investment in Cold War queer print culture. There was a new iteration of queer pulp in 1967, one that Isherwood followed with interest: gay pulp, published by straight "erotica" firms and marketed as both sex- and gay-positive. Gay pulp, though seemingly out of place, is essential to the plot and the structure of *A Meeting by the River.*

Isherwood had long been interested in dirty books. *The Last of Mr. Norris* featured a Swiss Family Robinson idyll of young boys that the baron read obsessively, much to the narrator's delight; Arthur's carefully protected collection of masochistic masterpieces includes one he wrote himself. Private obscene documents circulated in Isherwood's English circle for years, including pornographic poems from W. H. Auden. The final version of *Down There on a Visit* featured a dirty book on the ship in the "Mr. Lancaster" section; an early draft of *Down There on a Visit* includes an "artiste" who manages a pornography reading room:

> Peter . . . made out dimly in front of him a row of high desks, like the ones outside telephone-booths. . . . Peter's eyes got used to the gloom as he walked along the desks, glancing at the books and their titles. There were *David Copperfield Confidential, Moby's Dick, Inside Madame Bovary.* By the time he reached *Wuthering Heights and How He Got Up There,* Peter knew pretty much what to expect. Like the other volumes, it was a mimeographed typescript. He switched on his lamp and opened it at random:
>
> "You ready for it, Cathy honey?" "You bet your life I'm ready for it, Heathcliff sugar." "I'm going to give it to you, Cathy." "Okay, Heathcliff, you go ahead and give it to me. Let's see you give it to me. Just you quit your bragging and give it me right now—or else I'll get to start thinking you don't have it, Big Boy, maybe not any more than Edgar Linton does." "I'll show you if I have it, Cathy. I'll show you right this minute. Lookit, Cathy, lookit, lookit, lookit!" (Here a reader had scribbled on the margin of the page: "Dialogue most unconvincing and psychology poor. The

author obviously knows *nothing* about the English upper middle class.")[1]

Isherwood's comic send-up of battered and dog-eared paper books, existing parasitically on high culture, clearly sets up dirty books as slumming. The mock-literary titles of the dirty books, invoking Dickens, Flaubert, Melville, and Brontë, and the literary criticism at the end of the hilariously bad sex scene, becomes the basis for Isherwood's campy tone, even as the details suggest direct knowledge.

Books like these had been bubbling under the surface of mainstream publishing for quite a while. Philip Clark discusses gay samizdat (the Russian word for underground publishing): "manuscripts passed from hand-to-hand, from gay man to gay man, copied and distributed at high prices in the days when possession of such stories was illegal."[2] Quantifying how many of these manuscripts circulated, and how broadly, is difficult. In 1969, Guild Press published a pamphlet series titled Classics of the Homosexual Underground, which claimed to publish gay samizdat; Clark questions the authenticity of many of these pamphlets, but some appear to be genuine: "*A Night in the Hayloft* (1969) is surely based on an underground manuscript of the same title seized from Womack by the FBI during a 1960 raid, and a copy of the source material for *I Found What I Wanted!!* can be found among Cornell University's Gay Erotic Stories, c. 1930–1960."[3] But certainly, these clandestine documents, carefully circulated and protected, fed into the secret agent identity I discussed in chapter 6.

Until at least the 1970s, Isherwood read such books; he also wrote his own samizdat story in 1959, "Afterwards." Whether it is representative of other "classics of the homosexual underground" is debatable, but it does suggest, I think, Isherwood's private investment in dirty books. "Afterwards" has key similarities to gay pulp of the late 1960s, which Isherwood acknowledged and used in *A Meeting by the River*. "Afterwards" starts with the same premise as *A Single Man* would four years later: an older gay man's lover has died and he struggles to find his bearings "afterwards." From there, the story moves quickly to the narrator's friendship/

voyeuristic obsession with a young gay couple, Leonard and Forrest. The narrator has an affair with Forrest, moves away for a
year, and then, in the end, discovers that he is really in love with
Leonard. The story ends with their reunion, and a hopeful intima-
tion of their life together.

On the first page, Isherwood's narrator denounces heterosexuals:

> Fuck them.
>
> I loathe all heterosexuals of all ages everywhere. I loathe
> the poignant restrained heartbreaking books that are writ-
> ten about their nasty amours. Let them all rot. No—let
> them live. But I don't want to hear about them or read
> about them. I find them a bore. Worse than that. Disgust-
> ing. I find their love as disgusting as they find mine.
>
> And in the depths of my heart, I accuse them. Yes. I
> hold them guilty. Every one of them. Every one of them
> must bear a tiny fraction of responsibility for what hap-
> pened to Tom. (1)

This rant appears in a softened version in *A Single Man,* but here,
in a "queer story" written for friends and, presumably, fellow
queers, Isherwood's narrator is bitter and oppositional. This sense
of utter separateness even extends to the narrator's friendship with
a straight couple. Like George, the narrator is mortified for showing his grief to them. "Why do I feel I've exposed myself, betrayed
something? Must I be hostile, even at a moment like that? Must I
say, our feelings are not the same as yours—you can't, shan't understand them? Yes, apparently, I must. Do the Jews secretly feel
they suffer quite differently from the Goyim? On a different wavelength. Yes, I bet they do" (6). Queers are a separate fraternity;
straight people don't figure much into "Afterwards." It is an all-gay
milieu, dominated by gay bars and private queer parties.

Sex dominates "Afterwards" from the second page on. That
opening sex scene shows how much Isherwood held back in his
published novels during the Cold War:

> We both stood up and grabbed each other and began
> tongue-kissing. He was as hot as a monkey. He ground and

bumped his middle into me. He whispered "don't send me away", a line he doubtless got out of a queer novel, but I didn't care.

We went into the bedroom and stripped. He looked a lot better, naked. Olive brown, with strong little legs and a beard of black fuzz from throat to belly, and a huge thick meaty cock. He squatted down and started guzzling on my cock; then he pushed my thighs apart and stuck his tongue in my asshole and rimmed me. Something about him excited and disgusted me terrifically. I felt savagely sadistic. I started to wrestle with him, gripping his thighs between mine and really trying to hurt him. Also, I bit deep into his shoulder. But he seemed to want to play it that way, too. He fought back, wrestling and biting. The little bastard had muscles of iron, and if I'd let him he'd have broken my legs. It was like a fight to the death, between a pair of naked savages. We kept bracing ourselves, locking bodies and making superhuman efforts to overpower each other. Sweat and aggression was pouring out of me. Our flesh made wet rubbery sounds; the bed creaked and groaned. And, in the midst of this massacre, this boy kept panting 'oh darling—darling—it's so wonderful!' as if we were Romeo and Juliet.

At last, with a heave which nearly gave me a heart-attack, I managed to turn him over on to his belly. 'Now I'm going to fuck the shit out of you' I told him, playing the brute. He loved that. 'Yes, fuck me, darling' he gasped, 'fuck me, split me wide open, rape me!' I reached down to the drawer in the bedside table and took out the tube of KY. There was still some left. When we were both good and slippery, I rammed my cock into him with one push, but he didn't yell. His asshole must be really limbered up. He certainly has plenty of technique. He kept tensing his sphincter muscle to get me even hotter. I reached down under his belly and started jacking him off. The fucking made a great squelching and soon some shit began leaking out of his ass with the KY. I could smell it all over us. 'Darling,' he kept panting, 'darling, you're so wonderful to me!' Just before he came, he made a hideous braying noise like

a donkey. But I came and came, right out of the bottom of
my nuts. I ached all over, afterwards. (2–3)

For avid readers of Isherwood's fiction, where sex is rarely described, these sexual depictions may come as a bit of a shock. The
logistics of gay sex—K-Y Jelly, rimming, sphincter muscles, feces—
all are meticulously described, with careful attention to sounds
(squelching, braying), smells, and sensations (aching all over). Like
the gay pulp I describe later in this chapter, Isherwood's sex scenes
in "Afterwards" serve as a kind of how-to guide. Unlike many of
late-sixties "fuck books," however, the scene contains Isherwood's
camp humor as well. Isherwood juxtaposes the hilariously obscene
details of sex ("the fucking made a great squelching," for example, renders the act impossible to take seriously), and yet the trick
keeps trying to transform the one-night stand into an encounter of
grand passion: "this boy kept panting 'oh darling—darling—it's so
wonderful!' as if we were Romeo and Juliet" (2). Part of his serious
treatment of the essentially absurd act of having sex, Isherwood
suggests wryly, was influenced by "fagtrash": "He whispered 'don't
send me away', a line he doubtless got out of a queer novel, but I
didn't care" (2). Gay protest novels had a long afterlife.

Not all of the sex scenes are funny, of course. After another
sexual encounter, in which his sex partner "shoot[s] off in pints,
all over both of us," the narrator is disgusted with himself, because
"Deliberately, step by step, I'd excited him—I'd given him hot pants
for Tom's death" (15). But later sex scenes, especially the voyeuristic scene between Leonard and Forrest, involve more emotion:

Forrest came into the room, and there was Leonard standing by the bed, in his shorts. Forrest went over to him, a
little unsteady from the drink and put his arms around his
neck and began kissing him. . . . Still kissing Leonard, he
started to grope him and push his shorts down over his
hips. Leonard's eyes turned toward the window. He knew
I was watching. He put out his hand to turn off the lamp
by the bed. But it was just out of his reach and Forrest
held him, laughing. It was a show put on for me. Leonard
was drunk but still he was embarrassed. Forrest wasn't

embarrassed at all. And then Leonard couldn't help laughing, because by this time he was just as horny as Forrest. And his cockstand was just as big, or bigger. He started to grip Forrest's buttocks, digging his fingers into the flesh. Then their shorts fell on the floor around their ankles, and they were naked. Their great rigid cocks rubbed each other's belly-fuzz, slowly, getting every possible ounce of sensation out of it. They kissed as it they were slowly but gluttonously drinking from an enormous bottle. Their buttocks worked and their muscles bulged as they pressed closer and closer into each other. I felt as if I'd never seen them properly before, as they really are. My picture of them was intellectualized and much too complicated and all wrong, because a most important part of them was missing. What was missing was their two cocks. The cocks explained everything. They were a man and a boy who were crazy to have each other; it was as simple and as marvelous as that. (26–27)

When emotions are involved, Isherwood avoids graphic descriptions of sounds and smells and juxtapositions of sadism and corny sentimentality. The focus on "their two cocks" becomes the key to understanding these two characters. Although "two cocks" aren't ever so explicitly described in Isherwood's sixties fiction, they aren't completely absent, either. Isherwood gestures toward "their two cocks" emphatically throughout *A Meeting by the River.*

Isherwood ends "Afterwards" with gay domesticity that combines sex and romance. He even embraces the sentimentality he so disdains at the beginning of the story:

I can't write about any of that without being corny. So I'll be corny. Leonard fucked me, and God knows why—chemistry or compatible electric fields or something—but I felt like a little boy of seventeen being seduced by his daydream sailor, all body-fuzz and cock and muscles. I fairly melted, I swooned away in his arms, I opened my innermost ass to him, I belonged to him, I was his boy. And the fact that a tiny eye in my mind watched this and saw how ridiculous it was, only made it more absurdly marvelous. (56)

The narrator's ironic camp doesn't erase the faith in love that this passage represents; opening his "innermost ass," being with a fantasy sailor, is the height of gay romance. The story ends with them moving in together, and the lack of other journal entries tells the reader that this is a "happily ever after" story, "Because, if the rest of the pages were blank—if there were no further entries—then I'd know that this thing with Leonard had worked out, and was so perfect that there was nothing more to say" (58). Isherwood wondered whether "Afterwards" was "sheer pornographic sentimentalism," but concluded that it had "some emotion."[4] In any event, he chose to preserve it in his archive. It is striking to see how many of the features of "Afterwards"—the explicit descriptions of sex, the happy ending, the emphasis, in the end, on romance—recur in sixties gay pulp. "Two cocks" were about to make a dramatic entrance into print culture.

Queer pulp had been a prominent feature of the "paperback revolution" since the 1950s, of course, but in 1966, a new phenomenon emerged. Gay pulps were both explicit about sex and positive about gay identity. According to Michael Bronski, these books "almost always presented gay sex as horny, happy, and healthy. The 'shadows' had disappeared, and gay sex was now as bright and as clear as day."[5] The year 1966 was a banner time for this new publishing trend. Victor J. Banis's 1966 novel *The Man from C.A.M.P.* is satirical, hilarious, and irreverent. Richard Amory's *The Song of the Loon,* a self-described "pastoral," depicts a mythic Indian tribe that places man love at the center of its culture. Each chapter features an initiation in the "way of the loon," with a new sex partner. The pious, pedantic tone marks this novel as the new bible of gay life and the best-selling gay pulp of the sixties. Both these novels were published by Greenleaf Classics, as was Carl Corley's *My Purple Winter,* another 1966 pulp. Michael Bronski defines Corley's writing style as "idiosyncratic and compelling. Often an odd mixture of Erskine Caldwell (without the humor) and a naïve but startling folk style, all of the novels read unlike any other pulps of their time."[6] Many more gay pulp writers made their appearance in 1966.[7]

Gay pulp novels feature explicit sex scenes—usually one per chapter—but they also, like "Afterwards," feature romance. Indeed, Banis argues that pulp novelists' greatest contribution was love and commitment for gay characters:

> The choice to pursue a life together was not for the most part available to the characters in those earlier gay novels. . . . It was the gay paperback writers of the 1960s who first (and not without considerable risk) truly bridged that gap between frustrated love and the possibility of a long-term commitment. No longer did the characters in the novels of these writers have to be separated by the end of the book through tragedy or cure. "Happy ever after" became a possibility they could choose.[8]

"Pornographic sentimentality" was essential to gay pulp; not just explicit images of sex, but surrounding cultural narratives that authorize that sex, are essential. The two Adams no longer needed to be cast out of the Garden. *The Song of the Loon*'s dreamlike setting, on the frontier and up the river, is the prototype for this. In gay pulp, sex doesn't bring the fall; sex is what makes it paradise.

The transition from private circulation of homoerotic images to public production in the late 1960s came as a result of key court cases on obscenity. The application of these landmark cases in subsequent obscenity prosecutions was somewhat uneven in the 1960s; the requirement of "literary merit" meant that many companies were still vulnerable to judges who saw no value in smut. Still, the profits inspired a number of publishing companies to enter the field. Lynn Womack, for example, the publisher of physique magazines who won a key Supreme Court case in 1962, decided to focus on paperback erotica in 1963. Philip Clark terms this shift in the publishing conglomerate's focus a revolutionary moment:

> What Guild Press next attempted—serving as middle-man for less-arousing, often unillustrated gay books from a wide variety of publishers—was virtually unprecedented. . . .
>
> A distribution service. A reprint program. An original publishing house of both magazines and books. There were no small steps. Guild Press was launching the most

ambitious gay literary program the world had seen. And although various facets of the Guild's program would meet with varying degrees of success, the audaciousness of the plan is undeniable.[9]

Clark frames Womack as a pioneer of gay rights, one whose seedy publishing empire laid the foundation for gay liberation. Whether Womack's publishing agenda was really so "progressive" is questionable—Clark may be reading later gay separatism into an earlier time—but Womack's literary agenda was decisive in the emergence of gay pulp.

Most publishers of gay pulp, however, were established firms of heterosexual erotica. Earl Kemp, an editor for Greenleaf, claims that his entry into gay erotica was prompted by readers themselves:

> Contributors to the Gay category produced the most articulate of the fan mail, the writers having spent years pondering questions that plagued huge numbers of the rest of us. . . . The overt, active gays were frequently very specific with their literary requests. . . . What they wanted to read about was themselves, engaged in hot, forbidden romances that did not end in tragedy. They wanted vicarious little romps in the hay with their best buddies before heading home to bed with their anything-but-lover wives. . . . By the 1960s, the gay fan mail was coming in at a rate that could no longer be ignored. The time was right. *They were out there. If we published it, they would come.* And come they didn't, once we opened that fly and released the snorting beast within. . . .
>
> To a large extent, those gay fan letters sparked our overall success. We believed them when they told us what they wanted, and we proceeded to produce exactly that. We were a market-driven business, after all, and that market knew what it wanted.[10]

Kemp is writing a good forty years after the fact, so his recollections of an empowered horde of gay readers may be influenced by the gay rights movement and his long friendship with the irrepressible Victor J. Banis. Even so, his gay readers seem even more empowered than Isherwood's correspondents—and that is saying a lot. Rather than identifying with a particular writer, however, and imagining themselves in him, these gay readers openly desire fantasy with multiple authorial partners. They want positive endings, but even more important, they want "vicarious little romps" that represent an escape from their own lives. Explicit sex is a key component of this vision, but not the only one; unfraught, all-gay worlds were equally important. Gay readers wanted, not spy intrigue, but utopia. Michael Bronski notes in *Pulp Friction* that in the late 1960s, "There were now more men who were out and unafraid to purchase books with frankly homosexual themes from the racks in drugstores, bus stations, and in the newly emerging venue of the 'adult bookstore'" (193). These cultural conditions fostered the emergence of explicit gay pulp. "*If we published it, they would come*"—for Kemp, gay pulp was an incantation, conjuring empowered gay readers.

Recent assessments of gay pulp see it as a precursor to the Stonewall revolution—the "happy, horny, and healthy" version— but many gay activists in the 1970s saw the gay pulp phenomenon as exploitative and embarrassing, including best-selling writers such as Richard Amory. In a series of interviews with the gay press in 1970, Amory complained of low pay and editorial interference. Pulp writers had even more reason to complain than most writers, because pulp presses paid a flat rate (between $750 and $1,500), did not pay royalties, and kept all the rights for reprints and movie deals. *Song of the Loon* was the most egregious case; it sold, by some accounts, two million copies and was made into a movie, while Amory was paid only $750 and had no input into the content of the film.[11] Dirk Vanden, another pulp writer, wrote in a manifesto of sorts, "I think it is high time we let gay readers know just who gets the benefits of all that money they're spending on gay novels—and now on movies made from those novels (it sure as hell ain't the writers!)"[12]

Several pulp writers complained about editors making unauthorized changes to their writing. Amory called their editorial changes "Yahooism,"[13] and he thought they proofread poorly and corrected usage because they simply didn't understand it: "(Try, just once, to use the word 'shat' in a manuscript for Greenleaf. They'll change it to 'shit' immediately, as they did in *Naked on Main Street,* having no knowledge of the English language and no respect for *you.*)"[14] Dirk Vanden was even more critical: "I wish I had space to detail all of the cuts GC's editor made in my novels—whole sections of exposition cut out, vital parts of the climaxes sheared off—and then all the 'pulsating purple cockhead' *additions* he made to patch up the gaping holes—all without one word to me!"[15] Gay pulp editors insisted that the books be short, sex appear on every page, and titles and cover art be provocative.

So was gay pulp an anticipation of gay liberation, as new millennium critics claim, or an exploitative cultural embarrassment, as gay lib critics of the early 1970s accused? Probably neither. When one reads those seminal sixties gay pulps, one discovers that Michael Bronski's claim of a fundamental break is perhaps a bit overstated; the continuities with earlier queer pulp become apparent. These novels are not always healthy and happy. John Howard notes that many of Corley's novels have unhappy endings and define homosexuality in traditionally negative terms.[16] It is also true that gay pulp publishers made more than the writers, and probably often interfered. What the genre did, however, was make visible a hidden public of gay male readers, providing not just an enjoyable fantasy life but also a vision of gay identity. As I discuss later in this chapter, gay pulp was more than just one-handed reading.

Isherwood complained bitterly to his agent about the reprinting of *A Single Man* and *A Meeting by the River* by sixties pulp press Lancer Books, which placed his sixties fiction firmly within the new phenomenon of adult bookstores, next to other "fuck books." But Isherwood's investment in a public literary reputation didn't always match his private obsessions and enthusiasms. Though none of the groundbreaking 1966 pulps are in his library, his diaries show him reading gay pulps avidly, if not always approvingly, in 1967: "We spent a lot of the morning in two queer bookshops, the Adonis and Rolland's, where we bought *Sex Life of a Cop; Go Down, Aaron; Teleny; Like Father, Like Son; A Fool's Advice; The Beefcake Boys.* Buying such books is a sort of political gesture which is infinitely more satisfactory than actually reading them."[17] He also became friends with Samuel Steward in the early 1970s; Steward wrote gay pulp under the pseudonym "Phil Andros," and Isherwood not only read the Phil Andros novels but praised them.[18]

Isherwood did preserve one gay pulp in his library: Larry Townsend's 1971 *The Sexual Adventures of Sherlock Holmes.* Isherwood's longstanding love for Sherlock Holmes may explain why this novel made the cut. The novel is like *The Man from C.A.M.P.* in its queering of popular culture. In this version, however, Watson is just out of the army and making ends meet by turning tricks in the local pub. A friendly pimp sets him up with Sherlock Holmes, who takes him to his flat and beds him. A brief example should suffice to give a sense of this novel:

> My calves were shoved tightly into his armpits, my toes touching in the middle of his back. Then he released my penis and dropped his lips to touch my anus, grazing the scrotum with his tongue as he descended. This organ now probed gently at my puckered canal, dabbing hotly, wetly at the tight-closed opening as if asking permission to enter. Finally he inserted the tip, parting the sphincter as his tongue glided within, moistening and lubricating the passage as wave after wave of unbridled passion swept through my body. (n.p.)

This novel, plus Isherwood's diaries, letters, and novelistic references to gay pulp, authorizes a more thorough investigation of how the cultural phenomenon of gay pulp manifested itself in *A Meeting by the River.*

A Meeting by the River and Gay Pulp

Isherwood's last novel is structured as a series of journal entries written by Oliver, and letters from his brother Patrick to Oliver, their mother, Patrick's wife, and his lover, Tom. Oliver's impending ordination as a Hindu monk drives the plot of this novel, but Patrick's relationship with Tom provides a counterpoint. This cursory overview doesn't indicate how thoroughly pulp infuses the structure and plot of *A Meeting by the River,* however. Patrick has made a fortune pushing back the proprieties at his stuffy publishing firm; his first success in publishing was the memoir of "Anita Hayden . . . one of the leading musical comedy and film stars." Patrick's description of the affair shows his own investment in the lucrative pulp of the era, despite his employment by a reputable firm:

> Her memoirs were pretty hot stuff, as well as skating thinly over libel, and I, as a very junior partner, had to use all my arts of persuasion to get Uncle Fred and dear old G.B.V. to touch them with a barge-pole. G.B.V. said, referring to Anita, 'give me a good honest Piccadilly tart, any day of the week!' He asked me if I wanted to bring disgrace on a firm whose list had been adorned by the names of some of the noblest (and least-read) Edwardians. However, persuasion won the day, the memoirs were published and they made us such a shamefully large sum of money that the matter was never mentioned again. But that was only the first of my various ventures into vulgarity. (22)

Patrick has taken "vulgarity" to another level in his latest venture—overseeing a movie version of one of his novels. His publishers condemned the move publicly, but then "each has come to me behind the other's back and asked if he might make a small investment in the film out of his own pocket! Which will show you to what an extent I've already corrupted them. I sometimes feel slightly satanic" (23).

In other words, Patrick is an avid disseminator of trash, an enabler of the very trend in publishing that led to that "coverless and obviously much thumbed-through" gay pulp. His campy delight in "vulgarity," his pleasure in satanic corruption, and his interest in sex with men should have made gay pulp a welcome revelation. And yet, he is shocked that such things were being read openly. He writes to Tom:

> I know you weren't recommending it to me for its literary value and so your feelings won't be hurt when I say that it's probably the greatest trash I ever read in my life—and I'm speaking as a professional reader of trash, remember!—but

that doesn't make it any the less exciting. Admittedly I haven't had much experience of this sort of literature. I realize that it's being mass-produced nowadays, especially in your own enlightened country. Funny to think that, when I was your age, even, this book couldn't have been published openly and sold on the counter! (66)

Patrick's self-identification as "a professional reader of trash" is self-deprecating, but he still insists, like Isherwood did, that he can distinguish between the "literary" and "trash." His impressed observation that "when I was your age, even, this book couldn't have been published openly and sold on the counter" allows Isherwood to let his readers know about the new phenomenon of gay pulp, and highlights the generational conflict between Patrick and Tom. Tom represents the new, liberated consumer of gay pulp: bold, proud, and out enough to kiss his married lover at the airport in public. Tom even uses pulp as a sort of how-to manual. Patrick discovers that one of the most dramatic moments of his affair with Tom was a reenactment of a torrid pulp love scene:

You certainly must have intended me to get the stunning surprise I did get when I reached that chapter where they go to Tunnel Cove—otherwise you'd have prepared me for it in advance. Of course, I know that hundreds of tourists must have walked through that tunnel and out on to the reef, so it really isn't strange that some writer should have hit on the idea of setting a scene there in a book. But that particular kind of scene and those particular characters! Tom, I've got to know this, *did you deliberately make us re-enact it*? It would be just like you, yes, I can believe it of you, it's exactly the sort of wonderful sweet idiotic crazy thing you *would* do. . . . I love the romantic silliness of your doing it, but at the same time I can't help feeling, to put it mildly, embarrassed! (83–84)

Isherwood is winking at his gay readers in the know by suggesting how textual this emerging gay identity is. Authentic passion may just be a construction from new "mass-produced" texts.

Tom does more than reenact specific sexual acts, however. He also uses the gay pulps as a guide to finding love. Patrick becomes the romantic pulp hero incarnate for Tom:

> While I was reading the novel I suddenly remembered something—actually it was on the same night we got back from that trip, we were having dinner, and you told me that there was a character in a book you'd read that you used to think about a lot and hope one day you'd meet someone like him. The way you told me made it clear you meant that now you *had* met someone, and it was me. . . . But when I asked you about the book itself you smiled and got all mysterious. Now I realize that obviously the character was Lance in this novel. With all due respect to him, I must say I hope you consider me an improvement—because the way he talks is a bit overripe for my taste, and I don't greatly care to inherit the author's description of him as "faunlike"! (67)

Tom uses gay pulp as a model for his own romantic future, and projects those fantasies onto Patrick, finally calling him at the monastery in India to declare his undying love. It turns out that Patrick is not an improvement on Lance. Tom's mistake was simply this: Patrick was a character from a gay pulp, but he was the villain, not the romantic lead. Patrick emerges as a new version of Stephen Monk, and he was also based, at least partly, on Dell publisher Frank Taylor, the successful paperback editor who also branched into film, and was, incidentally, a bisexual who chased beautiful boys and waxed rhapsodic about hearth and home, often during the same conversation. One might suspect Isherwood of equating Patrick's literary and moral corruption, and the logic of the text supports this conclusion. Patrick is false, constructing multiple versions of himself for mother, wife, brother, and lover, and the reader discovers his elaborate lies, both self-serving and unnecessary.

Consider Patrick's attempted corruption of his brother. He first tries to lead Oliver back to the flesh by a display of his own naked body:

> I walked into the room and found him stark naked. . . . He proceeded to do a lot of pushups, forty at least, and then

about a dozen jumps, raising his arms and landing with
his feet apart, then jumping to bring them together again.
He did these jumps very deliberately, facing me and grinning at me, with his teeth looking whiter than ever in his
flushed brown face. And I couldn't help being aware of
his rather big penis slapping against his bare thigh as he
jumped. Patrick always had a beautiful body and it is still
in perfect shape, he must exercise all the time. You can tell
that he's been lying in the sun completely nude. (70)

Oliver is reminded of "some corny scene in an old Russian novel,
where the woman tempts the young monk" (71). But Isherwood's
readers may well be reminded of key scenes from the gay pulps,
where naked seductions, with a "rather big penis," are common.
Even the implied incest—Oliver later reveals that "When I was
going through my Freudian phase, I used to wonder if I wasn't actually in love with him, romantically and even physically" (115)—
has its counterpart in queer pulp.

Patrick reenacts his own gay pulp scene. Later, he appropriates
the language of pulps. Patrick's ostensible confession to Oliver
turns into another opportunity for corruption and seduction:

Then he launched into an immensely long account of how
he'd met this young American named Tom in Los Angeles and how they'd started having a love-affair with each
other. . . . If I was shocked, it wasn't by Patrick's story but
by the way he told it. When he started off, his language was
very restrained, in fact it was sometimes almost comically
formal. . . . But soon his tone changed and he began talking
very frankly and using four-letter words with a sort of aggressive relish. For instance, he told me how Tom and he had
driven to some deserted cove up the coast to the north for a
week-end, and how they'd been on a rock right above the sea
and Tom had grabbed hold of him and they had torn off each
other's clothes. I suppose it was really a relatively ordinary
scene of lust, but Patrick made it sound strangely horrible,
uncanny and bestial, like two animals devouring each other
alive. He described exactly what they did to each other, and I

noticed once again how fetishistic the words can be that we use for sexual acts. It was as if the mere uttering of them was nearly as exciting to Patrick as the act itself. (143–44)

When Patrick decides to come clean, as it were, telling Oliver, "I *need* to know that you know this about me" (143), he struggles with the right language. In the middle of his discussion, he shifts from formal to salacious, borrowing language directly from his well-thumbed gay pulp. With "four-letter," "fetishistic" words, Patrick transforms this potentially life-changing experience into a titillating tale that, like the novel itself, gave him "a personal thrill, a sexual kick" (145). A major purpose of gay pulp novels is to make the words as exciting as the act and to invite the reader to join in. Indeed, Oliver believes that Patrick is trying to entice him. Isherwood suggests something about the political and cultural effect of these novels, which provided a model of coming out that is provocative, challenging, and performative.

Yet Patrick isn't simply a villain and provocateur; he is also an embodiment of camp. He is superficial and facetious with everyone in his letters. His letter to Oliver about his wife is a good case in point:

She claimed that the news didn't surprise her in the least. Either she knows you a lot better than I do—from a different angle, *bien entendu*—or else she was showing off her feminine intuition! She sends you her love and says she hopes you'll return to England in due course and instruct her in The Way. She also asks if there's a Hindu order of nuns into which she may aspire to be received, because she wants to renounce the world as soon as the children have grown up. I accused her of simply wanting to renounce *me,* but this she denied hotly! (27)

Patrick's facetious tone here (exclamation points, capitalization, the mad camp of his wife leaving him) marks him as a camp character. Patrick is irreverent, gently mocking, flattering, and self-deprecating. He makes Oliver slightly ridiculous, solely through his facetious tone. His letters to his mother ("Certainly *my* prayers are no good to anyone, but my loving thoughts are with you as ever"; 101) show a gentler irony, while his letters to his wife are much more cutting ("I'm well aware that I'm making myself sound bitchy, not to say malicious"; 107). Despite the constructions of multiple personas, the camp tone is consistent.

In his letters to Tom, Patrick confides that camp is meant to protect his "true" self, which includes the self that loves men. This comes into conflict with the emerging ethos Tom represents, one that would, in the seventies, reject camp as self-hating:

> I know how you hate any sort of pretence and conceal-ment, and I admire you for that. But we must never forget, when we go against the majority, that we're forced to be like guerrillas, our chief weapon is cunning. We can't ever attack openly. That's just exactly what the enemy wants us to do, so he can destroy us. If we're bold and rash, we're simply putting a weapon into his hands. Defiance is a lux-ury we can't afford. (88)

The gay man as secret agent emerges again in this novel, but here, embodied by the deceptive Patrick, it becomes a suspect strategy, devious and ultimately false. Patrick's elaboration on his tech-nique emphasizes this:

> We have to be cunning. There's nothing dishonourable in that, it can even be a lot of fun. We'll play a game against them, Tom, and we'll outfox them and laugh at them while we're doing it. Do you know, I have a feeling that playing this game is going to be what binds us together more than anything else? It'll be you and me against the world! And although we're its enemies, we'll make this idiot of a world accept us and admire us, perhaps reward us, even—that'll be our triumph and private joke! (88)

This notion of deception as a mad camp aligns Patrick with an older version of gay identity. Patrick briefly rejects this game of outfoxing when he imagines a life with Tom and a more positive and open gay identity, which emerges simultaneously, from his exposure to gay pulp and to the monastery. The forces that would lead to gay liberation, and reject the dissembling of the "private joke," are bubbling in this novel, even if they do not win the day.

Conversely, Isherwood uses the structure and values of gay pulp to introduce his more serious pedagogical aims for Hinduism. For Isherwood, both Hinduism and homosexuality were minority consciousnesses. The two brothers must come out as cultural others, representing both Hinduism and homosexuality. *A Meeting by the River* provides encoded messages about gay pulp, but it is much more explicit in its primer about Hinduism. In fact, the novel spends considerable time defining Hindu terms: Swami, sannyas, gerua, Mahanta, darshan. It also defines key Hindu concepts, both through Oliver's journal, through letters "back home," and through dialogue between the two brothers. Patrick's letter to his wife gives a good example of the novel's pedagogical strategy:

> The Hindus believe that all one's work should be done symbolically, as though it was some kind of a religious ritual which has no practical usefulness, only intrinsic spiritual significance as an offering to the Supreme Being or whatnot—in other words, what's important is one's attitude to the performance of the action itself, not to its results—success and failure are regarded as equally irrelevant. (Forgive this clumsy exposition of what's probably kindergarten stuff to you; I only include it because it's part of the story.) (107)

Those asides justify definitions and theological explanations that Isherwood deemed essential to his story, but they also provide a road map of sorts for those interested in Hinduism. Readers learn how to greet an Indian holy man properly, what the colors of the robes mean, how key religious rituals happen and what they mean.

Victor Marsh argues that Isherwood's Hinduism was thoroughly enmeshed in his queer self-identification.[19] That enmeshment was, as Katherine Bucknell suggests, uniquely tied up in camp, in his appreciation of its rites, in its framing of guru/disciple relationships, even in its understanding of all human endeavor as ultimately trivial and meaningless. "In a sense," Bucknell argues, "*maya* itself is camp—it is the 'as if' world all in quotes."[20] In his diary, Isherwood attributed his understanding of Hinduism to "having been around Swami so much *and* understanding camp."[21] Similarly, Patrick's campy persona prepares him to understand and embrace Hinduism, and sets up Isherwood's explicit pairing of camp and Hinduism.

Hindus and homos are linked in other structural ways. Hinduism provides a model for symbolic paternal and fraternal bonds that Isherwood parallels and queers in the relationship between Patrick and Tom. This was a long-standing rhetorical gesture of Isherwood; Tom McFarland notes that Isherwood described his relationship with the Swami Prabhavananda and with Don Bachardy in almost precisely the same terms, an absolute devotion untouched by jealousy or expectations.[22] Isherwood had long been interested in younger men; Auden's letter to Isherwood in the 1940s, as they commiserated about their younger lovers, is revealing: "as you say, we Father-Shadows can only stand aside and pray."[23] But Hinduism transfigures that promiscuous coupling of fathers and sons from wolves and punks to gurus and disciples.

In his diary during the late sixties, Isherwood described his relationship with Don Bachardy in just this way: "How *can* love be profane if it really is love? In my own case, hasn't my relation with Don now become my true means of enlightenment?" (2:465). In a later entry, he mused that "a householder's life is not simply that he is not a monk but that he loves a human being rather than God. So he must learn to love God through that human being" (2:486). Isherwood later clarified this idea in a longer passage:

> I realize more than ever that this is IT. Not just an individual, or just a relationship, but THE WAY. The way through to everything else. This seemed to be obliquely confirmed by Swami this morning. . . . Vivekananda writes, "Religion is the practice of oneness with the infinite, the principle that dwells in the hearts of all beings, through the feeling of love." If you are tuned in on personal love, then you are on the same wavelength as infinite love. There may be terrific interruptions from the

static of egotism and possessiveness, but at least you *are*
on the right wavelength and that's a tremendous achieve-
ment in itself. (2:511)

Isherwood's insistence that a personal and sexual relationship is
a potential means to the divine elevates gay relationships to the
status of religious ritual.

In some of Isherwood's own writing about Hinduism, he insists on the spirituality of sex, even sex that was not monogamous.
Isherwood embraced devotion that must be devoid of possession
or jealousy: "The love of God described by Narada is a love in
which there can be no jealousy, no struggle of egos, no desire for
material advantage or exclusive possession, no dread of desertion;
a love which is incapable of unhappiness."[24] Isherwood's claim
that one learns divine love through physical and emotional love
pushes the boundaries of conventional morality. He imagined a
transcendence that constructed homosexuality not as sinful deviance but as natural, multiple encounters with the Absolute. He
insisted in an interview with Carolyn Heilbrun:

> Why shouldn't you be completely promiscuous? If you
> could only appreciate the sacredness of one-night stands—
> and realize that these are all God's creatures, you know,
> they're all my brothers or sisters. . . . I don't see, theoreti-
> cally, why there shouldn't be the most powerful sort of
> love, like St. Francis's, applied to one-night stands, where
> you really love a different person each night. But that's
> very advanced. . . . really, to have that feeling, that you are
> overwhelmed with empathy and with love, not to mention
> lust, for a person that you just meet for a few hours, that's
> surely a *very* advanced state to be in. I can imagine that it'd
> be very near a kind of enlightenment.[25]

Isherwood's reframing of one-night stands, not as narcissism or
exploitation but as a means to enlightenment, is one of the most
radical aspects of his camp Hinduism. It is also a version of camp
Hinduism that remained carefully veiled in his official statements
on his faith.

But perhaps Isherwood's gestures toward queer fraternal bonds are radical enough in *A Meeting by the River*. Oliver establishes a Platonic cross-racial relationship, and Patrick forms a sexual Anglo-American relationship. When Oliver became a believer, he set up house with his swami:

> A few weeks after I got back to Munich, I moved in with the swami. . . . It seemed odd to me at first, being in this relationship to an older man—partly, I suppose, because Father died when we were both so young, partly because I'd never lived with only one other person before, but always in institutions and communities, or by myself. The Swami took it quite for granted, however. And soon he began referring to me as his "disciple". . . —a disciple in the literal Hindu monastic sense, a novice monk who serves his guru and is trained by him like a son, and who will become a swami himself in due course. (20)

The father–son relationship is the model for the guru–disciple bond, one that can never be broken by the guru. Oliver's swami tells him this explicitly: "Don't you know the Guru can never run away from his disciple, not even if he wants to, not in this life, not in any other!' When he said this, I was kneeling beside his bed straightening the bedclothes, and he put his hand on my head, and patted it. He didn't do this very often. I always felt it was a special kind of blessing" (52–53). Oliver's homosocial bond is celibate but intimate, and it violates a number of cultural taboos about relationships between men.

Patrick describes his relationship with Tom in strikingly similar terms, as an idyllic fraternal bond:

> I've told you how I've always been very much attached to my brother Oliver. . . . Tommy, since I had that dream, I'm certain that *you* could be my brother—the kind of brother I now know I've been searching for all these years, without ever quite daring to admit to myself what it was that I wanted. I suppose I was frightened off by the taboos which surround the idea of brotherhood in the family sense—oh

yes, they encourage you to love your brother, but only as far as the limits they've set—beyond that, it's a deadly sin and a horror. What I want is a life beyond their taboos, in which two men learn to trust each other so completely that there's no fear and they experience and share everything together in the flesh and in the spirit. I don't believe such closeness is possible between a man and a woman—deep down they are natural enemies—and how many men ever find it together? Only a very few even glimpse the possibility of it, and only a very few out of that dare to try to find it. We are going to dare, aren't we? We must, Tom, or we shall never forgive ourselves. (131–32)

Patrick's articulation of a brotherly relationship as a model for gay partnership is close to Isherwood's own. It toys with incest taboos (remember Patrick's naked performance for Oliver) but more important, it insists that gay relationships are family relationships. Patrick's dream of a homosocial utopia parallels Oliver's own relationship with his swami.

Indeed, utopian dreaming becomes prophetic vision for both Oliver and Patrick. In *A Meeting by the River,* the visions are not individual but partnered, revealing a homosocial ideal between men. Patrick's comes first, and prompts his proposal to Tom:

This was much more than a dream, it was so intense it was a sort of vision. I mean, there was a burning pleasure and then an utter fulfillment with you, nearly as good as that shattering moment we had together at Tunnel Cove. But the whole experience went far beyond just sex, it was actually a glimpse of a life which you and I were living together! That's why I call it a vision. Tom, I'm certain this wasn't an ordinary dream-fantasy built up out of memories of the past. Explain it any way you want, *I know* I was experiencing something which hasn't happened yet and perhaps never will happened, but which *could. . . .* I *can* tell you one thing—this life I got a glimpse of was of such a closeness as I'd never even imagined could exist between two human beings, because it was a life *entirely without fear.* (130–31)

Patrick sees a life in which gay relationships are, as for Isherwood they were, a means to spiritual enlightenment. The insistence, twice, that this wasn't simply a sex dream but a vision gives it an import and sympathy that even Patrick's unreliable narration cannot undermine.

Oliver has his own homosocial domestic vision the night before his ordination, when he was struggling with the decision to become a monk:

> Presumably it was a few moments before waking that I saw Swami. Yes, I can say I did literally see him, although this wasn't a vision in the waking state. But seeing him was only a part of the experience of his presence, which was intensely vivid, far more so than an ordinary dream. Also, unlike a dream, it didn't altogether end when I woke up. . . . We were domestically together as we used to be in the old ways. . . .
>
> I knew that Swami was "dead," and I knew that nevertheless he was now with me—*and that he is with me always, wherever I am. . . .* Now we are never separated. I woke up actually *knowing* that. (172–73)

Oliver discovers through his vision that he has found the perfect father—one who will never desert him, even after death. His is also a life entirely without fear, with a partnership that transcends death.

For both Hindus and homosexuals, however, making the word flesh is treacherous. Oliver doubts the reality of his relationship with the guru and almost leaves the monastery. Patrick does reject his vision, dumping Tom and returning to his wife and the double life of camp. Even Christopher Isherwood's quest for a "home self" was sometimes cagey and contradictory. He refers to gay pulp, but he doesn't commit its indiscretion; we don't hear the four-letter, fetishistic words. Patrick is a character who lends himself to a number of conventional interpretations; Isherwood cannot quite bring himself to embrace Patrick as a lovable antihero, in the way he could Mr. Norris or Sally Bowles or Paul. By framing his positive descriptions of homosexuality through a deceptive, callous adulterer, Isherwood undoes many of the embedded "horny, happy, and healthy" images derived from the pulps. It is too easy, by the end of the novel, to dismiss "a life lived entirely without fear." Isherwood wasn't quite ready, in 1967, to claim that the relationship between Patrick and Tom could be as spiritually productive as the relationship between Oliver and his guru.

Nor was Isherwood ever entirely comfortable talking about his faith. Victor Marsh argues convincingly that Isherwood remained an ardent devotee and found in Hinduism a solution to the spiritual dilemma queer men face. But he did so privately; publicly, he struggled to articulate this notion, even when he wrote his spiritual autobiography *My Guru and His Disciple* more than fifteen years later (after his very public celebration as a gay writer had commenced). He wrote no fewer than eight versions of the afterword to the book, and one discarded paragraph suggests his difficulty:

> Having written it, my first reaction is a sort of defiant embarrassment. I realize how embarrassing, not to say gooey, this material will seem to many, perhaps most, of the people who read it. But then I become defiant and think, well, if it *isn't* embarrassing, that means it has no quality of shock. And if it's not shocking, then it can't really be any good, because nothing—no kind of so-called persuasion—could be as shocking as this material ought to be, if it really gets through to the reader in prime condition.[26]

"Defiant embarrassment" is a useful term to describe Isherwood's relationship to faith in his public persona. By this is also the term he uses in *Christopher and His Kind* to describe his relationship to his homosexuality. Coming out as both a Hindu and a homo was an ongoing struggle for Christopher Isherwood.

In *A Meeting by the River*, though, Isherwood redeems all the struggles of his characters—and perhaps his own. When Oliver's vision ends, he and the swami speak about Patrick:

> I'm to try to remember always, from this moment on, that Patrick is in Swami's care and in Swami's presence—even

though he himself may be utterly unaware of it now and
for some time to come. . . . No wonder Swami seemed
amused! If you look at this objectively, it's a pretty comic
situation. Poor old Paddy—he's in a state of grace! And he's
going to discover it the hard way. He doesn't dream what
he's in for, but he'll find out before long. (141–43)

Isherwood's notion of grace, as he explained in his lecture "Divine Grace," was not about forgiveness or redemption but about enlightenment, which could come in any number of ways. But the result of that discernment was to go beyond conventional notions of morality: "My master told me that when I see, when I am in that mood, I see God playing in so many forms, God as a saint, God as a sinner, God in the wicked, God in the diabolical. That God playing, as it were, with different masks."[27] God could even be found in a campy, bisexual seducer. Not many novels offer gay characters a state of grace, even one so vaguely threatening and ironic. Hindus and homos find a détente of sorts in *A Meeting by the River,* a state of grace that redeems both in their oppositional identities.

At the end of the novel, Oliver takes his vows and becomes a monk, and his brother Patrick bows down before him to take the dust from his feet. The final line unites homos and Hindus in a ritual of perfect acceptance and love: "And everybody was smiling and murmuring, as much as to say how charming it was of Patrick to play this scene according to our local Hindu rules, and how very right and proper it was that we two brothers should love each other" (191).

Christopher Isherwood, Gay Liberation, and the Question of Style

T HE APPEARANCE OF AN ARTICULATE, OUTRAGED, INSISTENT
public gay presence was the incarnation of Isherwood's most
fantastic queer fantasies. After the riots at the Stonewall Inn in
1969, gay liberation fronts emerged in a number of urban areas,
and political groups claimed public space vigorously. Gay liberation was a complex political and cultural movement; I am most
interested in gay liberation print culture, which was a central
means of creating gay and lesbian reading and writing communities. Gay pulp may well have created the audience for this explosion of print culture, but the shift from underground gay pulps
and adult bookstores to the visibility and volume of gay writing
in mainstream venues was dramatic. Gay bookstores appeared
in major urban centers across the country, including the Oscar
Wilde Memorial Bookstore in New York City, Giovanni's Room
in Philadelphia, Walt Whitman Bookshop in San Francisco, and a
Different Light bookstore in Hollywood;[1] as the 1970s progressed,
mainstream bookstores began to stock gay-themed books. While
mainstream publishers began publishing gay-themed work, independent gay presses like Daughters Inc., Naiad Press, Seahorse
Press, and Alyson Press published books intended solely for gay
and lesbian readers.[2] Gay-themed magazines and newspapers
emerged, including the *Advocate, Gay Community News, Gay
Sunshine,* and *Christopher Street;*[3] these publications reviewed
gay books and interviewed gay writers (including Isherwood,
on a number of occasions). Bibliographers such as Roger Austen
began recuperating forgotten gay writers; academic writers began
exploring the idea of a distinctively gay aesthetic, and the nascent
idea of a gay canon began to take hold. Isherwood's Cold War

experiments with gay content and camp middlebrow suddenly seemed prescient.

Gay liberation's new aesthetic was more open, more strident, and less playful than the Cold War gay print culture that spawned it; indeed, pre-Stonewall gay culture was rejected as inadequate, self-hating, and *closeted.* An ideal of transparency permeated gay liberation rhetoric, the desire to get beyond encoding and stereotypes to the pure unadulterated truth. Gay liberationists simultaneously rejected the past as inadequate and sought a gay heritage that mirrored, or, in that overused word, "anticipated" the gay liberation present. Nowhere is this split more evident than in the "new" gay novel. There was an explosion of gay novelists in the 1970s, dominated by American writers such as Andrew Holleran and Edmund White, members of "The Violet Quill."[4] This writing group sought models from the past, but its members thought very few worthy of consideration. Certainly, neither the Cold War gay novels from the forties and fifties nor the explicit gay pulp of the sixties was deemed worthy of their attention. They read André Gide, Jean Genet, and Christopher Isherwood's *A Single Man,* seen as a flawed but important precursor to the "new" gay ethos of books such as Edmund White's *A Boy's Own Story* and Andrew Holleran's *The Dancer from the Dance.*

Isherwood watched this new cultural phenomenon with delight. His library has many gay texts published in the late sixties and seventies: Angelo d'Acangelo, *The Homosexual Handbook* (1968); David Blamire, *Homosexuality from the Inside* (1973); Mark Freedman, *Homosexuality and Psychological Functioning* (1971); Martin Hoffman, *The Gay World: Male Homosexuality and the Social Creation of Evil* (1969); and Bruce Rodgers, *The Queen's Vernacular: A Gay Lexicon* (1972). These aren't the books that have come to be seen as most influential, like Guy Hocquenghem's *Homosexual Desire* or Dennis Altman's *Homosexual: Oppression and Liberation* (though he does have two subsequent books by Altman, one inscribed to him). They do, however, show his awareness of the cultural, political, and literary manifestations of gay liberation.

In the early 1970s, Isherwood could well have become a relic of the bad old days, since he was, after all, a gay man who refused to declare himself during the Cold War. But Isherwood worked hard to take advantage of this new reading and writing culture. In July 1970, he worried about whether to accept an invitation from the National Students Gay Liberation Conference, and declined only because he didn't want to embarrass Swami "by making a spectacle of myself which would shock his congregation and the women of Vedanta Place."[5] He admitted in his diary, however, that "I highly enjoy the role of 'the rebels' only uncle" and noted, "This is probably the last opportunity I'll ever have of becoming, with very little effort, a 'national celebrity.' And I hope I'm not such a crawling hypocrite as to pretend I wouldn't quite enjoy that, even at my age!"[6] By the next year, Vedanta no longer held him back.

His first participation in this brave new world was to participate in the new ritual of gay liberation: he came out in his 1971 memoir, *Kathleen and Frank*. His former friend Lincoln Kirstein found this "revelation" hilarious, giggling with his friend Dickie Buckle that Isherwood "had come out fearlessly, proclaiming himself an 'homosexual'; not a minute too soon."[7] Kirstein was a married gay man who never felt quite comfortable with gay liberation, but he had a point. Isherwood's Cold War novels were legible as queer novels to both reviewers and gay readers; if they weren't couched in the same style as gay liberation texts, they can't really be said to be closeted. Isherwood featured gay characters in all of his Cold War novels, and embedded arguments that justified them. "Proclaiming himself an 'homosexual'" was a bit of an overkill. On the other hand, Kirstein's suggestion that Isherwood was "out and proud" when he no longer had anything left to lose indicts Isherwood for cynical hypocrisy. In his diary, Isherwood detailed how he rewrote parts of *Kathleen and Frank* to make them more "aggressive" as a result of a visit from a gay activist:

Instead of:
　　Without even trying to decide between the relative disadvantages of alimony and police persecution, he is now quite certain that heterosexuality wouldn't have suited him. And he has always felt content and well-adjusted, being as he is . . .
　　I have written:

> Despite the humiliations of living under a heterosexual dictatorship and the fury he has often felt against it, Christopher has never regretted being as he is. He is now quite certain that heterosexuality wouldn't have suited him; it would have fatally cramped his style. (3:129)

Certainly, Isherwood's willingness to "come out" in a way clear to gay liberationists demonstrates his continued incorporation of American gay publishing trends into his own work.

The same year that *Kathleen and Frank* was published, Isherwood arranged for the publication of E. M. Forster's *Maurice*. Forster had written the openly gay novel in 1913, and despite circulating it privately among friends, he refused to have it published until after his death. The novel presented a positive view of gay life, with a happy ending, and it became an early artifact in recuperative gay identity. It was one of the earliest recuperations of canonical writers within a gay literary tradition, and one that Isherwood delighted in facilitating. Biographer Wendy Moffat described Isherwood's elation when he read Forster's gay short stories and revised ending to *Maurice* for the first time: "'Of course all those books [about Forster] have got to be re-written,' he said. 'Unless you start with the fact that he was homosexual, nothing's any good at all.'"[8]

This basic logic of gay liberation—"start with the fact that he was homosexual"—inspired Isherwood's next project, *Christopher and His Kind,* a memoir of his Berlin days. Isherwood was often asked to write articles and books about Berlin; in response to one such request from his agent, he wrote "No, I don't want to do another book about Berlin. Three is enough."[9] But the release in 1972 of *Cabaret,* a musical based on Isherwood's Berlin stories, brought him new visibility that he sought to exploit. *Christopher and His Kind* purported to be the "true" story of his time in Berlin, filling in details that the closet forced him to obscure. Isherwood introduced the memoir by claiming that "the book I am now going to write will be as frank and factual as I can make it, especially as far as I myself am concerned" (1). That honesty involves defiant rejections of "heterosexual middle-class propriety" (26), even in gay culture. He dismissively describes a friend's attempts to "introduc[e] him to some nice boy with steady habits who had clean fingernails and wore a collar and tie" as "nicey-nice third-sexism" (27). Instead, Isherwood embraces a world of working-class bars and multiple sexual encounters, and he intersperses his narrative with expressions of solidarity with his homosexual tribe.

Isherwood was prepared to leverage this tell-all memoir to re-introduce himself to the American reading public and attain the critical and commercial success he sought when he emigrated to the United States. He was hampered, however, by the fact that his books were all out of print, which embittered him toward both his agent and his publisher. In response to what seemed to Isherwood an inadequate offer for the paperback rights to *Kathleen and Frank*, Isherwood wrote Curtis Brown agent Perry Knowlton: "Hardly a day goes by without fan letters complaining to me how difficult it is to get my books; the fans have to wait for them at the public libraries, which does me no good financially. . . . I am getting all this publicity via Cabaret, and what good does it do me? Even the paperback of the Berlin Stories is hard to get. All I can get is praise—and assurances that I am 'the most neglected writer' etc. But why am I neglected? For purely commercial reasons."[10] Isherwood had long been angry with his agent, and the following year, he terminated his relationship with Curtis Brown. He wrote, tersely, "I began wanting to leave Curtis Brown about 20 years ago and only my own laziness prevented me—plus the usual author's reaction 'why change, they're all the same.' One thing I am sure of now—as far as I personally am concerned, it's better to be represented by one absolutely independent person than by any group, whatsoever."[11] He was being disingenuous, however; he may have wanted a smaller agent, but he also wanted a more skilled, prestigious agent who would increase his advances and his visibility.

Although Isherwood's initial choice of Irving Lazar didn't work out, he found the ideal agent in Candida Donadio. Donadio made her name discovering soon-to-be-famous writers, including Joseph Heller, Philip Roth, Thomas Pynchon, and Mario Puzo. In the early seventies, Donadio formed her own firm, and Isherwood managed to take advantage of her expansion and her considerable talents. Being represented by Donadio was quite a coup, one that friend Truman Capote was surprised he managed: Isherwood wrote to Donadio, "To hear what he would say, I told Truman Capote that I would like you to be my Agent. He answered, with some skepticism: 'If you can get her.' Then, with tremendous enthusiasm: 'She's the best—*anywhere.*'"[12] Certainly, for Isherwood, Donadio was the first step to his greatest critical acclaim and commercial success. (Isherwood wasn't able to terminate his relationship with Curtis Brown so easily; he ended up running the American rights through Candida Donadio, and the British and European rights through Curtis Brown.)

His next step was to leave Simon and Schuster. Isherwood had a close relationship with editor Peter Schwed, but he was unhappy that Simon and Schuster had allowed his books to go out of print. This was perhaps even more galling to Isherwood because Simon and Schuster owned Pocket Books and could have, one imagines, reprinted his novels rather easily. Simon and Schuster still held an option on his next book, and Isherwood instructed Donadio to release him from it. Peter Schwed was bewildered:

> I'd been under the impression that our relationship . . . had been one of mutual affection and admiration, and I could not conceive of any reason why . . . you could have any reason for wanting to leave us. Is your disappointment in us predicated completely upon the fact that after a period of time, on some of your books which haven't fared as well in the marketplace, we've allowed them to go out of print? If so, I can understand your feeling, but I have to point out that you may look long and hard before you'll find a publisher who reprints when the minimum printing means that he'll have an inventory of books that will sit in his warehouse for a decade.[13]

Schwed's distress was genuine, but his shock about reprints demonstrated a lack of attention that Isherwood deeply resented. He wrote Donadio: "I can understand that Peter Schwed's feelings are hurt. . . . I don't think he has ever gotten it through his head how important it is to me to have at least the better of my books back in print. I did write to him about this and he wrote back about other points in my letter, simply ignoring the republication question. The republication of my books is for me the top priority and I want to have the sort of publisher who can appreciate this fact."[14] Isherwood saw one last chance to consolidate his literary reputation, and Simon and Schuster's benign neglect was an impediment. His letter to Peter Schwed was more circumspect and sounds similar to his kiss-off letter to Curtis Brown: "There is little in all this that has to do with the relations between you and me. I must only contradict you when you identify yourself with Simon and Schuster and use the phrase 'mutual affection and admiration.' I have never felt the least degree of either emotion from any member of the firm except yourself. What I want is a publisher who convinces me that he really believes in my work."[15] Simon and Schuster, like Random House, fought to prevent Isherwood from leaving the firm. The newly installed editor Michael Korda, who became famous for being on the first wave of big media consolidations in publishing, wanted to increase the firm's fiction holdings, and keeping Isherwood became a matter of pride. Donadio's firm responses finally persuaded them to yield.

Free of the Simon and Schuster imbroglio, Isherwood signed a contract with Farrar, Straus and Giroux, a firm with an impressive literary reputation. Founded in 1946 by John Farrar and Roger Straus, the press gained its literary prestige in 1955, when Robert Giroux, former editor in chief of Harcourt Brace, joined the firm.[16] He brought seventeen authors with him, including T. S. Eliot, Flannery O'Connor, John Berryman, and Bernard Malamud. "With the impetus given it by Giroux," John Tebbel concludes in *A History of Book Publishing*, "the company firmly established its reputation as a 'quality' house in the sixties and seventies" (4:287). Other well-known authors included Isaac Bashevis Singer, Alexander Solzhenitsyn, Philip Roth, Susan Sontag, Tom Wolfe, Walker Percy, Donald Barthelme, and Peter Handke (4:287). Isherwood could join a prestigious publishing house as a valued, serious author. Roger Straus was also "known in the business as a fierce upholder of the independence of small houses and an aggressive foe of conglomerates and their acquisitions of publishing houses" (4:287). Indeed, Tebbel's final assessment of Farrar, Straus and Giroux demonstrates why the firm was a perfect fit for Isherwood, the congenital outsider: "Farrar, Straus & Giroux stood firm, one of a few small independents that were resolved to defend their publishing Alamo against the enemy" (4:288). FSG editor Michael di Capua enthusiastically pursued Isherwood's memoir and was willing to facilitate the reprinting of his previous novels as a condition of signing.

Farrar, Straus and Giroux accepted Isherwood's next book, notifying him by sending a fawning telegram and paying a twenty-five thousand dollar advance—by far the largest advance Isherwood had received. It nominated the book for a Pulitzer Prize, and this nomination gratified Isherwood to no end: "I was a bit staggered to hear of its nomination for the Pulitzer. Well, anyway, I value that as a gesture of solidarity from Farrar, Straus and Giroux. One which no former publisher has ever made."[17] Farrar, Straus and Giroux worked to reestablish Isherwood's literary reputation in other material ways, by acquiring the rights to all his novels and selling the republishing rights to Avon Press. This allowed Isherwood to take advantage of the publicity *Cabaret* brought him and to erase the lowbrow tinge that pulp presses gave him. Now, tastefully republished with Don Bachardy's drawings on their covers, Isherwood's novels were positioned as highbrow.

Of course, Farrar, Straus and Giroux, independent literary press though it was, was still a business, and it accepted Isherwood's book not only for its literary merit but also for its commercial appeal in the gay-friendly atmosphere of the seventies. Di Capua's decision about the cover of *Christopher and His Kind* shows how the firm decided to frame the book:

> I don't think this is what you and Don had in mind, but I hope you will both like it as much as I do. . . . I feel that a jacket has only one purpose: to be attractive, to make the casual browser have a favorable response when he picks up the book. To accomplish this, anything short of vulgarity is permissible, even a portrait of the author that shows him on his best day in the most favorable light. . . . Perhaps the portrait I prefer isn't as penetrating as the other, but it definitely presents a far more attractive Christopher and that's exactly why I ask you to let us use it. People do judge a book

by its cover, and I want them to see an author they'd like to take home with them.[18]

Di Capua's rationale suggests a commercialism that rivals the pulp publishers' more open appeal to "see an author they'd like to take home with them." By emphasizing a portrait that shows the author "on his best day in the most favorable light," the publishers were framing Isherwood as a prototypic gay man, one whose appeal is both wicked and attractive. No less than pulp novels, Farrar, Straus and Giroux used the cover to attract casual readers to this exotic "true story" of gay life. Isherwood, instead of railing at the exploitation of his work and image, seemed gratified by this construction of his work.

This careful cultivation of both his literary reputation and his image produced Isherwood's greatest commercial success. *Christopher and His Kind* made him a seventies gay cultural icon, but despite his best attempts to position himself in the mainstream, he was, more than ever, known as a gay writer. Apparently, this brave new world of gay liberation still had a remarkable number of continuities with the "bad old days," at least when it came to gay content. Take, for example, attempts to serialize the memoir. Isherwood, Donadio, and di Capua wanted to position it as a mainstream literary memoir; agents at Curtis Brown even objected to offering it to *Playboy,* for fear it would hurt sales in England. But as Donadio wrote to Isherwood, "All the other possible magazines have seen, and, alas, returned, with high praise, though not having found suitable excerpts."[19] The *Saturday Review* did end up excerpting four pages about Jean Ross, the model for *Cabaret's* Sally Bowles, but thought the rest of Isherwood's gay memoir wasn't "suitable." In the end, two publications agreed to extensive excerpts. Both were gay, and one was particularly provocative. In *Blueboy: The National Magazine about Men,* Isherwood's memoir is surrounded by suggestive photographs and advertisements. As FSG editor Michael di Capua commented when he mailed a copy to Donadio, "Here is the February/March issue of *Blueboy*—keep it away from the children."[20] I find it puzzling that a writer who did not want his books to be sold in adult

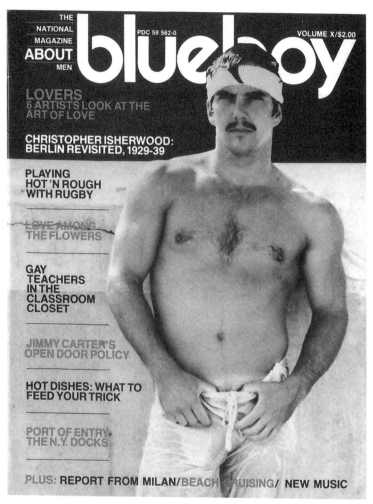

THE
NATIONAL
MAGAZINE
ABOUT
MEN

PDC 59 562-0

VOLUME X/$2.00

blueboy

LOVERS
6 ARTISTS LOOK AT THE
ART OF LOVE

CHRISTOPHER ISHERWOOD:
BERLIN REVISITED, 1929-39

PLAYING
HOT 'N ROUGH
WITH RUGBY

LOVE AMONG
THE FLOWERS

GAY
TEACHERS
IN THE
CLASSROOM
CLOSET

JIMMY CARTER'S
OPEN DOOR POLICY

HOT DISHES: WHAT TO
FEED YOUR TRICK

PORT OF ENTRY:
THE N.Y. DOCKS

PLUS: REPORT FROM MILAN/BEACH CRUISING/ NEW MUSIC

Blueboy: The National Magazine about Men, a new gay liberation publication, was one of only two magazines that agreed to serialize part of Isherwood's 1976 memoir *Christopher and His Kind.*

bookstores didn't object to photographic images of pubic hair
(one placed provocatively between a handsome man's lips) and
Crisco surrounding his work, but perhaps gay liberation made
him less uptight about dirty books.

The mainstream framing of Isherwood's queer manifesto, and

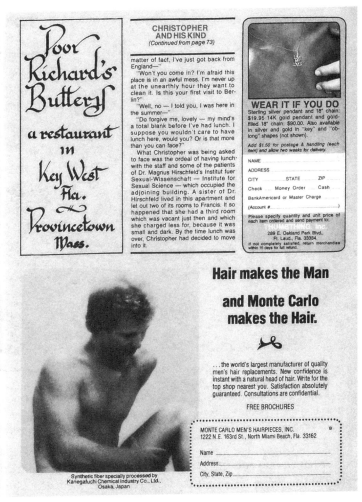

The excerpt of *Christopher and His Kind* in *Blueboy* was surrounded by gay advertisements. This publication of Isherwood's writing marked the first time he embraced gay print culture publicly.

his dependence upon gay cultures of letters for its success, suggest that it is impossible to distinguish subcultural authenticity from mainstream assimilation. Many images of queer defiance so proudly circulated as signs of the new millennium were recycled from "twilight" images of queer transgression in Cold War queer

Blueboy featured explicit gay images (including a color photograph series of men in sexually provocative poses) in the same issue that excerpted *Christopher and His Kind.* Previously, Isherwood had published excerpts of his writing in more literary venues such as the *New Yorker, London* magazine, and *Story* magazine.

pulp. Mainstream publishers had discovered what pulp publishers knew in the 1960s—gay writing sells. Isherwood's greatest commercial success in the United States came when he publicly targeted gay readers. Although there were some exceptions (Carolyn Heilbrun's special issue of *Twentieth-Century Literature,* for example), the majority of Isherwood's interviews were in gay publications. It was gay readers who lined up around the block at gay bookstores to hear him read from *Christopher and His Kind.* The triumph of a gay culture of letters, one might productively argue, was not a new creation but a natural outgrowth of Cold War queer print cultures. Both Cold War pulp and gay liberation publishing may be called "mainstream," but the term tells us nothing about the particular contingencies of audience, marketing, and form. Both are queer, but that term may be even more misleading, since contemporary queer theorists use the term as a utopian essence and an innate site of resistance,[21] rather than, as Christopher Nealon puts it, "a historical (rather than a metaphysical) contingency of identity."[22] Only the historical contingency of both mainstream and queer—or middlebrow queer—can make sense of the distinctive publishing phenomenon of *Christopher and His Kind.*

Isherwood's literary stardom coincided with his abandonment of fiction for memoir. Isherwood had written memoir before (notably, his memoir of the 1920s, *Lions and Shadows*), and he had always fictionalized his life. Still, Isherwood's American authorial incarnation had been grounded in fiction, and it is odd that at the moment of his triumphant gay Americanization, he abandoned fiction and his aesthetic of camp middlebrow.

Katherine Bucknell argues that Isherwood's happy relationship with Don Bachardy made fiction unnecessary to him.[23] As evidence, she cites a journal passage from 1953:

> —the nice smell of redwood as I lifted the garage door. And the feeling of impotence—or, what it really amounts to, lack of inclination to cope with a constructed, invented plot—the feeling, why not write what one experiences, from day to day? And then, as I slid my door back, this sinking-sick feeling of love for Don . . . and the reality of that—so far more than all this tiresome fiction. Why invent—when Life is so prodigious?
>
> Perhaps I'll never write another novel, or anything invented—except, of course, for money.
>
> Write, live what happens: Life is too sacred for invention—though we may lie about it sometimes, to heighten it.[24]

Curiously, this passage was written before the publication of Isherwood's Cold War novels, which suggests that Isherwood's evolution isn't as simple as Bucknell suggests. But the main issue for Bucknell seems to be style. Isherwood's camp style, which he merged with a middlebrow sensibility, is for Bucknell (and for many other post-Stonewall commentators) an unfortunate emblem of the closet. "During the 1930s," she claims, "the challenge of disguising his homosexuality perhaps gave his work an erotic charge that accounts for some of its special qualities: half-repressed hilarity, intensely cerebral linguistic enthusiasm, self-conscious charm. Then as the years went by, the same challenge had begun to twist his work out of shape."[25] Bucknell doesn't say "camp," but her description—"half-repressed hilarity, intensely cerebral linguistic enthusiasm, self-conscious charm"—suggests camp and dismisses it as a "twisted" mark of unhappy closet queens. The narrative Bucknell sketches in her brief article is pure gay liberation bravado: as Isherwood moves out of the "closet," he leaves the twisted camp tradition behind for a simpler, truer recounting of *what really happened.* Bucknell accepts the claim that fiction is false and memoir authentic.

Paul Piazza makes a similar claim about Isherwood's changes in style; his "later frankness about his personal life" led to "books [that] contain less posturing, fewer rhetorical gestures."[26] Although he sees a paring down of camp style even in Isherwood's sixties novels[27]—claiming that *"A Single Man* is more direct and honest" because "the writer has explored more deeply both the character and himself"[28]—Piazza finds the fruition of Isherwood's "direct and honest" style in his memoirs: "Intent on telling the truth Isherwood seems to regard the manner of his early works as a hindrance to revelation. The writing is energetic, subtle, but compared to that of his early works, austere and unembellished. The style here is nonstyle. In these books one meets the strict and adult pen of which Auden wrote, and sees realized the hope expressed in 1949 by a critic in the *Times Literary Supplement:* 'What could he do if he really tried.'"[29] Piazza sees the final evolution of Isherwood's style into "nonstyle" as a triumph over camp artificiality. Certainly, critics like Piazza and Bucknell are responding to changes in post-Stonewall gay fiction, but they are also following Isherwood's own triumphal narrative, repeated proudly for gay liberation audiences in the 1970s. I find it remarkable that so many critics accept these two premises: one, that Isherwood's style in the 1970s represents the "true" Isherwood

and, two, that Isherwood's gay liberation writing embodies art-
less, transparent nonstyle. Isherwood created multiple narrative
masks with ease, and often invented letters and adapted journals
in his novels. Furthermore, his conversion to Hinduism provided
a theological underpinning to his belief that all manifestations of
the self are equally false. So critics' trust in a memoir written forty
years after the fact as authentic is curious.

Despite Isherwood's liberationist bravado in *Christopher and
His Kind,* he had no such illusions about the truth of his narrative.
Take a look at Bucknell's passages more closely. Isherwood doesn't
promise the real story, but a mythic version of his life. After writing in his journal that "Life is too sacred for invention," he adds a
key disclaimer immediately afterward: "though we may lie about
it sometimes, to heighten it." In another passage quoted by Bucknell, Isherwood describes the difficulty he had writing *Kathleen
and Frank:* "The actuality of the experiences does bother me, the
brute facts keep tripping me up, I keep wanting to rearrange and
alter the facts so as to relate them more dramatically to my reactions. Facts are never simple, they come up in awkward bunches.
You find yourself reacting to several different facts at one and the
same time, and this is messy and unclear and undramatic. I have
had this difficulty many times while writing *Kathleen and Frank.*
For instance, Christopher's reactions to Kathleen are deplor-
ably complex and therefore self-contradictory, and therefore bad
drama."[30] Isherwood didn't allow himself to be so hamstrung by
"brute facts" in *Christopher and His Kind;* he manages to keep a
clear and dramatic narrative line—a brave sexual outlaw seeking
to save his lover from the Nazis, who tragically fails because of
structural homophobia. Bucknell tells us that Isherwood called
Christopher and His Kind "a 'non-fictitious novel,'"[31] and that description is much more accurate than the "true story" celebrations
of many critics. Isherwood was still fictionalizing in his memoirs,
but with a markedly different style, and for different purposes.

It's not that the heroic, mythic narrative of queer resistance
is wrong; Isherwood was always a rebel, even when he was circumspect in public. It's just that everything Isherwood wrote was
highly stylized. I tend to like the seventies Isherwood less than
his previous personas, and to mistrust his depiction of events. He

seems to me to be preening for his post–gay liberation audience—exaggerating his conquests, inventing a slumming Berlin past that matches a Rechy-like hustler view. He gives in to the cult of the past at the end of his life, inventing a simpler, defiant Christopher who feels no guilt, no self-doubt, no ambivalence. His style does change in the 1970s, as Isherwood notes in his journal: "When I reread my earlier work, I feel that perhaps my style may have lost its ease and brightness and become ponderous. Well, so it's ponderous. At least I still have matter, if not manner."[32] But this doesn't mean that his 1970s writing is "nonstyle"; rather, he abandoned the camp middlebrow style of his Cold War novels.

The assumption that "matter" can be transparent, that "nonstyle" is both possible and preferable, is an odd notion that emerges concomitantly with articulations of gay aesthetics. And its legacy continues to influence queer theory; although queer theorists no longer value transparency, they seem to agree that mainstream gay texts are formally uninteresting and ideologically suspect. "Queer" was recuperated in the 1990s as an innately oppositional term, and even as queer theory has been institutionalized, it insists on defining queer against the regime of the normal. But queer theory has its own regime of the normal, what critics like Judith Halberstam and Scott Herring call "metronormativity." In *Another Country*, Herring defines metronormativity as a preference not simply for the urban but for the aesthetics of queer urban existence. Indeed, he identifies the "violence of aesthetic intolerance" (29) as an essential component of metronormativity, and argues that "we have too often sidelined aesthetic arguments that refused to cultivate the polished meccas, and to continue to do so leave modernist studies . . . deeply impoverished" (61). Herring's argument ranges broadly across literature, visual culture, political magazines, and graphic novels, and his consideration of aesthetics includes fashion and advertising, but his argument has particular resonance when we consider queer theory's literary legacy.

Literary queer theory's thralldom to experimental aesthetics began with Eve Sedgwick's *Epistemology of the Closet*, not only because of Sedgwick's complex prose style but also because of the model of subtle genealogical excavation she provided. Those complex encodings of the closet were "so inexhaustibly and gorgeously productive . . . of modern Western culture and history at large" (68) that queer literary scholars came to prefer formal experimentation as well as texts that are encoded or closeted. This has left a number of texts—including pulp fiction, popular novels, and gay liberation and lesbian feminist novels—understudied and often undervalued by queer critics.

That there can be an aesthetics of accessibility, that "fatal readability" is as much an art as experimentalism—indeed, that the style of pre-Stonewall gay writing is diverse and not simply cowardly code—is rare in contemporary queer theory, enamored as it is by ahistorical readings of the "closet" in canonical works. The distinctive stylistic features that anchored diverse gay reading and writing communities have been overlooked, and that neglect hurts the appreciation of post-Stonewall gay literature just as much as that of Cold War literature that preceded it. *Middlebrow Queer: Christopher Isherwood in America* is just one contribution to what I hope will become a larger investigation of the contingencies and complexities of queer reading and writing communities. Isherwood, inveterate autodidact and enthusiastic supporter of gay novels and gay liberation, would doubtless concur. Gay life never stopped fascinating him, and his own distinctive literary contributions made that life all the more delightful.

Notes

Introduction

1. Austen, "Christopher Isherwood Interview"; Russo, "Interview with Christopher Isherwood."

2. Maupin, foreword to *The Isherwood Century*, xi.

3. Isherwood, *Diaries*, 1:243–44.

4. Love, "Modernism at Night."

5. Connolly, *Enemies of Promise*, 74.

6. Ibid., 71.

7. For a few examples, see Turner, *Marketing Modernism between the Two World Wars*; Morrison, *The Public Face of Modernism*; and Scandura and Thurston, *Modernism, Inc.*

8. Isherwood, *Isherwood on Writing*, 69.

9. Ibid., 73.

10. Ibid., 74.

11. Hutner, *What America Read*, 7.

12. Harker, *America the Middlebrow*.

13. Sedgwick, *Novel Gazing*, 23, 25.

14. Nealon, "The Ambivalence of Lesbian Pulp Fiction," 755.

15. Humble, "The Queer Pleasures of Reading."

16. Sedgwick, *Epistemology of the Closet*, 222.

1. Isherwood's American Incarnation

1. Berg, introduction to Isherwood, *Isherwood on Writing*, 20.

2. Isherwood, *Diaries*, 1:77.

3. Ibid., 183.

4. Ibid., 13.

5. Parker, *Isherwood*, 417.

6. Isherwood to Spender, 17 February 1940, Stephen Spender Collection.

7. Spender to Isherwood, 6 March 1940, Stephen Spender Collection.

8. Parker, *Isherwood,* 402.

9. Pease, *Visionary Compacts,* 3.

10. Isherwood, *Diaries,* 1:14.

11. Parker, *Isherwood,* 376.

12. Isherwood, *Diaries,* 1:428.

13. Ibid., 194.

14. See Saunders, *The Cultural Cold War.*

15. A few notable texts include Clark, *Cold Warriors;* Corber, *Homosexuality in Cold War America;* and Savran, *Communists, Cowboys, and Queers.*

16. Greenberg, "State of American Writing," 879.

17. Sherry, *Gay Artists in Modern American Culture,* 42.

18. Quoted in Parker, *Isherwood,* 483.

19. Ibid., 426.

20. Isherwood, *Diaries,* 1:20.

21. Moffat, *A Great Unrecorded History,* 113.

22. http://www.bartleby.com/142/135.html.

23. Isherwood's "On His Queerness":

> When I was young and wanted to see the sights,
> They told me: "Cast an eye over the Roman Camp
> If you care to.
> But plan to spend most of your day at the Aquarium—
> Because, after all, the Aquarium—
> Well, I mean to say, the Aquarium—
> Till you've seen the Aquarium you ain't seen nothing."
>
> So I cast my eye over
> The Roman Camp—
> And that old Roman Camp,
> That old, old Roman Camp
> Got me
> Interested.
>
> So that now, near closing-time,
> I find that I still know nothing—
> And am still not even sorry that I know nothing—
> About fish.

(http://wonderingminstrels.blogspot.com/2001/02 /on-his-queerness-christopher-isherwood.html)

24. Joseph LeSueur, an acquaintance of Isherwood's, catalogs the wide range of gay artists, writers, and musicians in New York during the 1950s and 1960s in *Digressions on Some Poems by Frank O'Hara.* See also Sherry, *Gay Artists in Modern American Culture.*

25. Wescott to Isherwood, 16 May 1949, Christopher Isherwood Collection, CI 2661.

26. Wescott, *Continual Lessons,* 307.

27. Kirstein to Isherwood, 31 August 1949, Christopher Isherwood Collection, CI 1562. Kirstein, referencing rumors of Wescott's sexual relationship with Kinsey, also wrote that he wished "there was an American Max Beerbohm who could draw 'Dr. Kinsey investigates the state of genitory contact on Mr. Glenway Wescott's brother's model artificial-insemination plan.'"

28. Isherwood to Kirstein, 19 December 1944, Lincoln Kirstein Collection.

29. Parker, *Isherwood,* 372.

30. Kirstein to Isherwood, 16 January 1945, Christopher Isherwood Collection, CI 1552.

31. Kirstein to Isherwood, 7 December 1944, Christopher Isherwood Collection.

32. Isherwood to Kirstein, 19 March 1945, Lincoln Kirstein Collection.

33. Kirstein to Isherwood, 7 May 1945, Christopher Isherwood Collection, CI 1577.

34. Hutner, *What America Read,* 243.

35. See Levin, *The Gay Novel in America,* and Austen, *Playing the Game,* for a detailed survey of gay novels from the period.

36. For a more detailed discussion, please see the afterword of my book *America the Middlebrow.*

37. Baldwin, "Everybody's Protest Novel," 10.

38. Ibid., 15.

39. Tompkins, *Sensational Designs,* 123.

40. Isherwood to Vidal, 19 December 1947, Christopher Isherwood Collection, CI 1369.

41. See Scully, *A Scarlet Pansy;* Niles, *Strange Brother;* Tellier, *Twilight Men;* Meeker, *Better Angel;* and Levinson, *Butterfly Man.*

42. Baldwin, "Reminiscences of James Baldwin," 101.

43. "Medicine: The Longergan Case."

44. Baldwin, "Reminiscences of James Baldwin," 101.

45. Isherwood, *Lost Years,* 140.

46. Ibid., 275.

47. Isherwood, "Young U.S. Writers," Christopher Isherwood Collection, CI 1188.

48. Motley to Isherwood, 24 May 1947.

49. Isherwood, *Lost Years,* 119–20.

50. Kirstein to Isherwood, 18 September 1944, Christopher Isherwood Collection, CI 1545.

51. Clarke, *Capote,* 130.

52. Kirstein to Isherwood, 28 November 1949, Christopher Isherwood Collection, CI 1656.

53. Parker, *Isherwood,* 501.

54. Kirstein to Isherwood, 21 December 1948, Christopher Isherwood Collection, CI 1559.

55. Wescott to Isherwood, 13 May 1949, Christopher Isherwood Collection, CI 2660.

56. Caskey to Kirstein, May 1949, Lincoln Kirstein Collection.

57. Linscott to Capote, 20 December 1950, Random House Collection.

58. Capote to Linscott, 10 April 1951, Random House Collection.

59. Isherwood to Kirstein, 14 April 1949, Lincoln Kirstein Collection.

60. Caskey to Kirstein, 11 April 1948, Lincoln Kirstein Collection.

61. Kirstein to Isherwood, 8 October 1952, Christopher Isherwood Collection, CI 1574.

62. Isherwood to Kirstein, 8 January 1948, Lincoln Kirstein Collection.

63. Isherwood to Vidal, 19 December 1947, Christopher Isherwood Collection, CI 1369.

2. "Too Queer to Be Quaker"

1. Quoted in Parker, *Isherwood,* 544.

2. Isherwood, *Isherwood on Writing,* 212.

3. Isherwood to Upward, 16 September 1956, Edward Upward Collection.

4. Parker, *Isherwood,* 550.

5. Jones, "Ambivalent Trio," 14.

6. Pritchett, "Books in General," 803.

7. Isherwood, *Isherwood on Writing,* 210.

8. Smith to Isherwood, 14 August 1953.

9. Parker, *Isherwood,* 518–19.

10. Isherwood, *Lost Years,* 169.

11. Ibid.

12. Ibid., 114n1.

13. Piazza, *Christopher Isherwood,* 170.

14. Isherwood, *Diaries,* 1:224.

15. Ibid.

16. Ibid., 210.

17. Atlas, *Bellow,* 201.

18. Ibid., 203–4.

19. Auden to Isherwood, 5 April 1944, Christopher Isherwood Collection, CI 2996.

20. Isherwood to Kirstein, 19 April 1946, Lincoln Kirstein Collection.

21. Isherwood, *The World in the Evening,* 111.

22. Isherwood to Smith, 1 December 1953, Dodie Smith Collection.

23. Isherwood, *The World in the Evening*, draft, Christopher Isherwood Collection, CI 1163.

24. Weeks, "The Peripatetic Reviewer."

25. Amis, "*The World in the Evening.*"

26. Hayes, "Pity Party."

27. Wilson, "The New and the Old Isherwood."

28. Leavis, *The Great Tradition*, 8–9.

29. Wilson, "The New and the Old Isherwood," 64.

30. Ibid., 64–65.

31. Kirstein to Isherwood, 17 October 1953, Christopher Isherwood Collection, CI 1577.

32. Isherwood, Writing Notebook, 28 March 1950, Christopher Isherwood Collection, CI 1158.

33. Ibid., 9 July 1950.

34. Ibid., 6 June 1950.

35. Ibid.

36. Isherwood, *The World in the Evening*, draft alternate version of chapter 5, Christopher Isherwood Collection, CI 1165.

37. Smith to Isherwood, 20 April 1947, Dodie Smith Collection.

38. Smith to Isherwood, 14 August 1953, Dodie Smith Collection.

39. Smith to Isherwood, 9 April 1953, Dodie Smith Collection.

40. Lamkin to Isherwood, November 1953, Christopher Isherwood Collection, CI 1623.

41. Linscott to Isherwood, 17 September 1953, Random House Collection.

42. Linscott to Isherwood, 24 September 1953, Random House Collection.

43. Isherwood to Linscott, 6 October 1953, Random House Collection.

44. Isherwood, *Lost Years*, 227.

3. "Fagtrash"

1. See, for example, Bonn, *Undercover*; Crider, *Mass Market Publishing in America*; Schlick, *The Paperbound Book in America*; Schreuders, *Paperbacks, U.S.A.*

2. Hench, *Books as Weapons*.

3. Bonn, *Undercover*, 103.

4. Ibid.

5. Bronski, *Pulp Friction*, 2–3.

6. Cowley, "Hardbacks or Paperbacks?," 122–23.

7. Cowley, "Cheap Books for the Millions," 98–99.

8. Earle, *Re-Covering Modernism*, 155.

9. Isherwood, *Lost Years,* 68.

10. Isherwood to Collins, 13 January 1954, Curtis Brown Collection.

11. Ibid.

12. Weybright, *The Making of a Publisher,* 170.

13. Crider, *Mass Market Publishing in America,* 183.

14. Weybright, *The Making of a Publisher,* 284.

15. Isherwood to Collins, 26 December [1951], Curtis Brown Collection.

16. Isherwood to Linscott, 13 April 1954, Random House Collection.

17. Ibid., 212.

18. Ibid., 276.

19. Weybright to Isherwood, 20 April 1954, Curtis Brown Collection.

20. Linscott to Isherwood, 9 April 1954, Random House Collection.

21. Isherwood to Knowlton, 22 May 1972, Curtis Brown Collection.

22. Isherwood, *Lost Years,* 275.

23. Foote, "Deviant Classics," 170.

24. Isherwood to Spender, 22 July 1954, Stephen Spender Collection.

25. Ibid.

26. John Collins to Isherwood, 1954, Christopher Isherwood Collection, CI 747. More is quoted from Collins's letter later in this chapter.

27. Mark Olson to Isherwood, 10 December 1976, Christopher Isherwood Collection, CI 1884.

28. John Collins to Isherwood; see note 26.

29. Tom Statham to Isherwood, 1962, Christopher Isherwood Collection, CI 2225.

30. Bachardy phone interview with the author, 23 September 2009.

31. Ibid.

32. Stanley Friedman to Isherwood, March 1951, Christopher Isherwood Collection, CI 879.

33. Jonathan Gear to Isherwood, 13 March 1978, Christopher Isherwood Collection, CI 919.

34. Craig Makler to Isherwood, 15 January 1974, Christopher Isherwood Collection, CI 1766.

35. Garth Fergeson to Isherwood, 27 January 1978, Christopher Isherwood Collection, CI 774.

36. Ibid.

37. Bergman, "The Cultural Work of Sixties Gay Pulp Fiction," 36.

38. Garth Fergeson to Isherwood; see note 35.

39. Hugh Bragan to Isherwood, 4 July 1973, Christopher Isherwood Collection, CI 654.

40. Isidro de Rieras to Isherwood, 5 February 1954, Christopher Isherwood Collection, CI 764.

41. Ibid.

42. Isherwood to Isidro de Rieras, 7 February 1954, Christopher Isherwood Collection, CI 1032.

43. Jenkins, *Textual Poachers.*

44. Schuster, *Passionate Communities,* 14.

45. Jenkins, "Fandom and/as Religion?"

46. Hochmann, *Getting at the Author.*

47. Don Bachardy, interview, 23 September 2009; see note 30.

4. Sixties Literature

1. Isherwood, *Diaries,* 2:142, 456.

2. McGurl, *The Program Era,* 197.

3. Isherwood, *Isherwood on Writing,* 133–34.

4. Isherwood, interview with Robert Robinson, 6 September 1959, Christopher Isherwood Collection, CI 3068.

5. Ibid.

6. Vidal to Isherwood, Christopher Isherwood Collection, CI 2617.

7. Isherwood, *Diaries,* 2:388.

8. Isherwood, Writing Notebook, 3 June 1955, Christopher Isherwood Collection, CI 1158.

9. McGurl, *The Program Era,* 205.

10. Morgan and Peters, *"Howl" on Trial;* White, *Pre-Gay L.A.;* Nealon, *Foundlings.*

11. Spender to Isherwood, 30 October 1960, Christopher Isherwood Collection, CI 2166; Rolph, *The Trial of Lady Chatterley.*

12. Isherwood, *Diaries,* 2:167.

13. DeKoven, *Utopia Limited,* 228.

14. McGurl, *The Program Era,* 198.

15. White, *Pre-Gay L.A.,* 17.

16. Ibid., 40.

17. Isherwood, *Diaries,* 2:354.

18. P. E. Britton to Isherwood, 1965, Christopher Isherwood Collection, CI 653.

19. Isherwood, *Lost Years,* 216–17.

20. P. E. Britton to Isherwood, 1965, Christopher Isherwood Collection, CI 653.

21. Isherwood, *Diaries,* 2:355.

22. Ibid.

23. Isherwood, interview with Clifford Solway, Christopher Isherwood Collection, CI 3072.

24. Ibid.

25. Cleto, *Camp,* 302.

26. DeKoven, *Utopia Limited,* 17.

27. McGurl, *The Program Era,* 217.

28. Whiting, *Pop L.A.,* 5.

29. Amaya was friends with both Isherwood and Don Bachardy, and

in 1974 he would feature Don Bachardy at the New York Cultural Center (Isherwood, *Diaries*, 3:691).

30. Berg and Freeman, *Conversations with Christopher Isherwood*, 96.
31. Whiting, *Pop L.A.*, 110.
32. Parker, *Isherwood*, 541.
33. Ibid., 542.
34. Collins to Isherwood, 10 January 1957, Curtis Brown Collection.
35. Ibid.
36. Ibid.
37. Tebbel, *A History of Book Publishing in the United States*, 3:155.
38. Ibid., 4:204.
39. Isherwood to Collins, 16 March 1957, Curtis Brown Collection.

5. "A Delicious Purgatory"

1. Vidal to Isherwood, Christopher Isherwood Collection, CI 2620.
2. Izzo, *Christopher Isherwood*, 209.
3. Baldwin, "Reminiscences of James Baldwin," 101.
4. Ibid., 107.
5. Tebbel, *A History of Book Publishing in the United States*, 4:307.
6. Hannon, "Jane Rule."
7. Ibid.
8. Burton L. Beals to Josephine Rogers, 18 December 1961, Jane Rule Collection.
9. Julian P. Muller to Josephine Rogers, 16 October 1961, Jane Rule Collection.
10. Kurt Hellmer to Rule, 2 May 1963, Jane Rule Collection.
11. Hannon, "Jane Rule."
12. Ibid.
13. Casillo, *Outlaw*, 120.
14. Rechy to Isherwood, 20 December 1960, Christopher Isherwood Collection, CI 1932.
15. Rechy to Isherwood, 1961, Christopher Isherwood Collection, CI 1933.
16. Rechy e-mail to Jaime Harker, 20 December 2011.
17. Casillo, *Outlaw*, 122–23.
18. Isherwood, *Diaries*, 2:482–83.
19. *Down There on a Visit*, draft, Christopher Isherwood Collection, CI 1059, 149.
20. Ibid.
21. Isherwood to Harry Heckford, 21 March 1967, Christopher Isherwood Collection, CI 1310.
22. Ibid.

23. Isherwood, *Diaries*, 1:212.

24. Isherwood to Upward, 21 August 1960, Edward Upward Collection.

25. Isherwood, Writing Notebook, 21 September 1959, Christopher Isherwood Collection, CI 1158.

26. Carr, *Queer Times*, 97.

27. Isherwood, *Down There on a Visit*, 12.

28. Carr, *Queer Times*, 102.

29. Vidal to Isherwood, May 1962, Christopher Isherwood Collection, CI 2620.

30. Isherwood to Smith, 27 December 1948, Dodie Smith Collection.

6. Secret Agents and Gay Identity

1. Bergman, *The Violet Hour*, 60.

2. Bristow, "'I Am with You, Little Minority Sister,'" 146.

3. Kackman, *Citizen Spy*, 76.

4. Ibid., 75–76.

5. Parker, *Isherwood*, 394.

6. Lewis, *Cyril Connolly*, 515.

7. Cleto, introduction to *The Man from C.A.M.P.*, ii.

8. Lewis, *Cyril Connolly*, 515.

9. Connolly, "Bond Strikes Camp," 12.

10. See Smith, *Hard-Boiled.*

11. Lewis, *Cyril Connolly*, 515.

12. Costello, *Secret Identity Crisis*, 19.

13. Isherwood, *Diaries*, 2:217.

14. Ibid., 202.

15. Ibid.

16. Fleming, *Moonraker*, 28.

17. Isherwood, *A Single Man*, 57.

18. Isherwood, Writing Notebook, 19 September 1963, Christopher Isherwood Collection, CI 1158.

19. Isherwood, *Down There on a Visit*, draft, Christopher Isherwood Collection, CI 1058, 2.

20. Banis, *The Man from C.A.M.P.*, 130.

21. Nealon, *Foundlings*, 110.

7. Spiritual Trash

1. Isherwood, *Down There on a Visit*, draft, Christopher Isherwood Collection, CI 3097, carbon copy of CI 1056.

2. Clark, "The First King of Pornography," 93.

3. Ibid.

4. Isherwood, *Diaries*, 1:822.

5. Bronski, *Pulp Friction*, 199.

6. Ibid., 226.

7. These writers include Christian Davies (Chris Davidson), George Davies (Lance Lester, Clay Caldwell, Ricardo Armory), Jan Ewing (Jack Evans), Richard Fullmer (Dirk Vanden), Dean T. Goodman (Douglas Dean), "Jay Greene," George Haimshohn (Alexander Goodman), Joseph Hansen (James Colton or James Coulton), Peter Tuesday Hughes, William J. Lambert III, Vincent Lardo (Julian Mark), "Michael Scott," Samuel M. Steward (Phil Andros), and Larry Townsend.

8. Banis, "The Gay Publishing Revolution," 117.

9. Clark, "The First King of Pornography," 87–88.

10. Kemp, "Strolling through Tumescent Town," 104.

11. Vanden, "Now Is the Time," 230.

12. Ibid.

13. Amory, *Song of the Loon*, 226.

14. Ibid.

15. Vanden, "Now Is the Time," 231.

16. Howard, *Men Like That*, 206.

17. Isherwood, *Diaries*, 2:485. The books he cites are Oscar Peck, *Sex Life of a Cop*; Chris Davidson, *Go Down, Aaron*; Oscar Wilde (attributed), *Teleny*; Dennis Drew, *Like Father, Like Son*; Carl Corley, *A Fool's Advice*; and Aaron Thomas, *The Beefcake Boys*.

18. Spring, *Secret Historian*, 362.

19. Marsh, *Mr. Isherwood Changes Trains*. For more on Isherwood's relationship to Hinduism, also see Copley, *A Spiritual Bloomsbury*, and Paine, *Father India*.

20. Bucknell, "Introduction," xxviii.

21. Isherwood, *Diaries*, 2:232.

22. McFarland, "'Always Dance,'" 243.

23. Auden to Isherwood, 23 June 1943, Christopher Isherwood Collection, CI 2992.

24. Isherwood, *The Wishing Tree*, 75–76.

25. Berg and Freeman, *Conversations with Christopher Isherwood*, 143.

26. Isherwood, *My Guru and His Disciple*, draft, Christopher Isherwood Collection, CI 1114.

27. Isherwood, "Divine Grace," Christopher Isherwood Collection, CI 1038.

8. Gay Liberation and the Question of Style

1. Pobo, "Journalism and Publishing."

2. Schell, "Book Publishers."

3. Pobo, "Journalism and Publishing."

4. See Bergman, *The Violet Hour.*

5. Isherwood, *Diaries,* 3:97.

6. Ibid.

7. Duberman, *The Worlds of Lincoln Kirstein,* 584.

8. Moffat, *A Great Unrecorded History,* 20.

9. Isherwood to Collins, 31 March 1965, Curtis Brown Collection.

10. Isherwood to Knowlton, 22 May 1972, Curtis Brown Collection.

11. Isherwood to Knowlton, 20 January 1974, Curtis Brown Collection.

12. Isherwood to Donadio, 19 February 1975, Donadio and Olson files.

13. Schwed to Isherwood, 30 May 1975, Donadio and Olson files.

14. Isherwood to Donadio, 13 May 1975, Donadio and Olson files.

15. Isherwood to Schwed, 4 June 1975, Donadio and Olson files.

16. Tebbel, *A History of Book Publishing,* 4:287.

17. Isherwood to di Capua, 27 July 1976, Farrar, Straus and Giroux Inc. records.

18. Di Capua to Christopher Isherwood, 20 August 1976, Farrar, Straus and Giroux Inc. records.

19. Donadio to Isherwood, 29 June 1976, Donadio and Olson Archives.

20. Di Capua to Donadio, 25 January 1977, Donadio and Olson Archives.

21. Lee Edelman's *No Future* and José Muñoz's *Cruising Utopia,* for example, take opposite views on the role of the future in queer theory, but each defines queerness as an innate, oppositional essence.

22. Nealon, "Invert History," 762.

23. Bucknell, "Why Christopher Isherwood Stopped Writing Fiction," 126.

24. Isherwood, *Diaries,* 1:455–56.

25. Bucknell, "Why Christopher Isherwood Stopped Writing Fiction," 132.

26. Piazza, *Christopher Isherwood,* 190.

27. Ibid.

28. Ibid., 192.

29. Ibid., 197.

30. Isherwood, *Diaries,* 3:120.

31. Ibid., 3:525.

32. Ibid., 3:400.

Bibliography

Archived Sources

Curtis Brown Collection, Isherwood Files. Rare Book and Manuscript Library, Columbia Library in the City of New York.

Donadio and Olson Archives. Donadio and Olson Inc., New York, N.Y.

Farrar, Straus and Giroux Inc. records. Manuscripts and Archives Division, New York Public Library. Astor, Lenox, and Tilden Foundations.

Christopher Isherwood Collection. Huntington Library, San Marino, Calif.

Lincoln Kirstein Collection. Lincoln Center, New York Public Library for the Performing Arts.

Random House Collection. Rare Book and Manuscript Library, Columbia Library in the City of New York.

Jane Rule Collection. University of British Columbia, Vancouver, Canada.

Dodie Smith Collection. Howard Gotlieb Archival Research Center, Boston University.

Stephen Spender Collection. Bancroft Library, University of California, Berkeley.

Edward Upward Collection. British Library.

Other Sources

Amaya, Mario. *Pop as Art: A Survey of the New Super-Realism.* London: Studio-Vista, 1965.

Amis, Kingsley. *"The World in the Evening." Twentieth Century,* July 1954, 88.

Amory, Richard. *Song of the Loon.* 1966. Reprint, Vancouver, B.C.: Arsenal Pulp Press, 2008.

Atlas, James. *Bellow: A Biography.* New York: Random House, 2000.

Austen, Roger. "Christopher Isherwood Interview." In Berg and Freeman, *Conversations with Christopher Isherwood,* 152–61.

———. *Playing the Game: The Homosexual Novel in America.* New York: Bobbs-Merrill, 1977.

Baldwin, James. *Another Country.* 1962. Reprint, New York: Vintage, 1992.

———. "Everybody's Protest Novel." In *Notes of a Native Son,* 13–23. 1955. Reprint, New York: Bantam Books, 1968.

———. *Giovanni's Room.* 1956. Reprint, New York: Delta Trade Paperbacks, 2000.

———. "Reminiscences of James Baldwin." October 9, 1963. Fern Marja Eckman, interviewer. Columbia University Center for Oral History Collection.

Banis, Victor. "The Gay Publishing Revolution." In Gunn, *The Golden Age of Gay Fiction,* 113–25.

———. *The Man from C.A.M.P.* New York: MLR Press, 2008.

Baym, Nina. "Melodramas of Beset Manhood: How Theories of American Fiction Exclude Women Authors." In *The New Feminist Criticism: Essays on Women, Literature, and Theory,* edited by Elaine Showalter, 63–80. New York: Pantheon, 1985.

Berg, James T. Introduction to *Isherwood on Writing,* by Christopher Isherwood, 1–33. Edited by James T. Berg. Minneapolis: University of Minnesota Press, 2008.

———. and Chris Freeman, eds. *Conversations with Christopher Isherwood.* Jackson: University Press of Mississippi, 2001.

———. and Chris Freeman, eds. *The Isherwood Century: Essays on the Life and Work of Christopher Isherwood.* Madison: University of Wisconsin Press, 2001.

Bergman, David. "The Cultural Work of Sixties Gay Pulp Fiction." In Smith, *The Queer Sixties,* 26–41.

———. *The Violet Hour: The Violet Quill and the Making of Gay Culture.* New York: Columbia University Press, 2004.

Bérubé, Allan. *Coming Out Under Fire: The History of Gay Men and Women in World War II.* New York: Free Press, 1990.

Bonn, Thomas L. *Undercover: An Illustrated History of American Mass Market Paperbacks.* New York: Penguin, 1982.

Bristow, Joseph. "'I Am with You, Little Minority Sister': Isherwood's Queer Sixties." In Smith, *The Queer Sixties,* 145–63.

Bronski, Michael. *Pulp Friction: Uncovering the Golden Age of Gay Male Pulps.* New York: St. Martin's Press, 2003.

Bucknell, Katherine. Introduction to Isherwood, *Diaries, Volume 2,* xi–xxxvii.

———. "Why Christopher Isherwood Stopped Writing Fiction." In *On Modern British Fiction,* edited by Zachary Leader, 126–48. Oxford: Oxford University Press, 2002.

Burns, John Horne. *The Gallery.* 1947. Reprint, New York: NYRB Classics, 2004.

Carr, Jamie M. *Queer Times: Christopher Isherwood's Modernity.* New York: Routledge, 2006.

Casillo, Charles. *Outlaw: The Lives and Careers of John Rechy.* Los Angeles: Advocate Books, 2002.

Clark, Philip. "The First King of Pornography: H. Lynn Womack and Washington, D.C's Guild Press." In Gunn, *The Golden Age of Gay Fiction,* 87–95.

Clark, Suzanne. *Cold Warriors: Manliness on Trial in the Rhetoric of the West.* Carbondale: Southern Illinois University Press, 2010.

Clarke, Gerald. *Capote: A Biography.* New York, Simon and Schuster, 2001.

Cleto, Fabio, editor. *Camp: Queer Aesthetics and the Performing Subject; A Reader.* Ann Arbor: University of Michigan Press, 1999.

———. Foreword to *The Man from C.A.M.P.,* by Victor J. Banis, i–xii.

Connolly, Cyril. "Bond Strikes Camp." *London* 2 (April 1963): 8–23.

———. *Enemies of Promise.* 1938. Reprint, New York: Macmillan, 1948.

Copley, A. H. R. *A Spiritual Bloomsbury: Hinduism and Homosexuality in the Lives of Edward Carpenter, E. M. Forster, and Christopher Isherwood.* New York: Lexington Books, 2006.

Corber, Robert. *Homosexuality in Cold War America: Resistance and the Crisis of Masculinity.* Durham, N.C.: Duke University Press, 1997.

Corley, Carl. *A Fool's Advice.* San Diego: Publisher's Export Company, 1967.

Costello, Matthew J. *Secret Identity Crisis: Comic Books and the Unmasking of Cold War America.* New York: Continuum, 2009.

Cowley, Malcolm. "Cheap Books for the Millions." In *The Literary Situation,* 96–114. New York: Viking Press, 1955.

———. "Hardbacks or Paperbacks?" In *The Literary Situation,* 115–23. New York: Viking Press, 1955.

Crider, Allen Billy, ed. *Mass Market Publishing in America.* Boston: G. K. Hall, 1982.

Davidson, Chris. *Go Down, Aaron.* San Diego: Greenleaf Classics, 1967.

D'Emilio, John. *Sexual Politics, Sexual Communities: The Making of a Homosexual Minority in the United States, 1940–1970.* Chicago: University of Chicago Press, 1983.

DeKoven, Marianne. *Utopia Limited: The Sixties and the Emergence of the Postmodern.* Durham, N.C.: Duke University Press, 2004.

Drew, Dennis. *Like Father, Like Son.* San Diego: Publishers Export Company, 1967.

Duberman, Martin. *The Worlds of Lincoln Kirstein.* New York: Alfred A. Knopf, 2007.

Earle, David M. *Re-Covering Modernism: Pulps, Paperbacks, and the Prejudice of Form*. Burlington, Vt.: Ashgate, 2009.

Edelman, Lee. *No Future: Queer Theory and the Death Drive*. Durham, N.C.: Duke University Press, 2004.

Fiedler, Leslie. "The Un-Angry Young Men: America's Post-War Generation." *Encounter* 20, no. 1 (January 1958): 3–12.

Fleming, Ian. *Casino Royale*. 1953. Reprint, New York: Penguin Books, 2002.

———. *Diamonds Are Forever*. New York: Macmillan, 1956.

———. *From Russia, with Love*. New York: Macmillan, 1957.

———. *Goldfinger*. 1950. Reprint, New York: Penguin Books, 2002.

———. *Live and Let Die*. 1954. Reprint, New York: Signet, 1964.

———. *Moonraker*. 1955. Reprint, New York: Signet, 1964.

———. *On Her Majesty's Secret Service*. New York: Signet, 1964.

Foote, Stephanie. "Deviant Classics: Pulps and the Making of Lesbian Print Culture." *Signs: Journal of Women in Culture and Society* 31, no. 1 (Autumn 2005): 169–90.

Greenberg, Clement. "State of American Writing." *Partisan Review* 15 (August 8, 1948): 876–79.

Gunn, Drewey Wayne, ed. *The Golden Age of Gay Fiction*. New York: MLR Press, 2009.

Hannon, Gerald. "Jane Rule: The Woman Behind *Lesbian Images*." *The Body Politic*, December 30, 1975. http://www.xtra.ca/public/viewstory.aspx?AFF_TYPE=1&STORY_ID=3980&PUB_TEMPLATE_ID=1

Harker, Jaime. *America the Middlebrow: Women's Novels, Progressivism, and Middlebrow Authorship Between the Wars*. Amherst: University of Massachusetts Press, 2007.

Hayes, Richard. "Pity Party." *Commonweal* 60, no. 17 (July 30, 1954): 421.

Hench, John B. *Books as Weapons: Propaganda, Publishing, and the Battle for Global Markets in the Era of World War II*. Ithaca, N.Y.: Cornell University Press, 2010.

Herring, Scott. *Another Country: Queer Anti-Urbanism*. New York: New York University Press, 2010.

Hochmann, Barbara. *Getting at the Author: Reimagining Books and Reading in the Age of American Realism*. Amherst: University of Massachusetts Press, 2001.

Howard, John. *Men Like That: Southern Queer History*. Chicago: University of Chicago Press, 1999.

Humble, Nicola. "The Queer Pleasures of Reading: Camp and the Middlebrow." In *Middlebrow Literary Cultures: The Battle of the Brows, 1920–1960*, edited by Erica Brown and Mary Grover, 218–30. New York: Palgrave, 2011.

Hutner, Gordon. *What America Read: Taste, Class, and the Novel, 1920–1960.* Chapel Hill: University of North Carolina Press, 2009.

Isherwood, Christopher. *Christopher and His Kind, 1929–1939.* New York: Farrar, Strauss and Giroux, 1976.

———. *Diaries, Volume 1: 1939–1960.* Edited by Katherine Bucknell. New York: Harper Perennial, 1998.

———. *Diaries, Volume 2: 1960–1969.* Edited by Katherine Bucknell. London: Chatto and Windus, 2010.

———. *Diaries, Volume 3: 1970–1983.* Edited and introduced by Katherine Bucknell. New York: Harper, 2012.

———. *Down There on a Visit.* New York: Simon and Schuster, 1962.

———. *Isherwood on Writing.* Edited by James J. Berg. Foreword by Claude J. Summers. Minneapolis: University of Minnesota Press, 2008.

———. *Lost Years: A Memoir, 1945–1951.* Edited by Katherine Bucknell. New York: HarperCollins, 2001.

———. *A Meeting by the River.* 1967. Reprint, Harmondsworth: Penguin Books, 1970.

———. "On His Queerness." http://wonderingminstrels.blogspot.com /2001/02/on-his-queerness-christopher-isherwood.html.

———. "The Problem of the Religious Novel." In *The Wishing Tree,* 164–68.

———. *A Single Man.* 1964. Reprint, New York: Book-of-the-Month Club, 1996.

———. *The Wishing Tree: Christopher Isherwood on Mystical Religion.* San Francisco: Harper and Row, 1987.

———. *The World in the Evening.* 1954. Reprint, New York: Ballantine, 1967.

———. "The Writer and Vedanta." In *The Wishing Tree,* 155–63.

Izzo, David Garrett. *Christopher Isherwood: His Era, His Gang, and the Legacy of the Truly Strong Man.* Columbia: University of South Carolina Press, 2001.

Jackson, Charles. *Fall of Valor.* 1946. Reprint, New York: Arbor House, 1986.

———. *The Lost Weekend.* 1944. Reprint, New York: Time Incorporated, 1963.

Jenkins, Henry. "Fandom and/as Religion? The Power of the Metaphor . . ." *Intensities* interviews Henry Jenkins. Matt Hills, interviewer. @Console-ing Passions, University of Bristol, July 7, 2001. http:// intensities.org/Essays/Jenkins.pdf.

———. *Textual Poachers: Television Fans and Participatory Culture.* New York: Routledge, 1992.

Jones, Howard Mumford. "Ambivalent Trio." Review of *The World in the Evening,* by Christopher Isherwood. *Saturday Review of Literature,* June 5, 1954, 14–15.

Kackman, Michael. *Citizen Spy: Television, Espionage, and Cold War Culture.* Minneapolis: University of Minnesota Press, 2005.

Kemp, Earl. "Strolling through Tumescent Town." In Gunn, *The Golden Age of Gay Fiction,* 103–11.

Leavis, F. R. *The Great Tradition: George Eliot, Henry James, Joseph Conrad.* New York: George W. Stewart, 1948.

LeSueur, Joe. *Digressions on Some Poems by Frank O'Hara.* New York: Farrar, Straus and Giroux, 2004.

Levin, James. *The Gay Novel in America.* New York: Garland Press, 1991.

Levinson, Lew. *Butterfly Man.* [1934]. Reprint, New York: Castle, 1964.

Lewis, Jeremy. *Cyril Connolly: A Life.* New York: Random House, 1997.

Love, Heather. "Modernism at Night." *PMLA* 124, no. 3 (May 2009): 744–48.

Macdonald, Dwight. "Masscult and Midcult." In *Against the American Grain: Essays on the Effects of Mass Culture,* 3–78. New York: Random House, 1962.

Marsh, Victor. *Mr. Isherwood Changes Trains: Christopher Isherwood and the Search for the "Home Self."* Melbourne: Clouds of Magellan, 2010.

Maupin, Armistead. Foreword to Berg and Freeman, *The Isherwood Century,* xi–xv.

McFarland, Tom. "'Always Dance': Sex and Salvation in Isherwood's Vedantism." In Berg and Freeman, *The Isherwood Century,* 236–46.

McGurl, Mark. *The Program Era: Postwar Fiction and the Rise of Creative Writing.* Cambridge, Mass.: Harvard University Press, 2009

"Medicine: The Lonergan Case." *Time,* April 3, 1954. http://www.time .com/time/magazine/article/0,9171,850442-1,00.html.

Meeker, Richard. *Better Angel.* [1933]. Reprint, New York: Alyson Books, 2000.

Moffat, Wendy. *A Great Unrecorded History: A New Life of E. M. Forster.* New York: Farrar, Straus and Giroux, 2010.

Morgan, Bill, and Nancy J. Peters, editors. *"Howl" on Trial: The Battle for Free Expression.* San Francisco: City Lights Books, 2006.

Morrison, Mark S. *The Public Face of Modernism: Little Magazines, Audiences, and Reception, 1905–1920.* Madison: University of Wisconsin Press, 2000.

Muñoz, José. *Cruising Utopia: The Then and There of Queer Futurity.* New York: New York University Press, 2009.

Nealon, Christopher. "Invert History: The Ambivalence of Lesbian Pulp Fiction." *New Literary History* 31, no. 4 (Autumn 2000): 745–64.

———. *Foundlings: Lesbian and Gay Historical Emotion before Stonewall.* Durham, N.C.: Duke University Press, 2001.

Niles, Blair. *Strange Brother.* [1931]. New York: Ayer, 2002.

Paine, Jeffrey. *Father India: How Encounters with an Ancient Culture Transformed the Modern West.* New York: HarperCollins, 1998.

Parker, Peter. *Isherwood: A Life Revealed.* New York: Random House, 2004.

Pease, Donald E. *Visionary Compacts: American Renaissance Writings in Cultural Context.* Madison: University of Wisconsin Press, 1987.

Peck, Oscar. *Sex Life of a Cop.* Fresno, Calif.: Saber Books, 1967.

Phillips, Thomas Hal. *The Bitterweed Path.* 1950. Introduction by John Howard. Reprint, Durham: University of North Carolina Press, 1996.

Piazza, Paul. *Christopher Isherwood: Myth and Anti-Myth.* New York: Columbia University Press, 1978.

Pobo, Kenneth. "Journalism and Publishing." In *The Gay and Lesbian Literary Heritage,* edited by Claude J. Summers, 444–49. New York: Henry Holt, 1995. Updated version: http://www.glbtq.com/literature /journalism_publishing.html.

Pritchett, V. S. "Books in General." *New Statesman and Nation* 47 (1954): 803.

Rechy, John. *City of Night.* 1963. New York: Grove Press, 1994.

Rolph, C. H. *The Trial of Lady Chatterley: Reginia versus Penguin Books, Ltd.* Baltimore: Penguin, 1961.

Rule, Jane. *Desert of the Heart.* 1964. Tallahassee, Fla.: Naiad Press, 1993.

Russo, Tony. "Interview with Christopher Isherwood." In Berg and Freeman, *Conversations with Christopher Isherwood,* 162–65.

Savran, David. *Communists, Cowboys, and Queers: The Politics of Masculinity in the Work of Arthur Miller and Tennessee Williams.* Minneapolis: University of Minnesota Press, 1992.

Saunders, Frances Stonor. *The Cultural Cold War: The C.I.A. in the World of Arts and Letters.* New York: New Press, 2001.

Scandura, Jani, and Michael Thurston. *Modernism, Inc.: Body, Memory, Capital.* New York: New York University Press, 2000.

Schell, Lindsey E. "Book Publishers." In *LGBTQ America Today: An Encyclopedia,* edited by John C. Hawley, 150–54. Westport, Conn.: Greenwood, 2009.

Schlick, Frank L. *The Paperbound Book in America: The History of Paperbacks and Their European Background.* New York: R. R. Bowker, 1958.

Schreuders, Piet. *Paperbacks, U.S.A.: A Graphic History, 1939–1959.* Translated from the Dutch by Josh Pachter. San Diego: Blue Dolphin Enterprises, 1981.

Schuster, Marilyn R. *Passionate Communities: Reading Lesbian Resistance in Jane Rule's Fiction.* New York: New York University Press, 1999.

Scully, Robert. *A Scarlet Pansy.* New York: Nesor, 1937.

Sedgwick, Eve Kosofsky. *Epistemology of the Closet.* Berkeley: University of California Press, 2008.

———. Introduction to *Novel Gazing: Queer Readings in Fiction,* edited by Eve Kosofsky Sedgwick, 1–38. Durham, N.C.: Duke University Press, 1997.

Sherry, Michael. *Gay Artists in Modern American Culture.* Durham, N.C.: University of North Carolina Press, 2007.

Smith, Erin A. *Hard-Boiled: Working-Class Readers and Pulp Magazines.* Philadelphia: Temple University Press, 2000.

Sontag, Susan. "Notes on Camp." *Partisan Review* 31 (1964): 515–30.

Spring, Justin. *Secret Historian: The Life and Times of Samuel Steward, Professor, Tattoo Artist, and Sexual Renegade.* New York: Farrar, Strauss and Giroux, 2010.

Tebbel, John. *A History of Book Publishing in the United States: The Golden Age Between the Wars, 1920–1940.* 4 vols. New York: R. R. Bowker, 1972.

Tellier, André. *Twilight Men.* New York: T. Werner Laurie, 1933.

Thomas, Aaron. *The Beefcake Boys.* San Diego: Greenleaf Classics, 1967.

Tompkins, Jane. *Sensational Designs: The Cultural Work of American Fiction, 1790–1860.* New York: Oxford University Press, 1985.

Townsend, Larry. [J. Watson, pseud.]. *The Sexual Adventures of Sherlock Holmes.* New York: Olympia Press, 1971.

Turner, Catherine. *Marketing Modernism between the Two World Wars.* Amherst: University of Massachusetts Press, 2003.

Vanden, Dirk. *"Now Is the Time, the Walrus Said, to Speak of Many Things . . ."* In Amory, *Song of the Loon,* 230–34.

Vidal, Gore. *The City and the Pillar.* 1948. Reprint, New York: Random House, 1995.

Weeks, Edward. "The Peripatetic Reviewer." *Atlantic* 194, no. 1 (July 1954): 78.

Wescott, Glenway. *Continual Lessons: The Journals of Glenway Wescott, 1937–1955.* Edited by Robert Phelps. New York: Farrar, Straus and Giroux, 1990.

Weybright, Victor. *The Making of a Publisher: A Life in the 20th Century Book Revolution.* New York: Reynal, 1966.

White, C. Todd. *Pre-Gay L.A.: A Social History of the Movement for Homosexual Rights.* Urbana: University of Illinois Press, 2009.

Whiting, Cécile. *Pop L.A.: Art and the City in the 1960s.* Berkeley: University of California Press, 2006.

Wilde, Oscar [attributed]. *Teleny.* North Hollywood, Calif.: Brandon House, 1967.

Wilson, Angus. "The New and the Old Isherwood." *Encounter* 11, no. 8 (August 1954): 62–68.

Index

JAIME HARKER is associate professor of English at the University of Mississippi. She is author of *America the Middlebrow: Women's Novels, Progressivism, and Middlebrow Authorship between the Wars* and coeditor, with Cecilia Konchar Farr, of *The Oprah Affect: Critical Essays on Oprah's Book Club*.